Fraudulent Evidence Before Public International Tribunals
The Dirty Stories of International Law

Domestic lawyers are, above all, officers of the court. By contrast, the public international lawyer representing states before international tribunals is torn between loyalties to the state and loyalties to international law. As the stakes increase for the state concerned, the tension between these loyalties can become acute and lead to practices that would be condemned in developed national legal systems but have hitherto been ignored by international tribunals in international legal scholarship. They are the 'dirty stories' of international law.

This detailed and contextually sensitive presentation of eight important cases before a variety of public international tribunals dissects some of the reasons for the resort to fraudulent evidence in international litigation and the profession's baffling reaction. Fraudulent evidence is resorted to out of greed, moral mediocrity or inherent dishonesty. In public international litigation, by contrast, the reasons are often more complex, with roots in the dynamics of international politics.

W. MICHAEL REISMAN is Myres S. McDougal Professor of International Law at the Yale Law School, New Haven, Connecticut.

CHRISTINA PARAJON SKINNER is an attorney with Zuckerman Spaeder LLP, New York.

Fraudulent Evidence Before Public International Tribunals

The Dirty Stories of International Law

W. MICHAEL REISMAN

CHRISTINA PARAJON SKINNER

CAMBRIDGE
UNIVERSITY PRESS

CAMBRIDGE
UNIVERSITY PRESS

University Printing House, Cambridge CB2 8BS, United Kingdom

Cambridge University Press is part of the University of Cambridge.

It furthers the University's mission by disseminating knowledge in the pursuit of education, learning and research at the highest international levels of excellence.

www.cambridge.org
Information on this title: www.cambridge.org/9781107063396

First published 2014

A catalogue record for this publication is available from the British Library

Library of Congress Cataloguing in Publication data
Reisman, W. Michael, 1984– author.
Fraudulent evidence before public international tribunals : the dirty stories of international law / W. Michael Reisman, Christina Parajon Skinner.
pages cm – (Hersch lauterpacht memorial lectures ; 21)
Includes bibliographical references and index.
ISBN 978-1-107-06339-6 (hardback)
1. Evidence, Criminal (International law) 2. Fraud. 3. International courts. 4. Arbitration (International law) I. Skinner, Christina Parajon, author. II. Title.
KZ7422.R45 2014
341.5′5 – dc23 2013048017

ISBN 978-1-107-06339-6 Hardback

For
Judge Stephen M. Schwebel

It is of course a commonplace that government officials dissemble. Reasons of States are often thought to justify statements which are incomplete, misleading or contrary to fact. Covert operations, by their nature, are intended to provide cover, to lend credibility to "deniability" . . .

Nevertheless, there can be no equation between governmental statements made in this Court and governmental statements made outside of it. The foundation of judicial decision is the establishment of the truth. Deliberate misrepresentations by the representatives of a government party to a case before this Court cannot be accepted because they undermine the essence of the judicial function.

Judge Stephen Schwebel (*Military and Paramilitary Activities in and Against Nicaragua [Nicaragua* v. *United States]*)

Contents

Preface

In "Dirty Story," Eric Ambler's celebrated *roman noir*, the British Vice-Consul in Athens pronounces judgment on one Arthur Abdel Simpson: "You're a disgusting creature, Mr. Simpson. Your life is nothing but a long, dirty story."[1] In fact, Simpson, struggling on the margins of society, is, at his worst, a petty criminal; the Vice-Consul's contempt derives in no small measure from a rap sheet that contains no great crimes, no memorable violations, only a serialization of sleazy misdeeds.

Much as it is thought indecorous to recite a dirty story in polite company, international law's custodians of etiquette seem to have decreed that their dirty stories, questionable uses or abuses of evidence before international tribunals, are not to be mentioned. Indeed, in spite of the serious forgery discovered in the *Qatar* v. *Bahrain* case,[2] the International Court's judgment does not call attention to it and the eighty-two forgeries, which Qatar withdrew, are not to be found anywhere in the court's records. It is as if the massive forgery never happened. But any short-term gains in revisionism came at a cost. A character in a novella says, "The past is never past. If you corrupt your past, you corrupt the present and everything you do in the future. You lie and your soul lies forever."[3] We leave it to our readers to decide whether, in narrating these international dirty stories, we have succeeded in provoking a useful discussion or merely breached *courtoisie internationale.*

[1] E. Ambler, *Dirty Story: A Further Account of the Life and Adventures of Arthur Abdel Simpson* (New York: Charles Scribner's Sons, 1967), p. 11.

[2] See Chapter 8 this volume.

[3] D. Shai, "Foolsbus" in *American Spectacles and Other Cultivated Illusions* (New Haven Press, 1993), p. 78.

Certainly, compared to the horrendous violations of international law committed in the past decades, cases of fraudulent evidence which have been practiced on public international courts and tribunals are, like the entries in Arthur Abdel Simpson's pathetic dossier, only dirty stories. But, for all that, we believe that they are not unimportant. They mar the noble vision and ennobling practice of sovereign States voluntarily submitting their disputes to courts and tribunals for peaceful resolution in accordance with international law; in raising doubts about the accuracy of international decision, they diminish the future willingness of States to resort to tribunals. Moreover, corruption of the truth often extends beyond the hearing room of a single case: in an interdependent world, lies which manage to distort judicial or arbitral decision in one case can contaminate many others. Judge Schwebel, to whom this book is respectfully dedicated, put it concisely: "they undermine the essence of the judicial function."

We firmly believe that the improvement of law and its procedures is an appropriate function of legal scholars, but we confess, at the outset, that we have no "magic bullet" to defeat the practice of fraudulent evidence practiced on international courts and tribunals. But we hope that recounting and analyzing these lamentable dirty stories and detailing the injury which fraudulent evidence can cause will provoke a more intense demand for clarifying the responsibility of counsel, for effectively policing and sanctioning the use of fraudulent evidence in public international tribunals, and in particular, for expanding the powers of international courts and tribunals to deal with it.

The text of this book is based on a Lauterpacht lecture which was delivered by one of the authors who was also counsel in *Qatar* v. *Bahrain*. The authors acknowledge with gratitude the assistance of the staff of the Yale Law Library, in particular Teresa Miguel-Stearns and the insightful comments on the manuscript of Eyal Benvenisti, Sir Elihu Lauterpacht, Robbie Sabel, and Jan Paulsson. Ms. Cina Santos supervised the production of the manuscript with her customary skill, patience, and good humor.

W. Michael Reisman
Christina Parajon Skinner
New Haven, Connecticut

1

The problem of fraudulent evidence before public international tribunals

Good decisionmaking presupposes the intelligence, craft skill, and character of those charged with making the decisions. It also presupposes accurate information. Without accurate information about what has occurred, even those endowed with character, skill, and focused energy are unlikely to produce a sound decision.

Because the business of government is making decisions, it is no surprise that governments undertake substantial efforts to secure reliable information. Executive branches and legislatures proactively obtain information through various methods, including intelligence services, testimony in hearings, and proprietary research services. Courts are an exception to this practice, for they continue to rely nearly exclusively on the litigants themselves for the information that is the predicate of their decisions. Externalizing the costs of assembling information is an economic and rational method for intelligence-gathering in cases and controversies. Parties and interveners have powerful incentives to collect and organize the relevant facts and all parties are assumed to have sufficient resources to do the job. In theory, oaths and perjury laws can be used to deter dishonest impulses and, failing those, parties can be expected to ferret out the truth in the theater of cross-examination.

However, some people, undeterred by fear of moral, professional, or state-imposed consequences, will try to mislead courts with fraudulent information. The adversarial system's equivalent of the invisible hand – the powerful incentives that motivate parties to flush out falsehoods and reveal the truth – is relied upon to make the system work. But the law's invisible hand is an imperfect mechanism. Various extrinsic factors may distort the dynamics of information gathering. Resource disparities between the parties may create informational imbalances. Political actors may inundate decisionmakers and adversaries with disinformation and propaganda. And where one of the parties is a government with control over whatever is in dispute, access to information vital to the decisionmaking process may simply go unknown.

Usually, factors intrinsic to the judicial process will temper disparities and equalize parties. But not always. Not all of the intrinsic features of the judicial process work to ensure that accurate information reaches decisionmakers. Only a novelist would have the courage to confess that "seldom, very seldom does complete truth belong to any human disclosure; seldom can it happen that something is not a little disguised, or a little mistaken."[1] The myth system of the bar holds that lawyers are officers of the court. Yet the competitive nature of the adversarial system follows an operational code of ethics that tolerates, justifies, indeed applauds, presentation of the relevant factual and legal data in the light most favorable to the client.[2] Precisely because the law presumes that the parties are in a situation of equality, neither counsel feels obliged to "argue" its adversary's case. Moreover, counsel often believes that the client is entitled to all the presumptions and potential arguments that the law avails; counsel may believe that she is under a professional ethical obligation to ensure that her client gets the benefit of those presumptions. The result is an arsenal of accepted practices that may sometimes distort the information provided to decisionmakers. These tactics may corrode the accuracy of information just as if counsel had consciously provided fraudulent evidence. Yet these tactics are not fraudulent.

One very basic dimension of the problem is thus identifying positively a "fraud." In grappling with it, one is reminded of Potter Stewart's resigned response to the intractable problem of defining "hard-core pornography": "I know it," he said, "when I see it."[3] Litigation, after all, is a competition for high stakes, for all its normative regulation. The representatives of the parties struggle to present versions of facts and authoritative policy in a light most favorable to their principals. Within the bounds of plausibility, advocates are expected to produce interpretations of the law, of custom and general principles, and relevant prior judicial and arbitral decisions in ways that support the parties' respective arguments. In some cases, unscrupulous lawyers intentionally misstate the law, either by commission or omission. But since *curia novit lex* (the court knows the law), the court

[1] J. Austen, *Emma*, reissue edn. (New York, NY: Bantam Classics, 1984), p. 374.
[2] W. M. Reisman, *Folded Lies: Bribery, Crusades, and Reforms* (New York, NY: Free Press, 1979).
[3] *Jacobellis* v. *Ohio*, 378 US 184, 197 (1964) (Stewart, J., concurring).

is expected – and more importantly, is able – to expose and correct such misstatements. It is the misrepresentation of facts that concerns us. And bear in mind that at international law, facts include national law. Thus, an intentional suppression of a secret decree by one of the litigants that would have been outcome-determinative in a case but was not disclosed might, depending on one's view of fraud, constitute fraudulent evidence. Similarly, the promulgation of a national decree after the fact but with intended retroactive effect, might constitute fraud from an international perspective. In terms of this sort of analysis, the suppression of a relevant and potentially outcome-determinative governmental decision by one party in circumstances in which the other could not, by its reasonable efforts, have learned of its existence, would also qualify as fraud.

Not all intentionally inaccurate facts constitute fraud in its strict legal sense. Where a controverted and determinative issue is "A" or "not-A" and each party adduces evidence to support its side of the issue, a decision by the tribunal will necessarily mean that one party's evidence is more credible than the other's, whatever the threshold of credibility may be. But the implication of that finding as to whether the losing party practiced fraud varies depending on the type of evidence adduced.

The determinative issue may turn on what we might call *evaluative* evidence, that is, evidence with respect to which both parties concede the existence of a person, thing or event, but disagree about some aspect of its relative meaning or value. In these circumstances, a tribunal's finding of "A" does not necessarily mean that the evidence adduced to support "not-A" was a lie or fraudulent evidence. If you and your attorney insist, in a proceeding before the Foreign Claims Settlement Tribunal, that your house in Havana was worth $50,000, but the tribunal holds that it was worth $15,000, the tribunal's finding does not necessarily mean that it believed you were lying (though you may have been) or, perhaps more pertinently, that the tribunal would use that term to describe the mix of greed and self-delusion that was motivating your testimony. Reasonable people (including arbitrators) may disagree as to the value of a thing and/or as to the criteria to be used in its evaluation.

The normative prism through which evidence is viewed may also color the evaluative conclusion. One party may claim that the other's manifestations of sovereignty over contested territory have no legal value because of an earlier critical date or because of the operation of some other legal principle; for example, *uti possidetis*. No matter how forced or implausible such a legal argument may be, it would not be characterized as fraud.

In contrast to evaluative evidence, a determinative issue may turn instead on what we might call *existential* evidence, that is, whether the person, thing or event exists, existed, or ever happened. In such cases, it is more likely that a tribunal's finding of "A" does mean that the evidence to support "not-A" was a lie or was fraudulent. When you attest, by affidavit, that you had a house in Havana at a particular address and the tribunal decides that no house ever existed at that site, the implication is that your evidence was a lie or was fraudulent. And, of course, if you produce documents such as deeds that state that you owned the house, a rejection of those documents must connote something more than unpersuasive evaluative evidence. When a decisionmaker rejects one party's existential evidence, it may say that it is "unpersuaded" or that it is not making judgments of truth or falsity or that you had failed to shift the burden of proof. But sometimes it is in effect holding that one allegation is false and, by implication, that the evidence supporting it is false. The rejection of evidence in this sense, therefore, is quite different from a rejection of evaluative evidence.

Whether evidence is existential or evaluative may sometimes be a close call. One might describe a two-room cottage as "palatial," and many tribunals would characterize the adjective as permissible puffing. To describe the two-room cottage as a ten-room house would surely be fraudulent. But to describe the structure as a "commodious residence" without indicating the number of rooms or square feet, in the hope that the other party or the tribunal will not insist on a specification, shifts our discussion from fraudulent evidence *qua* evidence to the question of what parties are expected to prove in order to prevail in a particular litigation. Even then, however, a relevant question may be whether the other party had a reasonable opportunity to secure the facts that would have corrected the misimpression created. In the *Tunisia/Libya* case, which we consider in Chapter 4, one might say that Libya's failure to submit to the court the coordinates for oil concessions had greatly exaggerated Libya's claim. Or, one might say that Libya's nonfeasance was a direct cause of the judicial "confirmation" of a boundary that did not exist legally. But indicative of the intellectual difficulty, one might also say that Libya was under no duty to volunteer the coordinates and that Tunisia's counsel should have checked the records in Tripoli to find or verify them.

Most cases contain existential and evaluative issues. With existential issues, by implication, the evidence of the losing party is false, even if the decisionmaker couches its conclusion in terms of not having shifted the burden of proof or not having established a preponderance of truth. Though the distinction may be difficult in some cases, it is important to bear it in mind, for how the claim is characterized will have a significant effect on how it is dealt with.

In international law, the knotty issues surrounding the definition and identification of "fraud" are intertwined with questions of how best to deal with its consequences. If processes of revision are available for allegations that the winner lied on existential issues, the loser may bring such claims after judgment when the alleged fraud is uncovered, opening the issues to a new proceeding. This has a potential for social and economic disruption, as third parties may have relied on the prior decision.

The issue is skirted but not really resolved if one says that arbitrators do not determine truth or falsity but, assuming the good faith of the litigants, simply record whether the burden of proving a particular fact is met or shifted. The explicit obligation in Article 53 of the Statute of the International Court of Justice which requires the court to "satisfy itself," when a party is absent, "that the claim is well founded in fact and law," might be read to suggest that there is no such obligation when the defendant is present; then, perhaps, the burden is on each party. But the general evolution of the notion of "equitable principles" and, particularly, after *North Sea Continental Shelf*, the idea that even a negotiated settlement must be equitable,[4] suggest that *a fortiori* the outcomes of a judicial process must also be equitable. This may import a more active role and burden on the court as suggested in the *Taba* award and in Judge Oda's opinion in *Tunisia/Libya*, both of which we will examine.

But in the absence of an international tribunal's more active role and an independent curial burden to determine the facts, fraud becomes relevant in judgment review only if there is an additional, independent assumption that a prohibition on the submission of fraudulent evidence is always implied in international adjudication and arbitration. However, in the international forum, the robustness of this implied prohibition is tethered to political forces which may sometimes overwhelm legal and ethical norms.

As compared to national legal systems, the international system is institutionally limited in its ability to prevent and punish fraudulent conduct. National legal systems may police the boundary between zealous advocacy and fraud through codes of professional conduct that both prescribe limits and sanction violations. These codes are applied by professional societies concerned with regulating the comportment of their members. In egregious

[4] *North Sea Continental Shelf (Germany* v. *Denmark/Germany* v. *The Netherlands)*, 1969 *ICJ Rep.* 3, para. 85 (20 Feb.), 41 *ILR* 29.

cases, courts themselves have an array of deterrent and punitive techniques to police the comportment of counsel.

The international system has nothing comparable to this arsenal of deterrent, preventive, and punitive weapons. There are, as yet, no international professional associations to which a measure of disciplinary jurisdiction has been delegated. Still, the absence of effective institutions does not mean that there can be no authoritative and controlling decisions, as the very operation of the international legal system demonstrates. Unorganized social systems or unorganized sectors within them may develop effective functional equivalents to the enforcement methods of domestic legal systems. In the rather turbulent political arena in the United States, for example, an electorate, dependent on information from political actors, runs risks comparable to those of courts which must depend on information from the litigants. Some observers believe that the system adjusts itself to these exigencies. Michael Kelly has written:

> Politics, in its own strange fashion, is an honest business. The rules of the game allow small lies of omission, waffling, fudging and any amount of hedging. But flat-out lying and acts of direct betrayal are much rarer than cynics believe, and greatly frowned upon. The survival of the system demands this.[5]

Others may have less sanguine assessments of the self-corrective mechanisms within American politics. But commentators across the political spectrum seem to agree that some sort of official or quasi-official "truth squad," along with a centralized sanctioning system, would impose collateral costs on the operation of the system that would outweigh any possible benefits. A respected conservative weekly in the United States, commenting on a perennial problem in American politics, opined that:

> [w]ithholding information from Congress, short of actual false statements or perjury, is a political phenomenon and part of the inevitable and indeed healthy interbranch rivalry. If witnesses go too far, they have committed a political sin and they should receive a political punishment, even up to losing their jobs; they should not be subject to criminal prosecution.[6]

Others may well disagree with this laissez faire approach.

In the international system, it would seem that a similar approach has been taken until now. Courts and tribunals follow the diplomatic practice of

[5] M. Kelly, "The President's Past," *NY Times (Magazine)* (31 July 1994), § 6, 20, 40.
[6] "Partisan Reflections," *Nat'l Rev.* (29 Aug. 1994), 15.

not "insulting" governments if it appears that they have engaged in fraud. Hence use of the term "fraud," international law's quintessential "f" word, is, as will be clear from the case studies, likely to be avoided, especially when the perpetrator of the fraud was a government official, acting in an official role. A document that is exposed as counterfeit will probably not be called fraudulent, but rather "inauthentic." The party that adduced it will not only not be sanctioned but may also still be permitted to prove its case by means of other documents. Perhaps international courts and tribunals are simply being realistic in taking for granted a certain amount of "sinning." It may be that they view their assignment as not to police the ethics of government practitioners in court, but to reach the right decision. Alas, this also incentivizes undesirable behavior.

An effort to submit fraudulent evidence that is exposed in the course of the arbitral process may arouse indignation or embarrassment, but, precisely because it is unsuccessful, it does not deform the decision. The fraud exposed prior to decision is simply disallowed legal effect.[7] The problem of fraudulent evidence is most acute where the fraud is effective: a decision, which would not otherwise have been made, has now been made as a direct consequence of one of the party's efforts to mislead the decisionmaker.

The problem of the legal treatment of the results of defrauding legislatures is different from that of courts. There is no modern doctrine of "*res legislativa*" parallel to *res judicata*. By contrast to the pretended finality of the decrees of the Medes and the Persians, modern legislation is accepted, as Pound put it, as an experiment in social organization. When legislatures discover that some of their factual assumptions were mistaken, whether as a result of someone's good or bad faith, they routinely amend, revise, or abrogate their handiwork. Like courts, they too recognize the importance of settled expectations and reliance, but these policies do not, apparently, raise the same specters as they do in the judicial arena.

[7] This is long-standing practice. The US Venezualen and Chilean Commissions of 1885 and 1892 allowed the tribunal on motion of a party to strike from the record "improper, irrelevant, immaterial, or scandalous" evidence. J. B. Moore, *History and Digest of the International Arbitrations to Which the United States has Been a Party*, 6 vols. (Washington DC: Gov. Printing Office, 1898), vol. III, p. 2228; D. V. Sandifer, *Evidence Before International Tribunals* (University Press of Virginia, 1975), p. 164. A similar power was asserted in the US Mexican Claims Commission of 1868 – from this Sandifer concludes: "Tribunals will disregard evidence shown to be forged or to contain perjured testimony, although in general they have no authority to punish the persons forging or swearing to the false documents." *Ibid.*, 163–64.

In international courts and tribunals, by contrast, the doctrine of *res judicata*, finality for courts' decisions, is accorded high deference. Even precedents, which are, after all, a form of judicial lawmaking, are rarely openly overruled. They are "distinguished."

Perhaps this stance is an acknowledgment of the absence of an enforcement mechanism in public international law. When domestic courts realize that the mistakes they have made are the result of the prevailing litigant's deliberate misrepresentations, rectification is a problem with which they struggle in ways that legislatures do not. This divergence in practice is curious, for a legislative change – of course – is likely to affect many more people than will the revision or invalidation of a "final" judgment. The reasons for the difference in treatment may be found in what Merriam called "miranda."[8] Whether one follows Holmes[9] or Kelsen[10] on this matter, the judgments of the courts are our law: law, as Holmes put it, is what the courts "do in fact."[11] In effective constitutional systems, we organize our lives and finances around the expectation that what courts have done is legal and right. We organize much of our national myth and rest much of our public conception of ethics and probity on the holdings of our courts. Perhaps, in light of this ethos, the custodians of the courts feel that too much – including their own legitimacy – is at stake.

One cannot consider the problem of fraudulent evidence in international law without relating it to the larger issue of loyalty in international politics. In national legal systems, the assumption is that there is a single authority to which loyalty is owed. In international politics, by contrast, there are competing loyalty systems. First and foremost, citizens still owe allegiance to their states, not to the world community. When individuals representing their states confront each other in an international tribunal or another international institution, their loyalty will be to the sovereign. In the competition for loyalty, international tribunals, with the fragility of

[8] C. H. Merriam, *Political Power: Its Composition and Incidence* (New York and London: Whittlesey House, McGraw Hill, 1934), pp. 102–13.

[9] O. W. Holmes, Jr., "The Path of the Law," *Harv. L. Rev.*, 10 (1897), 457, 461; see also O. W. Holmes, "The Path of the Law," address delivered at the dedication of the New Hall of the Boston University School of Law (8 Jan. 1897) in M. Lerner (ed.), *The Mind and Faith of Justice Holmes: His Speeches, Essays, Letters, and Judicial Opinions*, reprint edn. (New York: Modern Library, 1954), pp. 71, 75 ("The prophecies of what the courts will do in fact, and nothing more pretentious, are what I mean by the law.").

[10] H. Kelsen, *General Theory of Law and State*, A. Wedberg (tr.), (Cambridge, MA: Harvard University Press, 1945).

[11] Holmes, "The Path of the Law," p. 461.

their power base and, in ad hoc tribunals, their ephemeral existence, are a weak second.

***

As we will see, the international legal system encounters daunting challenges in dealing with awards and judgments that have been secured by means of fraudulent evidence. Precisely because of the weakness of enforcement mechanisms, international law elevates the principle of *res judicata* to a *grundnorm* on par with a *pacta sunt servanda.* As a result, when it confronts an international decision which has been secured by fraud, international law, rather than acknowledging that *res judicata* has its limits, inclines to stand by the decision but looks plaintively to national law for a remedy.

Consider the extraordinary incident of the *Weil* and *La Abra* claims before the Mexican Claims Commission.

In 1868, Mexico and the United States established an international claims commission for injuries that Americans were alleged to have suffered in Mexico in the civil war. In *Weil*, Benjamin Weil, a naturalized American, claimed $334,950 in compensation for nearly 2,000 bales of cotton he alleged had been seized and appropriated on September 20, 1864 by General Cortina of the Mexican Liberal forces. His sole evidence consisted of an affidavit he himself had executed in New Orleans in 1869 along with some other supporting affidavits made between 1869 and 1872.[12] According to the affidavits, the receipts for the cotton and travel expense vouchers had been lost.[13]

The American Commissioner, perhaps betraying his discomfort over the wispiness of the evidence, stated: "I am willing to give every opportunity in my power, as a commissioner, to the [Mexican] government to make a full and ample investigation of the claim, and respond to it, and very much wish that this might be done."[14] Mexico declined this invitation, apparently out of fear that it would allow Weil another opportunity to submit false evidence. The Mexican Commissioner observed the dubious credibility of the evidence and complained of the difficulty for Mexico to establish "negative proof."[15]

As the two national Commissioners did not agree, the decision fell to the umpire, Sir Edward Thornton. In his opinion, the claimant's version was "sufficiently proved" and "not disproved by evidence on the part of the

[12] Moore, *History and Digest*, vol. II, p. 1324. [13] *Ibid.*, 1325. [14] *Ibid.*, 1324.
[15] *Ibid.*, 1325.

defence."[16] According to his view, an international arbitrator assumes the credibility of the evidence and determines only whether burdens of proof have been met or shifted. Hence, Sir Edward awarded for the claimant.[17]

The *La Abra* claim was for the alleged dispossession of a mine and seizure of ores by the Mexican authorities.[18] As in the *Weil* claim, the Mexican Commissioner opposed the claim. He contested the authenticity of the evidence, pointing out several oddities. For example, the mine, which had been sold in 1865 for $50,000, was valued by the claimant in 1868 for $2.5 million, despite the mine's difficult history and no record of economic success.[19] In the view of the Mexican Commissioner, much of the evidence had been obtained by fraud. The umpire decided for the claimant, holding that Mexico had behaved in a hostile manner in order to drive the claimants out.[20]

Mexico requested rehearing based on new evidence.[21] The umpire refused on the grounds that under the Convention he had no competence to reconsider matters that the Commission (and he) had already considered, that in any event a reexamination would not lead him to change his mind, and finally, that the decisions had already been made public and thus reliance interests may have arisen.

> [T]he Mexican agent would wish the umpire to believe that all the witnesses for the claimant have perjured themselves, whilst all those for the defense are to be implicitly believed. Unless there had been proof of perjury the umpire would not have been justified in refusing credence to the witnesses on the one side or the other, and could only weigh the evidence on each side and decide to the best of his judgment in whose favor it inclined. *If perjury can still be proved* by further evidence, the umpire apprehends that *there are courts of justice in both countries by which perjurers can be tried and convicted*, and he doubts whether the government of either would insist upon the payment of claims shown to be founded upon perjury. In . . . 'Benj. Weil v. Mexico', the agent of Mexico has produced circumstantial evidence which, if not refuted by the claimant, would certainly contribute to the suspicion that perjury has been committed and that the whole claim is a fraud. For the reason already given *it is not in the power of the umpire to take that evidence into consideration, but if perjury shall be proved hereafter no one would rejoice more than the umpire himself that his decision should be reversed and that justice should be done.*[22]

Sir Edward's stance shows great reverence for finality of international awards. It assumes that the administrative consequences of allowing the

[16] *Ibid.*, 1326. [17] *Ibid.*, 1324–27. The award was for $479,975.95 in gold coin.
[18] *Ibid.*, 1327. [19] *Ibid.*, 1328. [20] *Ibid.* [21] *Ibid.*, 1329.
[22] *Ibid.*, 1329–30 (emphasis added).

reopening of awards would undermine the entire decisional process. It implicitly, in turn, acknowledges that although some mistakes will inevitably be made, there is no inherent corrective competence at the arbitral level. Remedies depend upon diplomatic or political means. Even Mexico acknowledged the finality of the award, only hoping that if and when evidence of the fraud was presented, it could count on "the sentiments of justice and equity of the United States" to remedy the injustice.[23]

In 1878, concerned over the possibility of fraud, the United States Congress requested the executive branch to investigate the cases.[24] The investigation, too, assumed the *international* system's inability to offer redress for an award secured by fraud. In 1879, after investigation, then-Secretary of State Evarts reported to the President that the conduct of the claims and the integrity of the tribunal and its procedures gave no ground for complaint:

> I conclude, therefore, that neither the principles of public law nor considerations of justice or equity require or permit as between the United States and Mexico that the awards in these cases should be opened and the cases retried before a new international tribunal.[25]

Even so, Evarts felt that there was some doubt of the "integrity of the claim of Benjamin Weil" and the extent of the damages claimed to have been suffered at La Abra. Accordingly, he counseled that:

> the honor of the United States does require that these two cases should be further investigated by the United States to ascertain whether this Government has been made the means of enforcing against a friendly power claims of our citizens based upon or exaggerated by fraud.[26]

Evarts took for granted that the authority for all such investigation had to come from Congress, as it did not exist in international law. (The Commission had long since dissolved, so the question of whether it could have corrected one of its own awards if both states agreed did not arise.)

It is noteworthy that Evarts assumed that a violation of procedure or a defect in the integrity of the tribunal – classic grounds of nullity – would have afforded Mexico a legal ground for reopening the cases *internationally*. Not so for an award rendered on the basis of fraudulent evidence. At the most, it generated a moral obligation on the part of the United States to ascertain, by its own internal procedures, whether one of its own citizens had exploited

[23] *Ibid.*, 1330. [24] *Ibid.*, 1333. [25] *Ibid.*, 1334. [26] *Ibid.*

it. Evarts, like Sir Edward, insisted on the principle of international finality of an award, even one tainted by fraud.

Over the next several years, both Congress and the Executive continued to question whether the awards had been obtained by fraud. Congress ultimately conferred jurisdiction on the Court of Claims to investigate the charge of fraud. In 1897, the Court of Claims held that the awards had been obtained by fraud.[27] And when the Supreme Court considered the *La Abra* decision, it affirmed this conclusion,[28] also assuming unassailable finality of the award at the international level. The United States subsequently returned the amounts Mexico had paid.[29] Because there was never any intimation that the award was null on the international level, it was the United States, acting on its "honor," that refused to enforce an unconscionable award. The issues of fraud and its consequences were determined domestically. The remedy was fashioned by Congress.

Weil and *La Abra* tell us something curious about this part of the process of international law. The initial uncertainty as to whether there had been fraud was followed by an increasing degree of concurrence, and finally unanimity that there had been fraud. Yet both Mexico and various branches of the United States government took for granted that an award based on clearly established fraudulent evidence was *not* null at international law. A remedy for the injustice had to come from the winning state as a matter of its internal law by a discretionary decision not to enforce the decision.

But our study will show that several other approaches have also been applied:

The *Weil/La Abra* approach views an international award as insusceptible to arbitral review for fraud because, according to this view, the tribunal and international law lack the competence to change an award once rendered. There may be compelling reasons for this approach. But it does little to discourage fraud. From a party's ex ante perspective the only risk (and cost) to attempting fraud is that it may lose the case (which it might regardless of its fraudulent submissions).

The *Sabotage Cases*, which we consider in the following chapter, illustrate a second approach: it views fraud as a per se violation that allows a continuing tribunal to reopen an award without the claimant having

[27] *United States* v. *Weil*, 35 Ct. Cl. 42 (1900); *United States* v. *La Abra Silver Mining Co.*, 32 Ct. Cl. 462 (1897).

[28] 175 US 423 (1899).

[29] R. E. McClendon, "The Weil and La Abra Claims Against Mexico," *Hispanic American Historical Rev.*, 19 (1939), 31–32.

to establish additional legal justifications. Some decisions from the Iran Claims Tribunal after the *Ram* decision[30] also resemble this approach, though there the principle may be more rhetorical than real.

In the *Tunisia/Libya* case, we can see a cumulative materiality approach. This third approach weighs the fraud in term of factors such as the extent of its effects on the award, the claimant's diligence, and third-party reliance before deciding whether to vacate the award.

Taba exemplifies a fourth approach: it abandons any assumption that each party is responsible for protecting its own interest and instead undertakes an active tribunal competence to redress an imbalance between the parties without regard to the possibility of fraud.

In still a fifth approach, the tribunal distances its legal analysis from the facts adduced by fraud, arguably as a method of preventing the fraud from contaminating the decision. We see this approach taken in *Nicaragua* v. *United States*, where the International Court relies on certain legal theories in order to circumvent the questions of whether and the extent to which Nicaragua had supplied arms to the insurgent groups. In *Qatar* v. *Bahrain*, the court's approach was one of denial: there is no mention of the fabricated documents in the court's final decision; the only inkling that fraud was practiced is found in ad hoc Judge Fortier's separate opinion. Again, in *Corfu Channel*, the court proceeds with its decisionmaking absent the factual contents of the document in question.

We do not undertake a comparative study of national practice, whose political dynamics are radically different from those of public international law. Rather than a codification of rules, our work comprises a study of separate incidents, whose participants were, nonetheless, aware of precedents and what one might call "subsequents," that is, the sense common to anyone who plays a decision role in international law and is thus attuned to the varying law-generative dimension of each decision.[31]

Since an overarching aspect of the problem is the clarity of the code of proper behavior of those functioning as counsel in international litigation, the problem cannot be considered without some reflection on the rules of professional ethics of counsel in an international legal system that is

[30] See Chapter 6 this volume for a discussion of the *Ram* decision, in which the Iran–US Claims Tribunal conceded that, in theory, a continuing tribunal has, "by implication," "the authority to revise decisions induced by fraud" until the tribunal's dissolution. *Ram Int'l Indus.* v. *Air Force of Iran*, 29 *Iran–US Cl. Trib. Rep.* 383, p. 390, para. 20 (1993).

[31] See *Glamis Gold, Ltd.* v. *United States (Canada* v. *United States)*, UNCITRAL Award, 8 June 2009, available at: www.state.gov/documents/organization/125798.pdf.

relying, more and more, on third-party decision. International law has yet to develop a clear and enforceable code of proper behavior for those seeking justice and those acting as counsel before the International Court or an arbitral tribunal. We hope that the stories we consider will bring attention to the ethical obligations incumbent on all when litigating in an international forum.

2

The *Sabotage Cases*: suborned witnesses

The so-called *Sabotage Cases* concerned certain acts of German sabotage in the United States, prior to America's entry into World War I. The German secret service had mounted covert operations against factories and shipping depots in the United States that were engaged in producing and shipping munitions to the Allies. The cases were tried before the post-war German–United States Claims Commission, which had been established to resolve the claims arising out of the war. The cases present the only instance, in our study, in which an international tribunal clearly condemned one of the states litigating before it for committing fraud and, moreover, acted on such a finding of fraud. (The claimant also produced witnesses the Commission characterized as liars.) Indeed, this continuing tribunal even reconsidered its theretofore limited conception of tribunal powers and pronounced itself competent to reopen a matter to deal with later-discovered fraud.

I

In this case, as in several of the stories that we study, context is key in framing the issues and understanding the decisions of tribunal and counsel alike. In particular, to better appreciate the desperate position in which Germany found itself, it is necessary to look more closely at America's neutrality practice at the beginning of the war.

After the formal declaration of war by the European Powers on August 4, 1914, the United States issued a Proclamation of Neutrality.[1] President Wilson, attempting both to "avoid and to reform the Old World,"[2]

[1] See L. E. Ambrosius, *Wilsonian Statecraft: Theory and Practice of Liberal Internationalism During World War I* (Wilmington, DE: Scholarly Resources, 1991), p. 35.

[2] See *ibid.*, 23.

described his approach as pursuing "our own honor and our obligations to the peace of the world."[3] Whatever that meant, the United States' neutrality was rather idiosyncratic, as it tilted in favor of the Allies.[4] Part of the tilt was due to the fact that the United States was allowing private groups to lend large amounts of money to the Allied Powers to enable their purchase of munitions from US manufacturers. It was difficult to criticize these actions in the domestic political arena because, whatever their primary intention, those foreign purchases were priming the pump and thus helping to pull the United States out of a depression.[5] But these massive credits had a hook: the fear that Britain might collapse under the weight of its debt burden, lose the war, and be unable to repay, leaving American financial institutions in desperate straits. So, along with the debt, US financiers acquired a vested interest in Britain prevailing in the war.

In theory, the Central Powers could also have taken advantage of the American markets. In actuality, they could not because of the dominance of the British Navy. Britain was able to blockade all enemy travel across the Atlantic,[6] stopping and searching even US vessels for contraband. Although this violated US neutral rights and President Wilson protested,[7] British violations were overshadowed by the German response to the British blockade: submarine warfare.[8]

For Germany, submarine warfare proved a two-edged weapon. Germany was eager to stem the flow of armaments to its adversaries, but it was also keen to keep the United States out of the war for as long as possible. And, while U-boats were effective at disrupting the Allies' monopoly over surface Atlantic traffic, the use of submarine warfare increasingly provoked American opinion to favor the Allied cause. When a German U-boat sank the *Lusitania*, a British passenger ship, 1,198 people (124 of whom were US citizens) died. Popular opinion in the United States, until then neutral at best, shifted toward the Allies.[9] Wilson dispatched notes to the German government stating that the *Lusitania* incident violated universal moral law, but he stopped short of barring Americans from traveling on

[3] See *ibid.*, 35.

[4] On theories of why the United States inclined against Germany, see C. C. Tansill, *America Goes to War* (Boston, MA: Little Brown, 1938), pp. 3–15.

[5] See *ibid.*, 54–55. The US policy of allowing private US interests to sell to belligerents did not comport with the contemporaneous neutrality policies of Spain, Italy, Denmark, Sweden, Norway, and Holland, all of which restricted exports to belligerents. See *ibid.*, 37, 57. Notably, from November 1, 1916 through February 2, 1917, J. P. Morgan and others raised $822,633,000 for Britain alone. *Ibid.*, 118.

[6] See *ibid.*, 37. [7] See *ibid.*, 192–97. [8] See *ibid.*, 199.

[9] See Ambrosius, *Wilsonian Statecraft*, p. 39.

belligerent ships, a step that would have largely resolved the domestic political problem.[10]

On August 19, 1915, the Germans sank the *Arabic*, a British freighter.[11] Only two of the resulting forty-four deaths were American, but Colonel House, Wilson's advisor, urged Wilson to sever diplomatic relations with Germany.[12] Germany averted that by pledging that, henceforth, when attacking passenger ships, it would give warnings and then rescue all passengers and crew.[13] When German agents were apprehended in the United States, Washington demanded the recall of Captains Boy-Ed and von Papen[14] from the German Embassy.[15] Their arrests swung popular opinion further against Germany.

The Allies were quick to take advantage of Germany's *Arabic* pledge to warn merchant ships before attack. Defensive guns had been mounted on the decks of Allied merchant ships,[16] which, while only defensive against traditional war ships, were lethal against submarines. Thus, while the US insistence on the *Arabic* pledge seemed humanitarian and even-handed, it would have effectively protected Allied shipping from German attacks, transforming the Atlantic into an open concourse for the carriage of Allied war material.[17] To redress this imbalance, Wilson and Secretary of State Lansing requested Allied commercial ships to disarm themselves. The Allies

[10] See *ibid.*, 40, 58. Indeed, when Congress began considering such measures in February 1916, Wilson deflected it with a characteristically moral argument: such a law would cost the United States its self-respect. See *ibid.*, at 58. Secretary of State Bryan, who had supported banning US travel on belligerent ships, resigned during the "*Lusitania* crisis," "adhering to the policy of impartial neutrality." See *ibid.*, 40. Secretary Lansing, who replaced Bryan, supported a policy more favorable to the Allies. See Tansill, *America Goes to War*, p. 168. Lansing's diary entry reveals that his outlook had been colored by the *Lusitania* sinking, which convinced him that Germany was hostile to all democratic nations. Ambrosius, *Wilsonian Statecraft*, p. 41.

[11] See Ambrosius, *Wilsonian Statecraft*, p. 44. [12] *Ibid.* [13] *Ibid.*

[14] The recall of the German military attaché, Captain Franz von Papen, was of special significance in the *Sabotage Cases* due to his involvement in sabotage activities generally. One telegram from Germany, dated January 26, 1915, that had been intercepted by the British, called for the German Embassy in the United States to pursue sabotage programs in both America and Canada. At the trial before the Mixed Claims Commission, the Germans claimed this was a low-level blunder that the Ambassador ignored and that it was, in any case, contingent, only intended for use if the United States actually entered the war. See H. Manchester, "The Black Tom Case," *Harper's Mag.* (Dec. 1939), 60, 64.

[15] Tansill, *America Goes to War*, pp. 388–89. [16] See Ambrosius, *Wilsonian Statecraft*, p. 59.

[17] "In effect, American insistence that German submarines abide by the rules of cruiser warfare to avoid the loss of American lives had protected Allied shipping from this new weapon." *Ibid.*

were unreceptive, in no small part because they thought that further German attacks could push America into war on the Allied side.[18]

Colonel House eventually asked Wilson to drop his insistence that Allied merchantmen disarm as a condition for peace discussions.[19] With this obstacle removed, on February 22, 1916, the British Foreign Minister and Colonel House agreed, in essence, that if the Allies' situation worsened, the United States would convene a peace conference; if the Central Powers did not attend, the US would enter the war to further the ends of peace.[20]

On March 24, 1916, the Germans torpedoed the British passenger ship *Sussex* in violation of the *Arabic* promises.[21] Lansing pushed for severance of diplomatic relations with Germany, but American popular opinion favored the idea of a collective security peace initiative.[22] Wilson settled for securing a renewal of German promises to warn merchant and passenger ships before attacking and to rescue all survivors.[23]

In December 1916, after his reelection, Wilson asked the belligerents to list their war objectives, in the hopes of finding a common ground on which peace negotiations could begin.[24] Germany, perhaps for strategic reasons, responded positively to American overtures; the Allies outlined what amounted to a "demand for victory."[25] Wilson's response was the "peace without victory" speech before the Senate. It set out his own vision of a post-war league of nations that would ensure an American conception of a lasting peace.[26]

Ultimately, it was Germany, smarting under a regime that included an effective Allied maritime blockade, while still allowing the Allies to supply themselves from North America, that effectively ended US neutrality. It was a situation that created a war of attrition which promised to bleed the Central Powers long before it bled the Allies. In these circumstances, on

[18] See *ibid.*

[19] See *ibid.* Wilson later renewed his protests against Allied violations of US neutral shipping rights, especially after Britain published a blacklist of American firms and individuals who traded with the Central Powers, and who, as a result, were not to be permitted to trade with British nationals. See Ambrosius, *Wilsonian Statecraft*, p. 73; Tansill, *America Goes to War*, p. 535. Britain also expanded the definition of contraband and, with France, seized German nationals from US ships. Tansill, *America Goes to War*, pp. 526, 571, 576–78. These conflicts, which were never resolved, were eventually eclipsed by US entry into the war. See *ibid.*, 584.

[20] See Ambrosius, *Wilsonian Statecraft*, pp. 51–53. Before agreeing to the House–Gray memo, Wilson inserted the word "probably" to qualify the American commitment to enter the war. See *ibid.*, 54.

[21] See *ibid.*, 68. [22] See *ibid.*, 70; Tansill, *America Goes to War*, p. 493.

[23] See Ambrosius, *Wilsonian Statecraft*, p. 70. [24] See *ibid.*, 76. [25] See *ibid.*, 79.

[26] See *ibid.*, 80.

January 31, 1917, Germany announced it would commence unrestricted submarine warfare on neutral and enemy ships the following month.[27] Wilson severed diplomatic relations with Germany and on February 26 asked Congress to authorize the arming of US merchant ships.[28]

On February 24, 1917, British intelligence gave the United States the Zimmerman telegram,[29] in which Zimmerman, the German Under-Secretary of State, offered to assist Mexico in a war against the United States and suggested that Mexico should also ask Japan to join the Central Powers.[30] On March 18, 1917, news arrived of the sinking of three US merchant ships by German U-boats. Wilson requested Congress to declare war on April 2, 1917. Four days later Congress complied and open hostilities between the United States and Germany commenced.[31]

II

It was in the period of technical US neutrality but de facto Allied support that the Black Tom explosion and Kingsland fire occurred. Unable to stop the flow of material to the Allies by its submarines without bringing the United States into the war, sabotaging that material by covert action, before it was shipped, may have seemed a strategy of last resort.

Black Tom Island was a shipping and warehouse complex of the Lehigh Valley Railroad located on a peninsula that juts into New York Harbor from the Jersey shore.[32] At 2:08 a.m. on Sunday, July 30, 1916, there was an explosion on the island; the blast was fueled by one thousand tons of shells and munitions that were being stored at the pier until they could be shipped to the Allies.[33] The explosion reverberated over a 100-mile radius, including parts of New York, New Jersey, Connecticut, Pennsylvania, and Maryland.[34] Investigators later concluded that the fire that ignited the explosions may have begun as early as 12:30 a.m. in two separate places: first in a munitions car, and then shortly thereafter, on the deck of a barge tied to one of the piers.[35]

The force of the explosion shattered many windows in Jersey City and New York City.[36] The blasts incited considerable distress among the nearby populations: people ran out into the streets in their nightclothes,

[27] See *ibid.*, 82. [28] See *ibid.*, 84. [29] See *ibid.* [30] See *ibid.*, 84–85.
[31] See *ibid.*, 85–87. [32] See Manchester, "The Black Tom Case," 60. [33] See *ibid.*
[34] "Munition Explosions Cause Loss of $20,000,000; 2 Known to be Dead, Many Missing, 35 Hurt; The Harbor Raked by Shrapnel for Hours," *NY Times* (31 July 1916), 1.
[35] See Manchester, "The Black Tom Case," 61–62.
[36] "Munitions Explosions Shake New York; Wreck $7,000,000 Jersey Storage Plant; Many Killed; Alarm and Damage Here," *NY Times* (30 July 1916), 1, 2.

"thoroughly frightened and unable to contain themselves."[37] The physical damage was also quite extensive. Several warehouses in the vicinity were destroyed and many barges in the harbor were sunk. Damage was estimated at thousands of dollars and there was even concern that the downtown Manhattan financial district would not be able to open.[38]

In the initial stages of the investigation that followed, the *New York Times* reported that, "On one point the various investigating bodies agree, and that is that the fire and subsequent explosions cannot be charged to the account of alien plotters against the neutrality of the United States."[39] Indeed, the first arrests in the case were made on charges of manslaughter against the superintendent of docks and the Lehigh Valley Railroad agent for violating a law prohibiting the overnight storage of munitions at the pier.[40] Numerous suits were brought against the Lehigh Valley Railroad for deaths and injuries stemming from the explosions, embroiling the railroad in litigation for the next twenty-three years.[41]

Theories of the origin of the explosions began to change when two Norwegian workers, thought to be German sympathizers, were found to have drawings of US submarine plans. The espionage theory was nourished by reports from Seattle, Washington of German plots to destroy ships that were docking there.[42]

The investigation soon centered on Michael Kristoff, a worker at the Eagle Iron Works. His aunt,[43] with whom he lived, and her daughter (Kristoff's cousin), with whom he sometimes stayed, had gone to the police to report that Kristoff had left the cousin's home early on the night of the explosion, saying that he was going to the Iron Works to collect back pay.[44] This had struck the women as odd because payroll departments were not ordinarily open on Saturday evenings. Kristoff had returned to his aunt's home late exclaiming, "What I do? What I do?"[45] Kristoff's family further reported that they had previously seen him with drawings of bridges and

[37] See *ibid.*, 2. [38] See *ibid.* [39] "Munition Explosions," 2. [40] See *ibid.*, 1.
[41] See Manchester, "The Black Tom Case," 61.
[42] See "Held as Plotters in Black Tom Fire," *NY Times* (10 Aug. 1916), 1, 2.
[43] There is some conflict as to whether Mrs. Rushnak was Kristoff's aunt or his cousin. The *Harper Magazine* article refers to her as his "cousin." A *New York Times* article refers to Mrs. Rushnak as Mrs. Chapman's "mother." Because the Commission decisions and opinions refer to her as his "aunt," so, too, do we.
[44] See Manchester, "The Black Tom Case," 62; "Held in Explosion Case," *NY Times* (3 Sept. 1916), 11.
[45] See Manchester, "The Black Tom Case," 62; "Cousin Pointed Out Black Tom Suspect," *NY Times* (4 Sept. 1916), 14 (though the *New York Times* account quotes Kristoff as having said "What'll I do? What'll I do?").

factories.[46] The cousin claimed to have seen a letter Kristoff sent to a mysterious person named Graentnor.[47]

Kristoff admitted to the police that he had worked for a man named Graentson, who paid him $5,000 "to do something."[48] At the trial before the post-war German–US Mixed Claims Commission, the United States would later press the view that Kristoff, assisted by two other German agents, named Witzke and Jahnke, worked for Graentsor.[49] "Graentsor," "Grantnor," or "Graentnor" was supposedly an alias for Frederick Hinsch, a man known to have fled from the United States to Mexico after America entered the war to serve as a German agent there.[50]

At the time of the explosion, however, investigators did not have enough evidence to hold Kristoff. The prison doctor found Kristoff to be of low intelligence and probably incapable of planning or executing the explosion.[51] Kristoff often rambled, leading investigators to suspect that he might be insane. After his release, the Lehigh Valley Railroad hired a private detective named Kassman to pose as an anarchist and befriend Kristoff. Kassman later claimed that Kristoff admitted to him that he had played a role in the Black Tom explosion. However, the Mixed Claims Commission would dismiss this evidence as incredible given various omissions and inconsistencies in Kristoff's alleged admissions and Kassman's report of them.[52] Kristoff, for his part, worked for a while at a chocolate factory and died before the Commission heard the damages case.[53]

46 See Manchester, "The Black Tom Case," 62. 47 See *ibid.*

48 See "Held in Explosion Case," 11.

49 During the first trial before the Mixed Claims Commission, the American Agent relied on the testimony of Officer Altendorf, who had captured Witzke while acting as a secret agent. Altendorf testified that Witzke had confessed his complicity in the Black Tom explosion to Altendorf, thereby proving German involvement in the event. The Commission, however, found Altendorf to be an incredible witness. *United States ex rel. Lehigh Valley RR* v. *Germany* (Mixed Cl. Comm'n 1930) (hereinafter *1930 Hamburg Decision*) in *Mixed Claims Commission, United States and Germany, Administrative Decisions and Opinions of a General Nature and Opinions and Decisions in Certain Individual Claims From October 1, 1926, to December 31, 1932, with Orders of March 25 and May 7, 1925 and Appendices* (Washington, DC: Gov. Printing Office, 1933), pp. 849, 980–81 (hereinafter *Mixed Claims Commission, Administrative Decisions and Opinions of a General Nature*).

50 See *1930 Hamburg Decision*, p. 983; *Certificate of Disagreement and Opinion of the American Commissioner* (15 June 1939) (hereinafter *Certificate of Disagreement*) in *Mixed Claims Commission, United States and Germany, Opinions and Decisions in the Sabotage Claims Handed Down June 15, 1939, and October 30, 1939 and Appendix* (Washington, DC: Gov. Printing Office, 1939), pp. 1, 110 (hereinafter *Mixed Claims Commission, Sabotage Claims*).

51 See Dep't of State, *Press Releases* 59 (15 Nov. 1930), 325, 360. 52 See *ibid.*, 362–65.

53 See Manchester, "The Black Tom Case," 62; "Washington Loses Black Tom Claims," *NY Times* (14 Nov. 1930), 1.

The Kingsland explosion was the second instance of massive sabotage. The Canadian Car and Foundry Company, which was located seven miles west of the Hudson in the Jersey Meadows, had guarded the plant with a staff of some 200 security personnel.[54] On January 11, 1917, an explosion occurred while the munitions plant was finishing an $83,000,000 order of shells for the Russian government.[55] Because the shells did not yet have detonating fuses installed,[56] the damage caused in the radius of destruction was less than at Black Tom, though it still exceeded millions of dollars and prompted nearby populations to flee from their homes.[57] Unlike the Black Tom explosion, which killed between two and six people, no deaths were suffered at Kingsland.[58]

The fire at Kingsland which caused the explosion began at the bench of Theodore Wozniak, in Building 30, where he and others were cleaning shell cases with denatured alcohol. What followed is disputed.[59] Early affidavits from workers at the plant claimed that the fire started from a spark from a machine, or perhaps a light bulb. According to this version of events, the spark landed in a tub of alcohol at Wozniak's bench and the fire spread rapidly.[60]

Separate investigations were launched by the company and by authorities in the United States and Russia.[61] Early reports stated that the most probable cause was an accident at Wozniak's bench. The company, however, suggested from the start that the fire could have been of an incendiary origin.[62] Wozniak himself, under suspicion, vanished.[63] Later reports claimed that up to twelve workers at Kingsland were German agents, who were also responsible for several other fires in the area.[64] Speculation about sabotage was further fueled by the fact that the day after the Kingsland explosion, 200 tons of powder blew up at the DuPont factory in Haskell, New Jersey.[65]

[54] See Manchester, "The Black Tom Case," 62; "Exploding Shells Rain Four Hours; $5,000 Loss," *NY Times* (12 Jan. 1917), 1.
[55] See Manchester, "The Black Tom Case," 62. [56] See *ibid.*; "Exploding Shells," 4.
[57] See "Exploding Shells," 1, 4.
[58] See Manchester, "The Black Tom Case," 61; "Munition Explosions," 1.
[59] See text accompanying notes 93–99 below. [60] See "Exploding Shells," 1, 4.
[61] See Manchester, "The Black Tom Case," 62.
[62] "Loss at Kingsland put at $17,000,000," *NY Times* (13 Jan. 1917), 1.
[63] See Manchester, "The Black Tom Case," 63.
[64] "Find German Agents in Munition Works," *NY Times* (18 Nov. 1917), 4.
[65] See Manchester, "The Black Tom Case," 63; "Du Pont Powder Plant Explosion Rocks 4 States," *NY Times* (13 Jan. 1917), 1.

III

The Treaty of Berlin of 1921, which reestablished peace between the United States and Germany,[66] determined that all the property of the German government that had been seized by the United States during the war would be held by the United States until Germany

> made suitable provision for the satisfaction . . . of all persons, wheresoever domiciled, who owe permanent allegiance to the United States of America and who have suffered, through the acts of the Imperial German Government, or its agents, since July 31, 1914, loss, damage, or injury to their persons or property, directly or indirectly, whether through the ownership of shares of stock in German . . . American, or other corporations, or in consequence of hostilities.[67]

A Mixed Claims Commission to settle all outstanding war claims between the two countries was established by the Agreement of August 10, 1922.[68] In accordance with Article I, the Commission was to settle three categories of claims:

1 Claims of American citizens, arising since July 31, 1914, in respect of damage to, or seizure of, their property, rights and interest, including any company or association in which they are interested, within German territory as it existed on August 1, 1914.
2 Other claims for loss or damage to which the United States or its nationals have been subjected with respect to injuries to person, or to property, rights and interests, including any company or association in which American nationals are interested, since July 31, 1914, as a consequence of the war;
3 Debts owing to American citizens by the German government or by German nationals.[69]

[66] Treaty of Peace, US–F.R.G., 25 Aug. 1921, 42 Stat. 1939 (hereinafter Treaty of Berlin), reprinted in W. Kiesselbach, *Problems of the German-American Claims Commission*, E. H. Zeydel (trans.), (Washington, DC: Carnegie Endowment for International Peace, 1930), app. A, p. 129.

[67] *Ibid.* The preamble of the Treaty incorporated the above language from a Joint Resolution of Congress, which had been approved by the President on July 2, 1921.

[68] Agreement for a Mixed Commission To Determine the Amount To Be Paid by Germany in Satisfaction of Germany's Financial Obligations Under the Treaty Concluded Between the Two Governments on August 25, 1921, US–F.R.G., Aug. 10, 1922, 42 Stat. 2200 reprinted in Kiesselbach, *Problems of the German-American Claims Commission*, app. B, p. 132.

[69] *Ibid.*, art. I.

The decisions of the Commission were to be "final and binding upon the two Governments."[70] With respect to the taking of evidence, the Commission had the authority to "consider all written statements or documents which may be presented to it by or on behalf of the respective Governments."[71] This narrowly drawn grant of authority did not allow for oral examination of witnesses; that had to be authorized separately through legislation in Germany and the United States.[72]

The Agreement conferred on the Commission especially broad jurisdictional powers *ratione temporis*. The United States was able to press claims dating from the start of the war and not just from the date it had actually entered the hostilities.[73] Claims could be brought against Germany by people damaged by acts of war, regardless of whether they were caused by Germany or the Allies.[74]

The Commission, composed of two national commissioners and an umpire,[75] did not operate by majority vote.[76] Article 2 provided that the umpire would act only if the national commissioners were unable to decide a certain issue "upon any cases . . . or upon any points of difference."[77] In practice, for reasons of economy, the national commissioners regularly invited the umpire to sit with them at arguments.[78] A special rule was adopted for the hearing of the *Sabotage Cases*, where the Commission specifically authorized the umpire to sit with the national commissioners throughout oral argument.[79] At the request of the German government, the

70 *Ibid.*, art. VI. 71 *Ibid.*

72 See C. P. Anderson, *Report of American Commissioner: Mixed Claims Commission United States and Germany* (Washington, DC: Gov. Printing Office, 1933), pp. 9–11. Germany passed a statute in 1923 that allowed German representatives of the Commission to file for subpoenas in German courts. In 1930, the US Congress passed a statute allowing international tribunals to issue subpoenas according to their own internal procedures. This presupposed that a tribunal had such competence whereupon US courts would assist. In the case of the German–US Commission, it proved ineffective because the German government refused to agree that the Commission itself had any inherent subpoena powers. Finally, Congress, in direct response to the *Sabotage Cases*, authorized the American Agent to subpoena witnesses without formal Commission action. *Ibid.*

73 See Kiesselbach, *Problems of the German-American Claims Commission*, pp. 33–34.

74 Agreement for a Mixed Commission, art. 1(2); see also E. M. Borchard, "The Opinions of the Mixed Claims Commission, United States and Germany," *Am. J. Int'l L.*, 19 (1925), 133, at 133–34.

75 See Agreement for a Mixed Commission, art. II.

76 See S. M. Schwebel, *International Arbitration: Three Salient Problems* (Cambridge University Press, 1987), p. 217.

77 See *ibid.*, 216–17. 78 See *ibid.*

79 See "Special Rules of March 20, 1929" in H. H. Martin, *Final Report of H. H. Martin Acting Agent of the United States Before the Mixed Claims Commission United States and Germany*

umpire was an American selected by the President of the United States.[80] Each government designated a national agent, who presented the cases before the Commission[81] with the assistance of counsel as necessary.

In order to deal with the large number of cases pending before it, some 20,433 claims,[82] the Commission adopted another economizing approach. It grouped similar cases in a category to which certain general rules would then be applied,[83] whereupon the national agents would decide the specific cases within that category, applying to the Commission for *pro forma* approval of their agreements.[84] Only when the agents disagreed, would formal adjudication take place with the agents prosecuting the individual claims.[85]

The professional quality of the personnel of this Mixed Claims Commission was high. The first umpire was Justice Day of the United States Supreme Court, who served for the first several months of the Commission's existence. After retiring for health reasons in the spring of 1923, he was replaced by the then American Commissioner, Judge Edwin B. Parker.[86] After Judge Parker's death in 1929, which occurred after the first arguments of the *Sabotage Cases*, Roland W. Boyden became umpire in January 1930. After his death in October 1931, Justice Owen Roberts of the United States Supreme Court was appointed umpire, in March 1932.[87]

(Washington, DC: Gov. Printing Office, 1941), p. 101; see also Schwebel, *International Arbitration*, app. II, p. 220.

80 See Schwebel, *International Arbitration*, p. 217. Schwebel notes that while this was rare, it was not unprecedented. *Ibid.*, n. 222.

81 Agreement for a Mixed Commission, art. VI.

82 Martin, *Final Report of H. H. Martin*, p. 94.

83 See K. S. Carlston, *The Process of International Arbitration* (Columbia University Press, 1946), p. 17. For example, one administrative ruling governed all of the claims brought under the sinking of the *Lusitania*. See Anderson, *Report of American Commissioner*, p. 6.

84 See Carlston, *The Process of International Arbitration*, p. 17.

85 *Ibid.*, 21; see Kiesselbach, *Problems of the German-American Claims Commission*, pp. 17, 21.

86 See *ibid.*, 8.

87 See *Mixed Claims Commission, Administrative Decisions and Opinions of a General Nature*, p. II. The first American Commissioner, Judge Parker, was followed by Chandler P. Anderson. See Kiesselbach, *Problems of the German-American Claims Commission*, p. 8. Upon Anderson's death, on August 2, 1936, the President appointed Christopher B. Garnett to replace him. See Martin, *Final Report of H. H. Martin*, p. II. The German Commissioner was initially Dr. Wilhelm Kiesselbach, who later resigned and was replaced by Dr. Victor L. F. H. Huecking, who "retired," as we will see, on March 1, 1939, in protest over the Commission's decision to reconsider the *Sabotage Cases*. See *ibid.* The first American Agent was Robert R. Morris, but Robert W. Bonynge was the Agent during most of the litigation of the *Sabotage Cases*. He served until his death on September 22, 1939 (about one month before the final decision in the *Sabotage Cases*). See Kiesselbach, *Problems of the German-American Claims Commission*, p. 10; Martin, *Final Report of H. H. Martin*,

Justices Day and Roberts and Judge Parker came to the Commission with substantial judicial experience. Judge Parker was praised for his "high degree of conscientiousness, impartiality and learning."[88] Yale Professor Edwin Borchard, who was actively involved in the litigation, observed that "[t]he skill with which his judicial duties have been performed commands respect and admiration and reflects credit upon . . . the institution of international arbitration."[89]

In addition to the quality of its personnel, the German–US Mixed Claims Commission differed in two other ways from other international tribunals that operated during the post-World War I era: first, the absence of neutral commissioners and, second, as mentioned earlier, a decisionmaking procedure that proceeded first by consensus, and only if it failed, by referral to the umpire.[90] The Mixed Claims Commission was also distinctive

pp. II–III. His assistant, H. H. Martin, then succeeded him. Martin, *Final Report of H.H. Martin*, p. II. Karl von Lewinski served as the German Agent. Kiesselbach, *Problems of the German-American Claims Commission*, p. 10. From October 1925, von Lewinski was assisted by Dr. W. Tannenberg, who later replaced him as the German Agent for much of the early stages of the *Sabotage Cases*. *Ibid.* An American, Thomas J. Healy, also assisted the German Agent. *Ibid.*, 11. Dr. Tannenberg was subsequently replaced by Dr. Lohmann in May 1933, who was replaced on May 16, 1934 by Richard Paulig. Martin, *Final Report of H. H. Martin*, p. II; *Mixed Claims Commission, Administrative Decisions and Opinions of a General Nature*, p. II.

88 E. M. Borchard, "Opinions of the Mixed Claims Commission, United States and Germany (Part II)," *Am. J. Int'l L.*, 20 (1926), 69, 80.

89 *Ibid.* The respective agents appointed by the two governments were of a comparable quality. The first American agent, Robert Morris, was a lawyer from New York and had been a member of the American–Venezuelan Commission. See Kiesselbach, *Problems of the German-American Claims Commission*, p. 11. His successor, Robert Bonynge, was also a New York lawyer. *Ibid.*, 10. Von Lewinski, the German Agent, had been the Privy Councilor of Justice and Legation and his successor, Dr. Tannenberg, had worked and trained with him on the Commission from October 1925. *Ibid.* This is in stark contrast to the Greco-Bulgarian and Greco-Turkish Mixed Commissions, whose neutral members were described as being borderline incompetent for the tasks with which they were confronted. See S. P. Ladas, *The Exchange of Minorities: Bulgaria, Greece and Turkey* (New York: Macmillan, 1932), pp. 52, 359.

90 See text accompanying notes 82–85 above. This was in contrast to the Greco-Bulgarian Mixed Commission, which decided issues by majority vote, having one member from each country, and two neutral members chosen by the Council of the League of Nations. See Ladas, *The Exchange of Minorities*, pp. 50, 60. Likewise, the Greco-Turkish Mixed Commission consisted of eleven members: four from each country, and three neutral members (a minority) chosen by the Council of the League of Nations. *Ibid.*, 353. They, too, were to decide issues by majority vote, but in practice, the neutral members insisted that all major decisions be unanimous, *ibid.*, 359, effectively depriving the neutral members of influence and paralyzing the Commission. The Mixed Arbitral Tribunals established to settle claims between Britain, Austria, Hungary, and Bulgaria generally consisted of a representative from each country, who selected a neutral third member as president; all

in its innovative use of administrative rulings to segregate claims into groups.[91]

decisions were decided by majority vote. See H. L. Hart, *The Mixed Arbitral Tribunals: An Experiment in Legal Procedure* (London and New York: Sir I. Pitman & Sons, 1932), p. 14.

91 The Greco-Bulgarian and Greco-Turkish Mixed Commissions generally employed three-member subcommissions to make initial determinations in the large numbers of cases, with a right of appeal or possible referral to the full Commission, respectively. Ladas, *The Exchange of Minorities*, pp. 65–73, 369–71. The Mixed Arbitral Tribunals often filtered claims through Clearing Offices in each country. If the Clearing Office could not settle the claim, it was referred to the Tribunal, which employed a streamlined pleading process. Hart, *The Mixed Arbitral Tribunals*, pp. 6–7, 15. This structure bore some similarity to the German–US Mixed Claims Commission in that these Clearing Offices functioned as mechanisms for reducing the caseload of the Tribunal. But the Mixed Claims Commission was viewed as taking this process one step further, actually grouping cases to speed the adjudication of masses of similar claims. Carlston, *The Process of International Arbitration*, pp. 15–17. The jurisdiction of the Mixed Claims Commission was somewhat similar to the Mixed Arbitral Tribunals in that both primarily focused on claims for contract and compensatory damages. Hart, *The Mixed Arbitral Tribunals*, p. 5. This similarity, however, did not hold for the Greco-Bulgarian and Greco-Turkish Commissions, which exercised what was in different ways both a broader and a more restricted authority legislatively, administratively, and judicially. These Commissions were more restricted in that they were charged primarily with the overseeing of the migration of minority populations across political borders. However, within this narrow category their authority was broader in that they directly supervised and facilitated the movement of these groups, and provided for the liquidation of their immovable properties. Ladas, *The Exchange of Minorities*, pp. 30, 353. In contrast, the German–US Mixed Claims Commission was primarily limited to the adjudication of damage claims stemming from the war.

Of course, one of the most central distinctions centers on the eventual success of the Mixed Claims Commission. Overall, the Commission was quite efficient at processing the 20,433 cases before it. Martin, *Final Report of H. H. Martin*, p. 94. Initially, the Commission had slightly over 12,000 claims. Carlston, *The Process of International Arbitration*, p. 15 n. 6. Awards were granted in 6,187 instances, totaling $186,813,901.56. *Ibid.* By agreement, on December 31, 1928, Germany and the United States decided that the Commission would hear additional claims brought on or before June 30, 1928, raising the total number of cases under consideration to 20,433, while excluding approximately 3,233 late claims totaling some $7,207,030. Martin, *Final Report of H. H. Martin*, pp. 96–97. Of these, only 154 cases were pending as of December 31, 1934; 153 of which were the claims under the *Sabotage Cases*. *Ibid.*, 4. Total amounts paid out by January 10, 1941 were $159,384,306.21. *Ibid.*, 93. The German government stopped paying on its bonds as of March 31, 1931, leaving it $109,340,000 in arrears by September 30, 1940. *Ibid.*, 95.

The total costs of the Commission through July 1, 1940 were valued at $1,486,000, a cost of $290 per day of work. *Ibid.*, 94. This resulted in a cost of just over four-tenths of one cent for each dollar the Commission awarded. *Ibid.* In contrast, the British–German Clearing Office processed 382,464 claims, about 10,000 of which were considered before the Mixed Arbitral Tribunal. Carlston, *The Process of International Arbitration*, p. 15 n. 6. £86,290,555 was paid on 78,378 claims. Hart, *The Mixed Arbitral Tribunals*, p. 8. By July 1931, the Greco-Bulgarian Mixed Commission had been presented with 138,000 claims, and created 48,000 files. The Mixed Commission examined 38,737 of these, and

The *Sabotage Cases* were argued six times for a total of sixty days, with over 50,000 pages of evidence. The United States submitted forty-one briefs, while Germany submitted thirty-four.[92]

IV

In the initial phase of the case, the United States alleged that eight men – Wozniak, Rodriguez, Witzke, Jahnke, Hinsch, Herrmann, Hilken (indirectly), and Thorne – had been involved in planning and executing the explosion at Kingsland.[93] It was clear that the fire had started at Wozniak's workbench, but it was unclear exactly how it had begun.

Herrmann and Hilken were two German agents who had planned German sabotage activities elsewhere in the United States. They initially claimed to know nothing about the explosion at Kingsland. But they later changed their testimony before the Commission and claimed that Herrmann had told Hilken that he had hired Wozniak and Rodriguez to destroy Kingsland by using incendiary "pencils" that contained flammable chemicals. Herrmann also claimed that Captain Hinsch had recommended both Wozniak and Rodriguez to execute the Kingsland fire. Charles Thorne, in the personnel department at Kingsland, corroborated Herrmann's story, testifying that he had, in fact, hired at least Rodriguez on Hinsch's orders.[94]

But the Commission branded both Herrmann and Hilken "liars" and discounted much of their testimony;[95] it also found Thorne's testimony incredible.[96] The Commission was skeptical of Herrmann's claim that Wozniak had fled to Mexico after the explosion, which the Commission found unlikely, given Herrmann's description of his casual encounter with him there, and the lack of more substantive evidence linking Wozniak to Mexico.[97]

approved 34,298 liquidations. Ladas, *The Exchange of Minorities*, p. 286. The liquidations were often long after the fact, and only 10 percent of the award was paid in cash, the rest in bonds that depreciated up to 30–50 percent of their face value. *Ibid.*, 47, 720. In 1927, the final balance of payment estimates were $22 million for Greece, and $15 million for Bulgaria. *Ibid.*, 322.

92 L. H. Woolsey, "The Arbitration of the Sabotage Claims Against Germany," *Am. J. Int'l L.*, 33 (1939), 737, 737.

93 See *1930 Hamburg Decision*, p. 970–71.

94 *Ibid.*, 973–74; see also Manchester, "Black Tom Case," 63.

95 See *1930 Hamburg Decision*, pp. 971–73.

96 See *ibid.*, 974; *Certificate of Disagreement*, pp. 115–18.

97 See *1930 Hamburg Decision*, p. 975. Later, during motions to reopen the case, the German government would contend that during the period in question, Wozniak was not in

Based on other testimony that sparks were coming from Wozniak's machine shortly before the explosion, and on the affidavits of other workers near him, the Commission concluded that Wozniak could not have been responsible for the fire. (This was despite the fact that Wozniak's own description of his actions was consistent with the use of the incendiary pencils to start the explosion.[98]) The Commission reasoned that if Wozniak had been the real culprit, he would not have placed himself in such a compromising position.[99]

The Commission also absolved Germany of blame in the Black Tom explosion. Ultimately, the Commission rejected the American Agent's theory that there was more than one fire, which would have suggested sabotage, and instead found the German Agent's theory that the fire was the result of spontaneous combustion quite plausible.[100] The chief suspects in the *Black Tom* case were Kristoff, Witzke, and Jahnke. Witzke was a proven German operative, who had been captured by a double agent named Paul Altendorf. Altendorf testified that Witzke had confessed to destroying Black Tom during their travels together in Mexico. But the Commission dismissed Altendorf's testimony as coming from "the chief liar who has appeared in the cases before us, a chief among competitors of no mean qualifications" (presumably referring primarily to the US witnesses, Herrmann and Hilken).[101] Germany, meanwhile, produced evidence showing that Witzke had been applying for US citizenship in San Francisco just prior to the accident, where Jahnke was also employed as a security guard at a bank.[102] Based on that evidence, the Commission eliminated the possibility of either Witzke's or Jahnke's active role in the fire.

The connection with Kristoff seemed similarly tenuous. The theory alleged was that the elusive Grantnor, Graentnor, or Grantsor was Kristoff's connection to the German sabotage operations.[103] Herrmann had claimed that "Grantnor" was an alias for Hinsch, but there was little to verify that claim and Herrmann was already considered to be a "wholly unreliable" witness.[104] Moreover, as the Commission noted, the police had released

Mexico, but rather at Tupper Lake, New York working in the timber industry. See "American Brief for Washington Argument of Nov. 1932" in *United States ex rel. Lehigh Valley RR* v. *Germany* (Mixed Cl. Comm'n 18 Nov. 1932) (No. 8103), pp. 75–78.

98 *1930 Hamburg Decision*, p. 976. 99 *Ibid.*, 977. 100 *Ibid.*, 979–80. 101 *Ibid.*, 981.

102 *Ibid.*; "Brief for Claimant" in *United States ex rel. Lehigh Valley RR* v. *Germany* (Mixed Cl. Comm'n 21 May 1928) (No. 8103), pp. 13–14; "Final Brief for the Underwriters" in *United States ex rel. Lehigh Valley RR* v. *Germany* (Mixed Cl. Comm'n 22 Mar. 1930) (No. 8103), pp. 64–67.

103 See *1930 Hamburg Decision*, p. 983. 104 *Ibid.*, 992.

Kristoff for lack of evidence, and the evidence of a detective named Kassman (hired by the Lehigh Valley Railroad to investigate Kristoff) was found unpersuasive.[105]

As for Hinsch, the Commission found it even more unlikely that he had been involved (under the alias Grantnor or otherwise), given his statements that he had ceased all sabotage activities when he began working on the commercial U–boat service[106] which had been established to transport goods from the United States to Germany as the means of evading the British blockade.

The Commission concluded:

> We cannot be sure that Kristoff did not set fire to Black Tom or take some part in so doing. We cannot be sure that Graentsor, or Grantnor, or Graentnor was not Hinsch, and that Hinsch did not employ Kristoff and others who are unknown. But it will sufficiently appear from the foregoing that, as we have said, the evidence falls far short of enabling us to reach the point, not merely of holding Germany responsible for the fire, but of thinking that her agents must have been the cause, even though the proof is lacking.[107]

Thus the first decision of the Commission, rendered by Umpire Boyden at Hamburg on October 16, 1930, dismissed the claims of the United States. While recognizing that there had been orders for general sabotage programs within the United States, the Commission found plausible the German Agent's theory that the German embassy had declined to pursue these orders.[108]

What is striking in this first phase of the case was the Commission's conclusion that witnesses for both parties were perjuring themselves. The Commission seemed to have taken for granted that it would simply have to work its way through the tissue of lies, woven by each of the parties, in order to reach the truth.

V

The American Agent filed several petitions for rehearing. The first, contending that the Commission had "misapprehended the facts and committed errors of law," was dismissed on March 30, 1931.[109] On the

[105] See *ibid.*, 984, 986–90; see also notes 52–53 above and accompanying text.
[106] *Ibid.*, 993. [107] *Ibid.*, 994. [108] *Ibid.*, 969.
[109] D. V. Sandifer, *Evidence Before International Tribunals*, rev. edn. (University Press of Virginia, 1975), p. 409; L. H. Woolsey, "The Sabotage Claims Against Germany," *Am. J. Int'l L.*, 34 (1940), 23, 27.

same day, the Commission issued a letter requesting the national Agents to brief the issue of whether the Commission had the jurisdiction to reopen the case for the admission of new evidence and, if so, what types of new evidence could be admitted.[110] This issue was briefed and the American Agent submitted a further petition for rehearing based on newly discovered evidence.

The new evidence consisted of: (1) affidavits purporting to show that Wozniak was a German agent; (2) certain letters written by Wozniak (under the name of Karowski) from St. Louis and Mexico City in August and September of 1917; (3) the infamous Herrmann Message; and (4) Hilken's diary and checkbook.[111]

The Commission was wary of this new evidence. A man named Baran had produced the Wozniak letters and sold them to the Canadian Car and Foundry Co. for $2,500. Umpire Roberts found the letters to be artificially aged and therefore of little value.[112] The Herrmann Message, which was presented as a major discovery and a virtual "smoking gun," was written with lemon juice in a *Blue Book* magazine dated January 1917. Allegedly, Herrmann wrote the message and had a man named Gerdts deliver it to Hilken in Baltimore.[113] The Commission agreed that if it were authentic, the message would show that: (1) Herrmann and Hilken knew that German agents were responsible for the Kingsland and Black Tom explosions (thus substantiating their previous testimony before the Commission); (2) Hinsch, Hilken, and Herrmann were German agents who were "privy thereto" (thereby discrediting Hinsch's earlier disavowals of his knowledge or participation in the plots); and (3) Kristoff and Wozniak had actively participated in these events.[114] But the Commission, recalling that Herrmann was a liar, concluded that the message said far too much about activities that these agents and operatives would have wanted to keep secret.[115] The Commission also noted the circumstances surrounding the "discovery" of the Herrmann Message – apparently, Hilken propitiously found the message, along with some other letters and correspondence, in the eaves of his attic around Christmas, 1930.[116]

[110] Sandifer, *Evidence Before International Tribunals*, p. 409.

[111] *Decision of the Commission Rendered by the Umpire, Honorable Owen J. Roberts* (3 Dec. 1932) in *Mixed Claims Commission, Administrative Decisions and Opinions of a General Nature*, pp. 1004, 1007, 1014 (hereinafter *1932 Decision of the Commission*).

[112] *Ibid.*, 1009–11. [113] *Ibid.*, 1019–21. [114] *Ibid.*, 1016. [115] *Ibid.*, 1020–24.

[116] *Ibid.*, 1018–19. The diary and checkbook were discounted as inconclusive. See *ibid.*, 1026–27.

With the two national commissioners unable to agree, Umpire Roberts dismissed the petition on December 3, 1932, finding that the new evidence would not be sufficient to reverse the Commission's original opinion. He therefore found it unnecessary to rule on the question of whether the Commission had the jurisdiction to allow the new evidence in the first place.[117]

On May 4, 1933, the American Agent filed another petition for rehearing, claiming: (1) certain witnesses for Germany had given fraudulent evidence and had colluded; (2) some of these witnesses were within the United States' jurisdiction, but could not be recalled without subpoenas; (3) Germany had misled the Commission; and (4) there was evidence of serious collusion between German and American witnesses.[118] In seeking to reopen the case on these grounds, the American Agent did not have an easy task. The prior case of *Philadelphia–Girard National Bank* presented a formidable obstacle, as it held that even when newly submitted evidence demonstrated that the underlying facts were not as the Commission had presumed, the Commission could not reopen the case.[119]

This time, however, the Commission granted the American Agent's petition and agreed, on December 15, 1933, to reopen the case. Due to a disagreement among the commissioners, Justice Roberts, as Umpire, rendered the Commission's decision, stating that, in reaching his decision, he had not considered the new evidence of fraud that had been filed since the last petition for rehearing.[120] After dealing with certain procedural issues, Justice Roberts turned to whether the Commission had the power to determine its own jurisdiction and, if so, whether it had the ability to reopen a case to admit evidence showing that the Commission had been deceived by submission of fraudulent evidence. The Umpire found that the Commission had the power to define the extent of its own jurisdiction because the Agreement of August 10, 1922 required the Commission to determine which claims it was entitled to hear, and both the United

[117] Sandifer, *Evidence Before International Tribunals*, pp. 409–10.

[118] See *Decision of the Commission* (15 Dec. 1933) in *Mixed Claims Commission: United States and Germany: Decisions and Opinions from January 1, 1933 to October 30, 1939 (Excepting Decisions in the Sabotage Claims of June 15, and October 30, 1939)* (Washington, DC: Gov. Printing Office, 1940), pp. 1115, 1118–19 (hereinafter *1933 Commission Decision*).

[119] *United States ex rel. Phila.–Girard Nat'l Bank* v. *Germany* in *Mixed Claims Commission, Administrative Decisions and Opinions of a General Nature*, pp. 939, 940; see also Sandifer, *Evidence Before International Tribunals*, p. 413.

[120] *1933 Commission Decision*, p. 1120.

States and Germany had agreed to accept such determinations as final and binding.[121] Thus, according to Justice Roberts, the internal procedures of the Commission were left to the Commission itself to define.[122]

But did the Commission have the power to reopen this case? The American Agent had argued that the case could be reopened because all of the claims before the Commission were actually multiple counts of a single suit. As the single case had yet to be closed, the question of whether it could be reopened did not even arise.[123] Germany contended that each claim was an individual case and a decision was final and binding on the parties when reached; thus it was impermissible to reopen any case in which the Commission had rendered an official opinion.[124]

Striking a middle ground, the Umpire held that the Commission was a continuing tribunal which heard discrete cases.[125] While recognizing that Article VI of the Agreement required that the decisions of the Commission be accepted as binding, it was left to the Commission to determine when its decision on a given claim was final.[126] Justice Roberts held that where the Commission had misinterpreted the evidence or made a mistake of fact or law, the Commission was under a duty to revise its decision – but it could not reopen a case for after-discovered evidence.[127] Although the Commission had been exceptionally lenient in closing the record, never having done so over the objection of either of the parties,[128] it would strain the bounds of reasonableness, the Umpire concluded, for the Commission to rehear a case simply for the American Agent to add new evidence to the record so as to persuade the Commission to reverse its prior ruling.[129]

But that did not mean that the Commission lacked the authority to reopen a case when it had been misled by the fraud and collusion of witnesses.[130] "Every tribunal has inherent power to reopen and to revise a decision induced by fraud," the Umpire stated.[131] "If it may correct its own errors and mistakes, *a fortiori* it may, while it still has jurisdiction of a cause, correct an error into which it has been led by fraud and collusion."[132] Accordingly, the Umpire ordered the case reopened in order to determine whether the American Commissioner's proof of deception, which had yet to be examined, proved that the Commission had relied on fraudulent evidence in reaching its initial decision.[133]

121 *Ibid.*, 1121–22. 122 *Ibid.* 123 *Ibid.*, 1122–23. 124 *Ibid.*, 1123.
125 *Ibid.*, 1123–24. 126 *Ibid.*, 1124. 127 *Ibid.*, 1124–25. 128 *Ibid.*, 1126.
129 *Ibid.*, 1127. 130 *Ibid.* 131 *Ibid.* 132 *Ibid.*, 1127–28. 133 *Ibid.*

Another long period of briefing, submission of evidence, and hearings followed.[134] This second phase of the *Sabotage Cases* revealed the extent to which fraudulent evidence had permeated the initial presentation of the cases. Ultimately, the Commission set aside its prior decision of October 16, 1930 and held Germany liable for the sabotage. Because the German Commissioner resigned in 1939, scarcely two weeks after the Commission had begun its final deliberations, the Umpire treated the case as a disagreement between the two national commissioners (who had been present for the presentation of all the evidence on which the decision was based) and rendered a short final opinion. He concurred with the American Commissioner's Certificate of Disagreement[135] which detailed the many frauds allegedly perpetrated against the Commission in the first proceeding. We will consider these incidents (or allegations) of fraud in some detail.

VI

In his *Certificate of Disagreement*, the American Commissioner accepted, as a starting premise, that the Imperial German government had authorized a sabotage campaign before the United States ever entered the war[136] and rejected the German explanation that any acts of sabotage were simply mistakes made by low-level members of the General Staff.[137] The American Commissioner then proceeded to review the evidence that had been presented in the initial phase of the case in light of later-discovered circumstances which cast much of that evidence into question.

134 Meanwhile, in the course of negotiating the Munich Agreement of July 1936, Germany offered to pay 50 percent of the principal, plus 5 percent interest, of the damages claimed from the two disasters. See Martin, *Final Report of H. H. Martin*, pp. 14, 30. The United States agreed in principle; all that remained was formal submission of the papers to the Commission. But protests were lodged by the award-creditors in sixty-five previous awards of the Commission (and three German nationals), *Ibid.*, 30–33, because the settlement proposal would have left insufficient funds in the Special Deposit Account at the US Treasury to pay all the claims. *Ibid.*, 32. For his part, the German Agent refused to sign the settlement documents because the agreement would no longer settle all outstanding liabilities. *Ibid.*, 36. Litigation eventually resumed and the Commission dismissed the US motions to enforce the Munich agreement on July 7, 1937. *Ibid.*, 44.

135 See *Decision of Commission Rendered by the Umpire* (15 June 1939) in *Mixed Claims Commission, Sabotage Claims*, p. 310; see also Schwebel, *International Arbitration*, p. 221. The German government contended that this vacancy made the Commission incompetent to decide the *Sabotage* claims. *Mixed Claims Commission, Sabotage Claims*, app., p. XIV.

136 *Certificate of Disagreement*, pp. 21–37.

137 "Oral Arguments" in *United States ex rel. Lehigh Valley RR* v. *Germany* (24 Sept. 1930) (No. 8103), pp. 202, 210–11; *Certificate of Disagreement*, pp. 21–37.

The Wozniak testimony

The Commissioner first considered the circumstances surrounding Wozniak's testimony, particularly, his compensation from the German government. Germany had paid Wozniak $450 for his two affidavits of April 24, 1929. Wozniak was then paid $500 in July 1930, $350 in September 1930 (for The Hague arguments), $200 when the German Agent returned from The Hague, and another $535 in April 1931.[138] This was in addition to $1,000 that Germany paid to secure his release from a criminal charge.[139] These payments were viewed as a response to a letter Wozniak had sent to the German Agent, Dr. Tannenberg, on October 26, 1929, demanding compensation for testimony favorable to the German case.[140]

The German Agent was suspected of a central role in this compensation scheme because his earlier statements to the Commission had described how Wozniak was to be compensated for reasonable expenses incurred in testifying.[141] The suggestion that these payments were limited to "reasonable expenses" was undermined by Wozniak's later testimony under subpoena, in August and September of 1933, that Tannenberg's assistant, Mr. Healy, had written to him, explaining that he was only to be compensated for his time and expenses. Wozniak, displeased, claimed that he then wrote to Tannenberg. Soon after the June examination, a letter of July 15, 1929 from Dr. Tannenberg was entered into evidence. There, Tannenberg assured Wozniak that Healy was not speaking for the German government, leading Wozniak to believe that additional payments could be arranged.[142]

There were other indicia that Germany had bought Wozniak's initial testimony. In 1932, Dr. Tannenberg informed the Commission that after Wozniak had submitted his initial evidence, he (Wozniak) had left New York for parts unknown, only returning in 1930.[143] Tannenberg volunteered that Wozniak had begun demanding more money from the German government in 1931, suggesting that these demands had just begun. The German Agent stated that after these demands, he "broke off [his] relations with Wozniak and ha[d] not seen him since."[144] Because of Wozniak's "new" demands, the German Agent indicated that Germany would oppose any future oral examination of Wozniak before the Commission, insinuating that any such testimony would likely have been bought by the claimants.[145]

[138] *Certificate of Disagreement*, p. 41. [139] *Ibid.* [140] *Ibid.*, 43. [141] *Ibid.*, 40.
[142] *Ibid.*, 40–42. [143] *Ibid.*, 43. [144] *Ibid.*, 61. [145] *Ibid.*, 62.

But the letters and communications later entered into the record showed that Dr. Tannenberg had in fact been communicating with Wozniak during this entire period. The letters demonstrated, at the least, a lack of candor toward the Commission and lent credence to the theory that it was Wozniak's initial testimony that had been bought outright.[146] This position was further bolstered by letters from Wozniak to Franz von Papen, the German Chancellor, which were returned, stating that Tannenberg and Dr. von Lewinski before him had offered to pay him for false testimony, especially if Germany won the case.[147]

That could explain why Wozniak changed his story after the initial October 1930 decision. He had previously denied having any role in the fire, denied that he was connected with any German agents, denied knowing Herrmann or Hinsch, and denied ever having any incendiary pencils.[148] After the October 1930 decision, Wozniak reversed himself on every one of these points, saying that he had met with and been paid by German agents.[149] In an examination before the Department of Justice, Wozniak admitted to knowing Hinsch. Before the Immigration and Naturalization Service, Wozniak admitted that he had met Herrmann while he was working at Kingsland.[150]

The American Commissioner also considered letters Wozniak had sent to the Russian embassy shortly before the Kingsland fire, in which Wozniak warned the Russians of dangerous conditions at the factories, which were, at the time, completing a major ammunitions order for that country.[151] This testimony had earlier been discounted as innocent or patriotic but, in light of the other revelations, was now taken as evidence of his involvement.[152]

The American Commissioner did not consider the letters that Wozniak supposedly sent from Mexico.[153] And for good reason! The American Agent had contended in his briefs that these letters, discovered in May 1931, discredited the German theory that Wozniak was at Tupper Lake, and showed instead that Wozniak had fled to Mexico in 1917, where he was generally known as a German agent.[154] The letters, purporting to

[146] *Ibid.*, 46–47. "If there was any decline in Wozniak's character which made him unfit as a witness, that decline began before Dr. Tannenberg's letter of July 15, 1929, and it continued on a fast-sliding scale following subsequent payments to Wozniak, all of which were known to the German Agent and not only concealed from the Commission but were the subject of misrepresentation at the 1932 Washington argument." *Ibid.*, 47–48.

[147] *Ibid.*, 48. [148] *Ibid.*, 53. [149] *Ibid.*, 53–54. [150] *Ibid.*, 54. [151] *Ibid.*, 51.

[152] *Ibid.*, 53. [153] *Ibid.*, 306.

[154] "American Brief for Washington Argument," pp. 75–78.

be from Wozniak to Baran and others, were sent while Wozniak was en route to Mexico. But apparently Baran had forged these letters to support the US theory and had then sold them to the Canadian Car and Foundry Co. for $2,500.[155] The forgery was discovered through the examination of the watermark on the paper, which was not used by that stationery company until 1926, and through stains on the letters, which had been added to give the appearance of age.[156] Neither side in the *Sabotage Cases*, it appears, was innocent of the taint of false evidence, though the level of responsibility at which the fraud was initiated, designed, or endorsed may have varied.[157] Certainly, the German Agent seemed directly implicated while it was arguable that the American claimants may have been victims of unscrupulous witnesses.

The Lyndhurst testimony

The so-called Lyndhurst testimony consisted of the affidavits of several workers at the Kingsland plant, who had observed the events leading up to the fire at Wozniak's workstation. Some of these affidavits stated, as the German Agent emphasized, that the machines in the factory sparked frequently and that it was a source of general concern among the workers. In arguments leading up to the October 1930 decision, the German Agent had argued persuasively that these sparks, not an incendiary pencil, could have started the fire.[158] Yet several of these affiants later changed their stories.

Domenico LaScola, a worker near Wozniak at the time of the fire, had submitted an affidavit that described sparks from the machine landing on Wozniak's table and his attempt to extinguish them with benzene-soaked rags.[159] But on April 26, 1933, a new affidavit was taken from LaScola, calling into question his prior testimony. In the new affidavit, he stated that Healy, an assistant to Tannenberg, had come to his house at night

155 *1932 Decision of the Commission*, pp. 1009–10. 156 *Ibid.*, 1009–13.

157 Aside from the Wozniak letters, the German Agent had tried to impeach other evidence that Wozniak was in Mexico. Prior to the October 1930 decision, the German Agent had proposed evidence purporting to show that Wozniak was in New York in late July and early November 1917. "Oral Arguments," pp. 354–62. Yet the two witnesses who identified Wozniak in Mexico placed him there in early August and November, respectively. Given the distance and travel time, the German Agent argued it was impossible for Wozniak to have been in Mexico at the relevant time. *Ibid.*, 358–62. None of these arguments were persuasive to the American Commissioner.

158 *Ibid.*, 326–45. 159 *Certificate of Disagreement*, p. 65.

with a translator (LaScola only spoke Italian) to ask him about the fire.[160] He said that later that night, at about 11 p.m., Healy returned and paid him $50. The next night, LaScola signed the affidavit, which he could not read because it was written in English. He stated, for his efforts, he was then paid an additional $100 in irregular installments over the next six months.[161]

In his new affidavit, LaScola testified that he had worked in that particular building of the Kingsland Plant (Building No. 30) for six months and had never seen any fires started by sparks or otherwise. He said that he had never claimed that the machine threw sparks and that he had not actually seen the fire start. He only became aware of the situation when he saw Wozniak trying to put out the small fire with a benzene-soaked rag.[162]

Another affidavit, by a worker named Ruggiero, had described the unsafe working conditions at Kingsland, which, he stated, led him to quit in December 1916. But the company payrolls showed that he had actually not worked there since August 26, 1916, calling into question the validity of his testimony about safety practices at the plant.[163]

An affidavit submitted by Urciuoli was also called into question. The factory had employed Urciuoli to take care of all the machines and to ensure that they did not throw any sparks. He had testified to having had to put out several sparks with his overcoat while in Building No. 30.[164] Later evidence demonstrated that Urciuoli had not been in the building for the entire week preceding the explosion and that he was attending his father's funeral at the time of the fire.[165]

The credibility of both Urciuoli and Ruggiero was further called into question by the testimony of the notary public who had executed their affidavits. The notary stated that he had heard that both men had been paid large sums of money for their testimony and that three people giving affidavits for the German government had told him that they also had received money for their affidavits.[166]

Another Lyndhurst witness, Victor Frangipane, testified that he was paid $50 for his statement, another $50 for his signature, and had received a

[160] *Ibid.*, 66. Healy later stated that he was told that the claimants were pressuring these witnesses to change their stories, and as a result, paid them additional sums of money to prevent this from happening. *Ibid.*, 71.

[161] *Ibid.*, 66. [162] *Ibid.*, 66–67. [163] *Ibid.*, 67. [164] *Ibid.*, 68–69.

[165] *Ibid.*, 69; "A Brief of the American Agent Supplementing the Oral Argument had at Boston, Mass., July 30–Aug. 1, 1931" in *United States ex rel. Lehigh Valley RR* v. *Germany* (Mixed Cl. Comm'n 15 Sept. 1931) (No. 8102), p. 6.

[166] *Certificate of Disagreement*, p. 69.

promise that if Germany won the case, he would receive at least an additional $500.[167] This seemed to be confirmed by letters between Tannenberg and Carella, a lawyer retained by Tannenberg to help secure the affidavits. The letters contained statements such as: "the witnesses . . . refused to sign any statements . . . they are holding me to the *promise* that I had made to them namely, *that they will receive some pecuniary advantage after the case has been finally adjudicated*."[168]

Hinsch's role

One of the main indications that Germany had practiced fraud was the increasingly manifest falsity of many of Hinsch's statements. Amidst all the fraud in this case, this was especially important because Hinsch's testimony had served to discredit Herrmann. And it was Herrmann's testimony that he had hired Wozniak and Rodriguez, on a German agent's (i.e., Hinsch's) orders, to perpetrate the Kingsland fire.

Hinsch's early connections with the German sabotage program were quite clear. He had been closely associated with a notorious German agent, Franz von Rintelen, who had written a book about his exploits entitled *The Dark Invader*.[169] Hinsch also admitted to having injected horses and mules with anthrax germs and to having planned to sabotage various munitions shipments.[170] But he claimed that he ended all such activities after April 1916, when he went to work on the German commercial U-boat team, with Hilken,[171] in Baltimore and New London. That claim was initially believed.

It now appeared, however, that Hinsch had not abandoned his sabotage activities, as he had claimed. The statements of Carl Dilger, a fellow German agent, were entered into evidence before the October 1930 decision. Dilger claimed to have delivered a trunk containing incendiary pencils to Hinsch well after Hinsch claimed to have given up his sabotage activities.[172] Other evidence confirmed that Hinsch had continued his sabotage activities. Letters between Hilken and Hinsch, which were entered into evidence on September 13, 1938, described the destruction of the Canton elevator in Baltimore, which destroyed two ships with munitions on board.[173] Further proof of Hinsch's involvement in the Canton fire was provided by an affidavit from one Felton, who claimed that Hinsch had hired him to plant small bombs on ships, docks, and in warehouses.[174] Additional

[167] *Ibid.*, 71. [168] *Ibid.*, 70. [169] *Ibid.*, 88. [170] *Ibid.*, 94. [171] *Ibid.* [172] *Ibid.*, 97. [173] *Ibid.*, 102. [174] *Ibid.*

witnesses, Turner, Grant, and Young, who were hired by Felton to participate in these activities, corroborated his account.[175] Letters and cables between Hilken and Arnold, the German agent in Havana, contained yet more evidence of Hinsch's continued sabotage activities. While testifying about these letters under subpoena in September 1933, Hilken stated that both he and Hinsch had continued their sabotage activities during the submarine work.[176]

There was also evidence that Hinsch had been absent from Baltimore both before and after the Black Tom explosion,[177] which countered Hinsch's earlier affidavit that he had not left Baltimore at all during this period, due to his work on the submarine *Deutschland*.[178] In fact, it now looked as though he had been in New York at the time: there were letters addressed to Hinsch in New York from the treasurer of the submarine company that were dated around that time, and Hilken's diary confirmed that Hinsch was at a party at the Hotel Astor on August 4.[179]

Hinsch was also absent from New London both before and after the Kingsland fire, despite his repeated claims that he had no time to travel because of his work on the submarines. Ahrendt, a co-worker, had initially supported Hinsch's testimony, but Ahrendt's affidavit was also called into question, as we shall see below.[180] Other letters from Hilken mentioned Hinsch's absence during this period and several port officials testified that Hinsch was absent on several occasions.[181]

Hinsch's credibility was further damaged when another of his affidavits, questioning Thorne's description of certain events, was impeached. Thorne had stated that on September 17, 1916, the Germans in New London were eagerly awaiting the arrival of the *Bremen*, another submarine. Hinsch claimed this was false because the submarine was already late, a cause of concern for everyone. But Hinsch's version of events was contradicted by reports in the local press dated September 16 through September 20, which stated that this was in fact the exact period in which the submarine was expected, that there had been one false sighting, and that the entire city was eagerly awaiting the *Bremen*'s arrival.[182] Hilken's diary (found in 1931), meanwhile, corroborated Thorne's description.[183] This all lent credibility to Thorne's central allegation that he had hired Wozniak at the Kingsland plant on Hinsch's orders.

175 *Ibid.*, 103. 176 *Ibid.*, 103–05. 177 *Ibid.*, 105–06. 178 *Ibid.*, 106.
179 *Ibid.*, 106–07. 180 *Ibid.*, 107. 181 *Ibid.*, 108–09. 182 *Ibid.*, 115–16.
183 *Ibid.*, 117.

Other German witnesses: Ahrendt and Woehst

Other witnesses key to the German defense were likewise shown to be incredible. Ahrendt had worked closely with Hinsch and Hilken on the submarine service. He had testified that Hinsch was in Baltimore continuously during the work on the *Deutschland* and later in New London for work on the *Bremen*. As mentioned, that no longer seemed true.

Also proven false was Ahrendt's earlier claim that he knew nothing about sabotage activity undertaken by Hilken during this period. A letter dated January 19, 1917, found in the files of the submarine company on September 13, 1938, contained a suspicious postscript in Ahrendt's handwriting:

> Yours of the 18th just received and am delighted to learn that the von Hindenburg of Roland Park won another victory.
>
> Had a note from March, who is still at McAlpin. Asks me to advise his brother that he is in urgent need of another set of *glasses*. He would like to see his brother as soon as possible on this account.[184]

The American Commissioner found this to be a crude code, saying that the victory was the Kingsland fire, which had occurred only one week earlier, that von Hindenburg referred to Hilken, that March was Herrmann, and that the emphasized word "glasses" referred to the incendiary "pencils" the German agents used to start fires.[185] The German Agent insisted that "brother" referred to Paul Hilken.[186] He claimed that the emphasized word "glasses" meant that Herrmann needed more money. This interpretation was said to make sense because Hilken had cash, not necessarily incendiary pencils.[187] It should be obvious to the reader that the contested facts were complicated.

Ahrendt was also caught contradicting himself when he claimed (in an earlier affidavit) that he knew nothing of Hinsch's activities in Mexico (where Hinsch had fled to avoid arrest) when he was forced to testify under subpoena.[188]

The American Agent also submitted evidence impeaching the testimony of Willie Woehst. Woehst had denied that he had ever been a German agent; that he had ever planned or possessed the materials needed for sabotage activities; that Hinsch had ever been linked to the Black Tom

[184] *Ibid.*, 85. [185] *Ibid.* [186] *Ibid.*, 140. [187] *Ibid.* [188] *Ibid.*, 82–84.

explosion; and that he had ever known Witzke, Jahnke, Kristoff (of the Black Tom explosion), or Wozniak (of the Kingsland fire).[189] But US agents, suspecting that Woehst was a German operative, found a letter to him from Herrmann that referred to developing letters written in lemon juice.[190] The letter not only implicated Woehst as a German agent, but also verified Herrmann's direct testimony of Woehst's activities.[191]

Affidavits by Mary Hildegarde Jacobsen, Woehst's first cousin, further undermined his prior denials. She stated that she had been with Woehst after the fire at Kingsland and that she had suspected that Woehst was involved in the explosion there.[192] Letters from Woehst to Hilken, which had been in evidence as of December 7, 1928, also connected Woehst to the activities of the German agents.[193]

Woehst's testimony had other inconsistencies that suggested an effort to downplay his affiliation to Hinsch and sabotage activities. For instance, hotel registers showed that Woehst had not been at the Mohican Hotel in New London from November 20 to 25, which was the only time and place he claimed that he had met Hinsch. Other records showed that he was on the *SS Frederick VIII* under a false passport, arriving in the United States on November 27, 1916.[194] Woehst's accounting was also impeached. He had claimed that, at the most, he had gotten $1,000 from Hilken to cover living expenses and pocket money for himself and Herrmann.[195] But Hilken's check stubs documented that at least $3,900 was disbursed to Woehst.[196]

The Arnold letters

Recall that Hilken had allegedly rediscovered the Arnold letters, along with the Herrmann Message, in his attic in 1930.[197] Those letters undermined the contention that the German government had not authorized sabotage activities in neutral countries. The earlier evidence of German sabotage efforts had been dismissed as a low-level bureaucratic mistake. But these letters between Hilken and Arnold (the German agent in Argentina) provided compelling proof to the contrary. They showed that Arnold had engaged in extensive sabotage activities in Argentina, especially by injecting livestock with diseases. The letters also confirmed that Hilken, with Hinsch, Herrmann, and Woehst, was also injecting animals with disease germs and was responsible for other acts of sabotage as well.[198]

[189] *Ibid.*, 125–26. [190] *Ibid.*, 128–29. [191] *Ibid.*, 129. [192] *Ibid.*, 131–33.
[193] *Ibid.*, 134–35. [194] *Ibid.*, 130. [195] *Ibid.*, 138. [196] *Ibid.*, 138–39. [197] *Ibid.*, 190.
[198] *Ibid.*, 145.

In light of all this evidence, the American Commissioner concluded, and the Umpire agreed, that German agents did engage in sabotage in neutral countries, including the United States, and that, through Wozniak, German agents played a direct role in the Kingsland fire.[199]

The Commissioner then turned to the evidence in the *Black Tom* case. The three primary suspects in that case had been Kristoff, Witzke, and Jahnke. At the time of the Hamburg Decision, the Commission had been unable to say that any of these people had acted in the explosion. Because subsequent evidence, especially the Herrmann Message, linked Kristoff to the explosion at Black Tom, the Herrmann Message became the major focus of the inquiry.

The Witzke and Jahnke alibis

New evidence also linked Witzke and Jahnke to the explosion, but the Commission did not expressly rely on it. Witzke was clearly a German agent and was arrested as such when attempting to reenter the United States from Mexico during the war.[200] Paul Altendorf, an agent for the United States, had met with Witzke in Mexico City and claimed that Witzke had told him about his involvement in various sabotage activities, including Black Tom. Witzke reportedly made more incriminating statements to various prison officials at Fort Sam Houston, where he was held.[201] The German Agent had argued against the reliability of Witzke's statements, at least in part because of the stress Witzke was under while facing the death penalty.[202]

In any event, upon closer examination, Witzke's San Francisco alibi – initially believed – did not withstand scrutiny. The Germans had earlier claimed that a notebook of Witzke's would support his alibi. They never produced it and finally admitted that it had no entry for the date in question.[203] The American Agent questioned the reliability of two letters

199 *Ibid.*, 154–56; 312–13 (Umpire's decision).

200 "Reply Brief for the Underwriters" in *United States ex rel. Lehigh Valley RR* v. *Germany* (Mixed Cl. Comm'n 15 Mar. 1929) (No. 8102), p. 16.

201 "Oral Arguments," pp. 284–86. He was eventually tried and sentenced to death as a spy, but President Wilson commuted his sentence to life imprisonment. Witzke was later released to Germany in a prisoner exchange. See "Reply Brief for the Underwriters," pp. 22–23.

202 "Oral Arguments," pp. 286–87. As to Jahnke, the writer known as British Operative No. 45 claimed that Jahnke had offered to sell him information about Black Tom. "Brief of the American Agent Supplementing the Oral Argument," p. 20.

203 "Petition for Rehearing" in *United States ex rel. Lehigh Valley RR* v. *Germany* (Mixed Cl. Comm'n 12 Jan. 1931) (No. 8102), p. 42.

from Witzke, which had been mailed from San Francisco at the time, because anyone could have actually posted them.[204] In addition, the United States pointed out in its briefs that even if Witzke had applied for citizenship in San Francisco on July 25, 1916, as the German Agent had alleged, he could still have made it to New York fifteen hours before the fire.[205]

Jahnke's alibi also proved weak. He said that he had been a security guard at the Anglo and London Paris Bank in San Francisco. The company did have Jahnke on its records, but the records did not say whether Jahnke had actually worked on the job or had gotten someone to cover his shifts for him. People who would have seen him daily at his job did not recognize his picture, suggesting that he could have been on the East Coast at the time of the Black Tom explosion.[206] However, as mentioned, neither the American Commissioner nor the Umpire referred to this evidence in their respective opinions. The American Commissioner focused instead on the Herrmann Message.[207]

The Herrmann Message

The American Commissioner recalled the Umpire's December 3, 1932 opinion that the Herrmann Message, if true, would have proved that the Kingsland and Black Tom explosions were the work of German agents; that Hinsch, Hilken, and Herrmann were involved; and that Wozniak and Kristoff were directly responsible for carrying out the acts. "I may utterly disregard all the new evidence produced," the Umpire stated, "and still, if I deem this message genuine, hold Germany responsible in both of the cases."[208] Given the import of that message, we will consider the circumstances surrounding it with some care.

According to Herrmann's account,[209] he had sailed with Gerdts from New York to Cuba and then to Vera Cruz, Mexico in February, and then March or April, 1917.[210] While in Mexico, Herrmann had orders to destroy the Tampico Oil Fields. To do so, Herrmann needed $25,000. In order to obtain it, he wrote the message in an issue of the *Blue Book* magazine. The message was dictated by a fellow agent named Siegel, and eventually delivered by Gerdts to Hilken.[211]

[204] *Ibid.* [205] *Ibid.*, 41. [206] *Ibid.*, 43–45.
[207] For the text of the Message, see *Certificate of Disagreement*, p. 157.
[208] *Ibid.*, 158 (quoting *1932 Decision of the Commission*, p. 1016).
[209] *Ibid.*, 165–67. [210] *Ibid.*, 164. [211] *Ibid.*, 167–68.

The American Commissioner determined that the Herrmann Message consisted of seven objectives:

1 To enlist Hilken's aid in convincing von Eckardt, the German Minister to Mexico, of Herrmann's *bona fides* and his mission in Mexico.
2 To persuade Hilken to send Herrmann $25,000.
3 To persuade Hinsch and Hilken to leave the States and come to Mexico, or, in the case of Hilken, to go to South America.
4 In connection with Hinsch to promote the destruction of enemy commerce on the West Coast.
5 To warn Hilken where he might expect trouble from co-saboteurs and their friends.
6 To awaken memories of past sabotage acts.
7 "[B]earer will relate experiences and details."[212]

As was quite clear from the Umpire's opinion of December 3, 1932, the Herrmann Message, if genuine, constituted convincing proof of German complicity in the acts. But its authenticity was uncertain, especially given that Hilken had suddenly discovered it in his attic sometime over Christmas of 1930. The American Commissioner's opinion thus focused on demonstrating the authenticity of the Herrmann Message.

To that end, the Commissioner pointed to the testimony of Herrmann, Siegel, Gerdts, and Hilken. Herrmann had admitted to recruiting Wozniak and Rodriguez for the Kingsland fire[213] and implicated Hinsch and Hilken in Black Tom. His testimony, as noted, also described the circumstances surrounding the writing of the message and identified the *Blue Book* magazine in the evidence as being authentic.[214]

Siegel's affidavits presented a more interesting conflict. On March 14, 1932, Herrmann had visited Siegel's office on his way from Chile to the United States. There he said that Germany and the United States were trying to clear up the *Sabotage Cases* and that he was to testify before the Commission at Germany's request. Siegel assumed that Herrmann wanted him to clarify his role to the German government and that the requested affidavit would be used for diplomatic purposes only.[215] He wrote out the affidavit and had it attested at the German Consulate. In this affidavit, Siegel provided some details about the Herrmann Message: he stated that the message was written crosswise in lemon juice in an American magazine and coded through the use of pinpricks on different

[212] *Ibid.*, 197. [213] *Ibid.*, 159, 162–63. [214] *Ibid.*, 165–67. [215] *Ibid.*, 172.

pages; he claimed that he dictated the message to Herrmann and that Gerdts had delivered it.[216] After learning that the affidavit was to be used against Germany, Siegel attempted to retract several of his more incriminating statements.[217] He still remembered the basics but was now uncertain about whether the message had been written in a book or a magazine and whether the sheets were the same size and number as those of the *Blue Book* magazine.[218]

Gerdts' testimony also supported the message's authenticity, but it, too, posed some difficulties. When lawyers for the claimants attempted to take his affidavit, Gerdts, it seems, demanded a $10,000 reward for his testimony.[219] After the American agents stated that their office had no objection, the claimants paid the reward.[220] With cash in hand, Gerdts stated that the message was written in lemon juice in a book of poetry, not a magazine, and had been delivered to Hilken.[221] The fact that Gerdts stated that the message was in a book, and the fact that he had claimed that much of the message had been verbally transmitted to him, conflicted with some of Herrmann's testimony. The American Commissioner minimized these inconsistencies, attributing them to faulty memory of an event that had happened over ten years earlier.[222] In any event, the message had referred to additional verbal orders.[223]

Hilken testified that Gerdts delivered the Herrmann Message to him and described the events surrounding it; apparently, Hinsch also told him that he (Hinsch) would personally delivered the bulk of the $25,000 to Herrmann.[224] Importantly, Hilken also offered testimony to explain the late "rediscovery" of the Herrmann Message and other critical information. It developed that an assistant to the American Agent had asked Hilken to look for his diary in the attic of his estranged wife's home on December 9, 1931.[225] She later found the diary and Hilken claimed he had discovered the magazine and other objects over Christmas 1930.[226] This account was verified by affidavits from Hilken's estranged wife and others.[227] Hilken also explained that he had taken so long in delivering the evidence to the American Agent because he feared further publicity in the media.[228] That excuse was plausible, considering that other claimants' lawyers had spoken with the press, and several articles had been published.[229] And Hilken had attempted to see Agent Boyden personally several times even though he did

[216] *Ibid.*, 171–73. [217] *Ibid.*, 173. [218] *Ibid.*, 173–74. [219] *Ibid.*, 181. [220] *Ibid.*, 182.
[221] *Ibid.*, 182–83. [222] *Ibid.*, 184. [223] *Ibid.*, 185. [224] *Ibid.*, 186–87; 209.
[225] *Ibid.*, 193. [226] *Ibid.*, 192, 195. [227] *Ibid.*, 193–95. [228] *Ibid.*, 195. [229] *Ibid.*, 194.

not submit the evidence until April 27, 1931. Other witnesses, including Boyden's secretary, confirmed Hilken's attempts to deliver the evidence earlier.[230]

The German Agent did his best to undermine the message and produced several witnesses to attack its authenticity. Ahrendt, for example, claimed that he had never before heard of the Herrmann Message and that Hinsch was continuously present in New London (implying it would have been impossible for Hinsch to have met Hilken to discuss the message).[231] Given Ahrendt's other credibility problems, the Commission concluded that his claims were fabricated.[232]

Hinsch also challenged the authenticity of the message in evidence. He claimed that the "real" message was only one page, not four; that it had a written description of Gerdts, because he and Hilken did not know who he was; and that Gerdts relayed most of the message verbally because the details had not been written down.[233] Hinsch also said that the message had been destroyed, and that it had been written in invisible ink, not lemon juice, which had become outdated.[234]

The Commission dismissed Hinsch's claims, for several reasons. For one, there was Siegel's testimony which, at least initially, strongly suggested that the message had been written down. Second, there was evidence showing that, despite his claims to the contrary, Hinsch and Hilken must have known Gerdts before the Herrmann Message was delivered.[235] Third, a shipmate of Gerdts' recalled him speaking about a message in lemon juice in a *Bluebook* magazine,[236] and someone specifically remembered seeing the magazine while eating with Gerdts in New York prior to his departure for Baltimore (the place of delivery to Hilken). Apparently, Gerdts had the magazine sitting by him on a dining table and a waiter serving food had accidentally ripped the cover.[237]

230 *Ibid.*, 195–96. 231 *Ibid.*, 216–17. 232 *Ibid.*, 215, 217.

233 See *ibid.*, 218–19. Even the Commission in an earlier hearing to reopen observed the "absurdity of sending this unnecessary information into an enemy country to a suspected spy then under surveillance." 1932 Decision of the Commission, p. 1024.

234 See *Certificate of Disagreement*, p. 219. Correspondence from the files of the Eastern Forwarding Company (which ran the submarine service), which was introduced on September 13, 1938, and Hilken's diary and testimony under subpoena demonstrated that Gerdts had previously dined with Hilken and Hinsch and that the two regarded him as more than just a new acquaintance whom they suspected might be an agent of the United States. They paid him $1,000 and sent him back to Mexico stating that more money would follow. *Ibid.*, 120–22.

235 See *ibid.*, 228, 231. 236 See *ibid.*, 227. 237 See *ibid.*, 233.

The German Agent also adduced expert testimony to challenge the provenance of the magazine. Germany's chief expert witness, Osborn, claimed that the January 1917 magazine which contained the Herrmann Message came from Abraham's Book Store in New York City and was purchased in 1931 to forge the "evidence."[238] Osborn prepared an affidavit in which a store clerk, Meyers, stated that he had in fact sold two copies of the January 1917 *Blue Book* magazine in March or April of 1931.[239]

But there were a few problems with Meyers' statement and Osborn's sworn account of it. For one, it was odd that the German Agent, Tannenberg, told the Commission that Osborn had given him a verbal report of Meyers' statement, but did not mention that Osborn had at the same time mailed him three written copies of it.[240] And there were discrepancies between the verbal and written accounts. For example, as recounted by Tannenberg, Meyers stated that the first customer in question specifically requested a *Blue Book* magazine from early 1917; but Meyers' written statement claimed that there had only been a general request for a magazine eleven or twelve years old.[241] There was also reason to question Osborn's impartiality. Tannenberg claimed that he had returned to the bookstore after Osborn's first visit and interviewed Meyers alone, without Osborn. But Osborn's diary showed that he went with Tannenberg to the store for this interview.[242] Also curious, the German Agent claimed Osborn was paid only $5,000 for his services when, in actuality, Osborn's bill had already been approved for $7,500.[243]

In view of this and other testimony,[244] it seemed increasingly clear to the American Commissioner that the Herrmann Message was

[238] See *ibid.*, 234. [239] See *ibid.*, 236. [240] See *ibid.*, 240. [241] See *ibid.*, 240–41.
[242] See *ibid.*, 244–45. [243] See *ibid.*, 270–71.
[244] Horace and John Qualters, two brothers who had sold the old *Blue Book* magazines to Abraham's Book Store, in 1930, also testified. They stated that Horace Qualters would often put a horizontal dash in the table of contents next to the title of articles he had read. His brother, John, would then put a vertical slash through the horizontal dash when he had finished reading the article. The brothers identified several other issues of the *Blue Book* magazine from Abraham's Book Store as bearing these marks. See *ibid.*, 247–48. The brothers initially identified the magazine containing the Herrmann Message as bearing their marks; however, they later thought that the marks in that issue differed from the brothers' distinctive style. See *ibid.*, 248–49. Other experts testified that the slashes in the January issue had had the vertical line drawn first, followed by the horizontal dash (the exact opposite of the Qualters brothers' method). See *ibid.*, 249. As a result, the Commissioner did not find the Qualters' testimony persuasive. See *ibid.*, 250–51.

authentic[245] and that it implicated Germany in the incidents at Kingsland and Black Tom.[246]

Additional expert testimony confirmed that view. Each side retained experts to address the issue of when the pinpricks (which were part of the cipher) were made – when the magazine was old or when it was relatively new. Osborn, for the Germans, testified that the abrasions from the pen were only in the margin, showing the paper had aged before it was written on. Looking at the extent to which the lemon juice had soaked through the pages, Osborn also testified that the juice had soaked through at the margin, again, showing that the magazine was written on when it was old.[247] By contrast, the US experts testified that the pricks had been made when the magazine was new.[248] They found abrasions throughout the page[249] and claimed that the lemon juice had spread fluidly, as was typical of newer

[245] One interesting side-light involved a charge by Stein, a handwriting expert, that a report he had prepared on June 10, 1931, which questioned the validity of the Herrmann Message and Wozniak's letters from Mexico, had been suppressed by the United States. But there was no evidence in his diary that he had worked on any report on that date and, perhaps more tellingly, there was no evidence that he had ever billed for the report. See *ibid.*, 253–54, 258–59. Also, the record suggested that Stein had not seen the Wozniak letters until June 16, 1931. See *ibid.*, 260. The Germans also claimed that the United States suppressed a Bureau of Standards report saying that the Herrmann Message was a forgery. The American Commissioner dismissed this argument because the Germans had only produced a short letter saying that the Bureau could not determine the age of the Herrmann Message one way or the other. See *ibid.*, 307–08.

[246] At this point, the American Commissioner noted that the situation had been established as follows:

1 It is admitted that Herrmann sent a written message by Gerdts to Baltimore.
2 The *Blue Book* magazine of 1917, produced by Hilken, contains a message admittedly written in the handwriting of Herrmann.
3 Herrmann, who wrote the message, has identified the same.
4 Siegel, who dictated it, identified the message in a statement written in his own handwriting.
5 Gerdts, the bearer of the message, has identified the message in the *Blue Book* as genuine.
6 Hilken, to whom the message was sent, has produced and identified the message.
7 Herrmann and Hilken, after first being unwilling to admit their responsibility for the Black Tom and Kingsland disasters, have either directly admitted their responsibility or have made admissions whence their responsibility must follow.
8 Arendt, Woehst and Hinsch, whose affidavits have been brought forward by Germany for the purpose of discrediting Hilken and Hermman, have themselves been discredited and have been proven to have been guilty of perjuries of the worst character.

Ibid., 262.

[247] See *ibid.*, 288–89. [248] See *ibid.*, 275. [249] See *ibid.*, 285–88.

paper.[250] Attention was also drawn to the fact that the "t"s in the message had been crossed by Herrmann in his old style of handwriting, not his new one.[251] Admiral Sir William Reginald Hall, while not a scientific expert, had been the Director of Naval Intelligence in Britain during the war, and his office had intercepted and decoded over 15,000 German messages. In Hall's opinion, the Herrmann Message was genuine.[252]

Relying on the Herrmann Message, the American Commissioner found that the German government was liable for the destruction of Kingsland and Black Tom. The Commissioner specifically noted that other evidence, such as the Wozniak letters and whether Wozniak was in Tupper Lake or Mexico after the Kingsland fire, did not matter.[253] The American Commissioner apparently followed the Commission's decision of December 3, 1932, which had stated that if authentic, the Herrmann Message showed fraud, and the decision of October 16, 1930 would have to be set aside.

Umpire Roberts concurred with the American Commissioner's *Certificate of Disagreement* and ordered that the decision of October 16, 1930 be set aside. He rested his decision on the "statements of Wozniak to Department of Justice agents and to the Bureau of Naturalization; the testimony of Herrmann, Hilken, Wozniak, Ahrendt, Thorne, and Hilken, Sr., taken in open court, under the statute; and the material drawn from the files of the Eastern Forwarding Company, and the evidence as to the so-called Lyndhurst testimony."[254] This proved that "the Commission was seriously misled" in its initial determinations.[255] The Umpire entered an award, with interest, of $31,400,000 for the claimants.[256]

[250] See *ibid.*, 291–92. [251] See *ibid.*, 303. [252] See *ibid.*, 300–01. [253] *Ibid.*, 306.
[254] *Decision of the Commission Rendered by the Umpire*, p. 312. [255] *Ibid.*
[256] Some efforts were then mounted to block the decision. See Martin, *Final Report of H. H. Martin*, p. 84. The Z&F Assets Realization Corporation filed a complaint to enjoin the defendants (the Secretaries of State and Treasury) from paying the award, and it was soon followed by the American–Hawaiian Steamship Company. These objections were filed primarily because the amount of the *Sabotage* claims effectively kept these companies from receiving full payment on their own awards from the Mixed Claims Commission. The District Court dismissed these suits, stating that the claims before the Commission were those of the United States and that any improprieties surrounding the withdrawal of the German Commissioner could only be brought by one of the contracting parties – one of the two governments. *Z. & F. Assets Realization Corp.* v. *Hull*, 31 F. Supp. 371, 373 (DDC 1940). The Supreme Court, sitting without Justice Roberts, affirmed, holding that while the parties had standing under the Act, they were bound by the Act's provisions, which allowed only the Secretary of State to certify claims. *Z. & F. Assets Realization Corp.* v. *Hull*, 311 US 470, 485–90 (1941).

The claims on the *Sabotage Cases* were not paid in full until 1953, when the Federal Republic of Germany settled all outstanding claims from the Mixed Claims Commission for a total of $97,500,000.[257]

VII

When the revised opinion in the *Sabotage Cases* was issued, the German press decried what was, in effect, a verdict that the German government had engaged in sabotage and fraud. Earlier, in the initial decision of the Mixed Claims Commission, official German statements had praised the Commission's impartiality in investigating the situation, praise which was all the more impressive due to the presence of two Americans on the three-person tribunal.[258] There was, however, little notice of this event in the German popular press because the public had not closely followed the entire proceedings.[259]

In contrast, when the revised opinion reversing the earlier decision was issued, Germany's official news agency stated that the Commission violated the regulations of the Commission by sitting without a German Commissioner and that the decision was merely an embodiment of "a new anti-German campaign in America."[260] The editor of the *Hamburger Fremdenblatt* said that the decision was a violation of the law and that Umpire Roberts was "openly prejudiced against Germany."[261] The editorialist dismissed it as an attempt by the United States to keep control of the $20,000,000 of German assets it was holding as security for German war claims[262] and an attempt to raise once again the bogeyman of German agents that had been used to mobilize the United States populace in World War I.[263] The *Völkischer Beobachter*, the Nazi organ, echoed these complaints, and claimed that Germany had not been given any opportunity to state its case, demonstrating that this decision was merely an attempt to injure Germany's reputation in the eyes of the world.[264]

The specter of activity by German agents was indeed sweeping through the United States at the time the Commission rendered its final decision. One article describing the Black Tom and Kingsland explosions after the final decision of the Commission concluded: "In 1914 the [US] government

257 Schwebel, *International Arbitration*, p. 224.
258 See "Black Tom Decision Praised in Berlin," *NY Times* (16 Nov. 1930), 9.
259 See *ibid.*
260 See "Black Tom Ruling Rejected by Reich," *NY Times* (17 June 1939), 1.
261 See *ibid.* 262 See *ibid.* 263 See *ibid.* 264 See *ibid.*

was slow to believe that a foreign power would resort to such tactics in a neutral country. To-day the Federal Bureau of Investigation is prepared for the worst."[265]

The controversy surrounding these events was soon eclipsed by the onset of World War II.

VIII

One may read the final chapters of the *Sabotage* decision of the Mixed Claims Commission as infected with war fever. But whatever the subjectivities of the American Commissioner and the Umpire, the substantive decision was probably sound. By the end of the long procedure, there was little question that there had been German orders to commit sabotage acts within the United States. Given Germany's acute dilemma at the time, covert action was a logical, if desperate and perilous tactic to stem the flow of American support to the UK and Russia while concealing Germany's role in it. If successfully concealed, Germany might prevail in what had become a war of attrition; if exposed, it would probably bring the United States into the war, to Germany's detriment. Herrmann and Hilken had both admitted to being German agents, and even Hinsch had conceded that, for at least a time, he had been involved in sabotage activities.[266] In a completely different matter, Witzke had been sentenced to death for activities as a German spy in both Mexico and the United States.[267] In the Commission, Germany's Agent had finally been compelled to contend that the orders were a simple bureaucratic blunder, which had been ignored by the German ambassador in the United States.[268] It is true that the Wozniak letters had been fraudulent, and that nothing could guarantee the authenticity of the Herrmann Message. On balance, however, given the huge amounts of evidence submitted in the case, it appears that the Commission did in fact take the relevant factors into account and reached a defensible conclusion.

Because the decision issued from a continuing commission, reopening an award before the Commission concluded all of its activities was an option. Yet one cannot discount the anticipation of another war that was rife by the time of the final decision. Six years earlier, when substantially

[265] See Manchester, "The Black Tom Case," 69.

[266] See *Certificate of Disagreement*, p. 94.

[267] See "Brief on Behalf of the Underwriters' Committee" in *United States ex rel. Lehigh Valley RR* v. *Germany* (Mixed Cl. Comm'n 10 Mar. 1925) (No. 8102), p. 50.

[268] See Certificate of Disagreement, p. 143.

the same procedural question had arisen, the Commission in *Philadelphia–Girard National Bank* had reached the opposite conclusion, though only on the question of subsequently discovered evidence with no indication of its fraudulent suppression by one of the parties. In denouncing the fraud, the Commission registered its indignation in stinging terms but Germany, once exposed for submitting fraudulent evidence, was not non-suited or otherwise sanctioned. By the time the Commission was operating, the fact of German sabotage during the war was not shocking, it was long well known. The only question was whether sabotage had proved to have been committed in the two cases at bar.

The context in which a case is decided is rarely recorded in a judgment itself, but it is a critical factor in assessing whether the decision is an aberration or represents a considered shift in policy that is likely to be perpetuated. We will not be able to determine whether these decisions were the start of a new policy until we have surveyed the major decisions that succeeded them. As for the critical factor of the continuing character of the tribunal that was reopening its prior award, other continuing tribunals after the German–US Commission have seemed reluctant to build upon the precedent of the *Sabotage Cases*.

3

Corfu Channel: suppressed vs. forged documents

In 1945, on the heels of World War II, relations between the United States and the Soviet Union, erstwhile allies but now competing superpowers, cooled, then chilled into what soon became the Cold War. In contrast to the conventional wars of the first part of the twentieth century, the superpowers mostly avoided direct confrontations, resorting instead to fomenting or assisting in proxy wars fought outside their territories.

The Greek Civil War was one early example of this pattern. At the end of World War II, the UK withdrew its support from the leftist group it had supported during the war, which had resisted the German occupation. Throwing its support to the exiled Greek government, Whitehall facilitated its return to power. The Communist Party mobilized, with the aim of expelling the new government.[1] The Communist government in Albania supported its counterpart in Greece.

In 1947, the United States entered the fray, as it became clear that war-torn Britain could not support the Greek government.[2] President Truman's efforts to garner congressional agreement for an aid package became a pivotal moment in US foreign policy. Truman committed the United States "to support free peoples who are resisting attempted subjugation by armed

We are indebted to Professor Carty's study, A. Carty, "The Corfu Channel Case – And the Missing Admiralty Orders," *L. & Prac. Int'l Cts. & Tribunals*, 3 (2004), 1, which first discovered the essential facts in this incident.

1 See generally P. Papastratis, *British Policy Towards Greece During the Second World War, 1941–1944* (Cambridge University Press 1984), pp. 218–25; N. Clive, "British Policy Alternatives 1945–1946" in L. Bærentzen, J. O. Iatrides and O. L. Smith (eds.), *Studies in the History of the Greek Civil War, 1945–1949* (Copenhagen: Museum Tusculuanum Press, 1987).

2 J. L. Gaddis, *The Cold War: A New History* (New York: Penguin Books, 2005), p. 31; see generally A. Gerolymatos, *Red Acropolis, Black Terror: The Greek Civil War and the Origins of Soviet-American Rivalry, 1943–1949* (New York: Basic Books, 2004).

minorities or outside pressures," and ushered in the Truman Doctrine with a $400 million support package for Greece and Turkey.[3]

It was against this backdrop of geopolitical tension that the Corfu incident unfolded. Relations between Britain and Albania began to deteriorate on May 15, 1946, when an Albanian battery around the region of Saranda fired upon the British ships *Orion* and *Superb* as they transited the straits.[4] The Albanians actually began firing after HMG ships had passed the battery and were heading away.[5] With scant explanation, the UK inferred that Albania intended to require notice and prior authorization for passage of warships and merchant vessels alike through the Straits of Corfu.

Even after the May shootings, the UK government preferred a peaceful approach. The Admiralty was instructed to forgo use of the channel while the dispute was handled diplomatically. The May hostilities thus triggered a series of terse notes exchanged between the two states, debating whether Britain enjoyed a right to innocent passage through the strait. In a note on May 21, Albania flatly denied that foreign warships had a right to pass, unauthorized, through an international strait, a portion of which is in the territorial waters of the littoral state.[6] The British response on May 31 protested the Albanian decision to "ignore the right of innocent passage."[7] Albania's reply reiterated its stance, insisting that it was entitled to require both permission and non-aggression for use of the strait.[8]

In July, the Admiralty expressed its frustration; it not only found Albania's posture inconvenient and impracticable but also regarded Albania's attitude as an affront to British naval mores. The First Lord of the Admiralty, Albert Victor Alexander, petitioned the Prime Minister, Clement Attlee, for permission to resume use of the channel and for authorization to return fire in the event of another attack. Alexander argued that the "Albanian attitude is unsatisfactory. It indicates a view of the international law on the subject which is quite unacceptable, and would impose restrictions on navigation of a nature which this country has for generations taken a lead in opposing."[9] Further, it was clear that the Albanian notes

3 W. D. Miscamble, *From Roosevelt to Truman: Potsdam, Hiroshima, and the Cold War* (Cambridge University Press, 2007), p. 310.

4 *Corfu Channel Case (United Kingdom* v. *Albania)*, 1949 *ICJ Rep.* 4, p. 27 (9 Apr.), 16 *ILR* 155.

5 *Ibid.*

6 *Ibid.*; "Application Instituting Proceedings" in *Corfu Channel Case (United Kingdom* v. *Albania)*, 1949 *ICJ Pleadings* 8, pp. 11–12 (13 May 1947).

7 *Ibid.* 8 *Ibid.*, para. 10.

9 Letter from Albert Victor Alexander, First Lord of the Admiralty, to Clement R. Attlee, Prime Minister (July 25, 1946).

could not be dismissed as mere braggadocio. The fact that Greek and Turkish vessels suffered similar attacks confirmed that Albania intended to enforce the notice and authorization policy without exception. In a final note in August, Britain declared in no uncertain terms that His Majesty's Government would resume use of the channel: British ships would continue to pass through the strait in a non-aggressive manner, with guns trained fore and aft.[10] If provoked, however, British ships would return fire.[11]

The Prime Minister authorized resumption of the use of the channel with the proviso that the channel should be used only "when necessary."[12] Essential or not, the Commander-in-Chief Mediterranean relayed his intention to traverse the strait on October 22 – which would be the first passage since Albania's receipt of the August note.[13] On that day, according to plan, a squadron of HMG warships, including the *Mauritius* and *Leander* and the destroyers *Saumarez* and *Volage*, left port at Corfu and proceeded northward through the channel. While proceeding through the strait and in Albanian territorial waters, *Saumarez* and *Volage* struck mines. Both destroyers were damaged and forty-four lives were lost.[14]

Prior to the October passage, the Admiralty had no cause to doubt the safety of the Corfu route. For one, the strait had been swept in 1944 and declared free of mines. The Admiralty had also relied on the Medri Charts, a series of charts and pamphlets produced by the International Routing and Reporting Authority, which had reestablished the strait as a "maritime highway" safe for usage. The channel had been check-swept again in February 1945 and declared safe for passage. The absence of any record of enemy or allied mines laid in the channel since February 1945 gave rise to what the UK would later call an "irresistible inference"

[10] ADM 1/22504, Telegram from Admiralty to Commander-in-Chief Mediterranean (Aug. 10, 1946).

[11] ADM 1/22504, Admiralty Message 061551, from Admiralty to the Commander-in-Chief Mediterranean (Aug. 1, 1946).

[12] ADM 1/22504, Minute 196/48, from Clement R. Attlee, Prime Minister, to Hartley Shawcross, Attorney General (4 Nov. 1948). However, the Admiralty argued that there was no such restriction and that the "when necessary" proviso had actually been added by the Admiralty in its orders to the Commander-in-Chief Mediterranean. Carty, "The Corfu Channel Case," pp. 7–8 (citing ADM/1/22504, Lang, to the First Lord. (2 Nov. 1948)).

[13] ADM 1/22504, Admiralty Message 211106A/September, from Admiralty to Commander-in-Chief Mediterranean (22 Sept. 1946).

[14] "Application Instituting Proceedings," p. 9.

that the mines had been recently laid, either by Albania or with its connivance.[15]

Claiming exigent circumstances and a self-defense-based right to intervene to secure the *corpora delicti*, Britain announced it would execute Operation Retail, a sweep of the channel for any remaining mines.[16] Although the International Central Mine Clearance Board had agreed that there should be further sweeps of the channel, it stipulated that such sweeps be accomplished pursuant to Albanian consent. However, Britain dispensed with the Board's prescription for Albanian consent and carried out Operation Retail on November 12 and 13; it later argued that this was a matter of self-preservation and, hence, permissible according to the right of self-defense.[17] The operation recovered twenty-two German Y-type mines.

After Operation Retail, positions hardened on both sides. The larger political implications of the dispute were stark: they included the East–West divide and superpower spheres of influence, not to speak of the consequences for the Greek Civil War. For Britain, the stakes were greater than the convenience of using the Corfu route. Securing a favorable ruling for the Royal Navy on the right of innocent passage for warships had worldwide implications. (The Albanian government, for its part, likely desired affirmation of its sovereignty in its waters.)

In December 1946, the British government demanded that Albania apologize, assure Britain that such attacks would not recur, and pay reparations for the damage to the ships as well as to the relatives of the deceased servicemen.[18] If Albania failed to meet these demands within two weeks, Britain would have "no alternative but to bring the matter before the Security Council of the United Nations as a serious threat to, and a breach of, international peace and security, showing criminal disregard of the safety of innocent seamen of any nationality lawfully using an international highway."[19]

The British were confident that they would prevail at the Security Council. Britain's Agent in New York, Sir Alexander Cadogan, relayed the Attorney General's opinion that they "had a sound case on which [they] could

[15] "Memorial of the United Kingdom" in *Corfu Channel (United Kingdom* v. *Albania)*, 1949 *ICJ Pleadings* 17, para. 76 (30 Sept. 1947).

[16] *Corfu Channel*, 1949 *ICJ Rep.*, pp. 33–34.

[17] "Reply of the United Kingdom" in *Corfu Channel (United Kingdom* v. *Albania)*, 1949 *ICJ Pleadings* 241, para. 82(a) (26 Mar. 1948).

[18] "Application Instituting Proceedings," para. 20. [19] *Ibid.*, para. 21.

safely go to the Security Council."[20] In New York, Cadogan emphasized the UK's right to innocent passage, while Albania claimed ignorance of the mines and challenged the lawfulness of the warships' passage.[21] Cadogan explained that the ships had been proceeding through the strait as part of their normal autumn exercises to rendezvous with the remainder of the fleet for harbor exercises. Regardless of the ships' purpose, he added, the Albanians, whether directly responsible, complicit, or merely cognizant of the laying of these mines, had violated international law by failing to warn the encroaching ships of their presence.

After hearing both sides' contentions, a majority of the council members concluded that a minefield did exist in the swept channel on October 22 and that this minefield could not have been laid without the Albanian government's knowledge.[22] But a draft Resolution stating as much failed because the USSR, a permanent member, voted against it. The Security Council concluded its deliberation on the Corfu incident in April 1947 and referred the matter to the International Court at The Hague.[23] From the UK's perspective, this was a desirable outcome. The British had entertained no illusions about the Security Council's ability to provide "any clear endorsement of [Britain's] views on the issues of international law involved" in the case.[24]

In September 1947, the UK applied unilaterally to the Court. The Attorney General, Sir Hartley Shawcross, and the Solicitor General, Sir Frank Soskice, were the main Law Officers involved; the Legal Advisor to the Foreign Office, Sir Eric Beckett, and the Lord Chancellor, William Jowitt, also participated as legal advisors to the government. In its Memorial, the UK maintained, as it had in the Council, that Albania laid, connived or knew of the mines, and had violated its duty to warn of the danger.[25]

[20] LCO 3/3217, Telegram No. 2012, from United Kingdom Delegation to Council of Foreign Ministers, p. 1 (26 Nov. 1946).

[21] "Memorial of the United Kingdom," para. 74 (noting that Albania had made these assertions in diplomatic notes and before the Security Council).

[22] Australia, Belgium, China, Colombia, France, and the United States. "Memorial of the United Kingdom," para. 58.

[23] "*Having considered* statements of representatives of the United Kingdom and of Albania concerning a dispute between the United Kingdom and Albania arising out of an incident on 22 October 1946 in the Straits of Corfu . . . *Recommends* that the United Kingdom and Albanian Governments should immediately refer the dispute to the International Court of Justice in accordance with the provisions of the Statute of the Court." SC Res. 324, UN Doc. S/RES/324 (9 Apr. 1947).

[24] PREM 8/406, Telegram No. 2412, from Permanent United Kingdom Representative to the UN (22 Nov. 1946).

[25] "Memorial of the United Kingdom," para. 92.

Albania filed a Preliminary Objection, but after a six-month delay, the parties concluded a Special Agreement in March 1948, which included Albania's counter-claims. The Special Agreement asked the Court to decide: first, whether "Albania [is] responsible under international law for the explosions which occurred on the 22nd October 1946"; and second, "Ha[d] the United Kingdom under international law violated the sovereignty of the Albanian People's Republic" on October 22 and on November 12 and 13.[26] Albania submitted its Counter-Memorial in June of that year, with British and Albanian Replies following in July and September respectively.

In their Counter-Memorial, the Albanian government denied responsibility for the mines.[27] As one explanation, Albania suggested that the mines were German, left over from World War II, and were unknown to the government on October 22. For Britain, this was an "impossible supposition":

> The Government of the United Kingdom submits that the existence of an unknown German minefield right across a channel of navigation in common use, and only discovered eighteen months after the conclusion of hostilities, when all the evidence available goes to show that the channel had been swept, and remained swept at the conclusion of hostilities, is an impossible supposition, contrary to common sense and the facts of general experience.[28]

Albania also accused the UK of itself laying the mines on November 12, so that they would then be uncovered on November 13.[29] For Britain, the allegation "implie[d] on the part of the Government of the United Kingdom an almost incredible naïveté and the reckless taking of risks extraordinarily disproportionate to the end desired."[30]

Regardless of who had laid the mines, the evidence strongly suggested Albania had at least *known* they were there. Expert examination of the mines recovered from Operation Retail reported that the mines were free from marine growth, freshly painted and greased, and contained little sign of rust, indicating that the mines were laid only very shortly before the October explosion.[31] In addition to the newness of the mines, the UK argued that it would have been impossible "for over twenty of such mines to be laid without the laying of the mines and the engines of the craft

[26] "Special Agreement" in *Corfu Channel (United Kingdom* v. *Albania)*, 1949 *ICJ Pleadings* 8, p. 29 (25 Mar. 1948).

[27] "Reply of United Kingdom," para. 37. [28] *Ibid.*, para 13.

[29] *Ibid.*, para. 54 (citing the Counter-Memorial of Albania, pp. 59–80) (UK translation).

[30] *Ibid.*, para. 55. [31] "Memorial of the United Kingdom," para. 23.

laying the mines being heard by the look-outs and coastguards around Saranda."[32]

On the key issue of law, innocent passage, the UK challenged Albania's contentions in diplomatic notes and at the Security Council that the ships' passage had been unlawful. The UK asserted that the right "is in full accord with the established rules of international law and the practice of civilised States."[33] As a factual matter, contrary to Albania's allegations, the UK contended that the ships' conduct had not been provocative: they had proceeded in passage and not battle formation and that maintaining crews at action stations was a reasonable precautionary measure in light of the May firings.[34]

The UK contended that challenging the lawfulness of the passage was an inappropriate response to the charge of mine laying. An unlawful passage would not justify the "grave measure of war taken by the Albanian Government, in allowing the secret minefield to be across the swept channel and letting His Majesty's ships run into it."[35] The UK's submission was "that the passage of His Majesty's ships was innocent in its intention and was taken in the *bona fide* belief of their possessing a legal right of passage through the Corfu Strait as an international channel of navigation."[36] Albania, the UK submitted, violated "the ordinary dictates of humanity" and even "breach[ed] . . . the rules which establish a minimum standard of conduct applicable in time of war to belligerents and neutrals."[37]

Back in London, the conviction with which Britain pleaded its case gave way to uncertainty and anxiety, as it became clear that both the Foreign Office and the Admiralty had withheld from the lawyers information regarding the Corfu operation. Consequently, the lawyers had not incorporated key facts into the UK's presentation which had been made at Turtle Bay and The Hague. After the case had gone to the International Court, the lawyers discovered that "Exercise Corfu" (i.e., the October passage) had been planned to test Albania's reaction to an *unauthorized* passage through the strait and to see whether it had learned its lesson from the May shootings. Although the Admiralty and, apparently, the Foreign Office had known this fact, neither department had shared it with the Law Officers before they approached the Security Council with Britain's claims. When Sir Hartley Shawcross found out, he complained that he had not

[32] *Ibid.*, para. 24. [33] *Ibid.*, para. 82. [34] *Ibid.*, para. 87. [35] *Ibid.*, para. 91.
[36] *Ibid.*
[37] "Application Instituting Proceedings," para. 3; "Memorial of the United Kingdom," paras. 4, 65.

"appreciated that . . . the passage was never part of the autumn cruise at all but was a separate full scale naval operation with an aircraft carrier in attendance and aircraft actually airborne."[38]

But the Admiralty's and the lawyers' accounts differ as to who knew what and when. The Admiralty claimed it had apprised the Foreign Office in a telegram that the passage had been a test: "Th[e] fact, therefore, was known to the Foreign Office before the decision to go to the International Court was taken."[39] Shawcross claimed the message was unclear. Even if he had seen such a telegram, this point "would [not] have occurred to me and I doubt if it can have been realised by Cadogan" while he was handling the matter in New York.[40]

Shawcross' assumption of Cadogan's ignorance was curious. Internal telegrams show that soon after the proceedings at the Security Council had begun, Cadogan sent to London for guidance. He anticipated that he might be asked why the ships had been passing through the straits, and thus inquired whether it could "be confirmed that they had recently been carrying out Fleet regatta South of Corfu in accordance with pre-war practice and that the 1st C.S. had then foregathered near Corfu prior to making passage through North Corfu Channel?"[41] In reply, the Foreign Office informed him that "the real reason for using the North Corfu Channel was to test Albanian reactions in view of the incident on the 15th of May and subsequent exchanges of notes."[42] The Foreign Office ended with an admonishment "to avoid discussing this point if at all possible."[43] If Cadogan saw this telegram, it is unlikely that he could have misunderstood its meaning.[44] But there is no indication that he, and others in the Foreign

38 ADM 1/22504, Minute from Hartley Shawcross, Attorney General, to Clement R. Attlee, Prime Minister (6 Nov. 1948).

39 ADM 1/22504, Minute from Clement R. Attlee, Prime Minister, to Hartley Shawcross, Attorney General (4 Nov. 1948).

40 ADM 1/22504, Minute from Hartley Shawcross, Attorney General, to Clement R. Attlee, Prime Minister (6 Nov. 1948).

41 PREM 8/1312, Telegram from Permanent United Kingdom Representative to the United Nations to Foreign Office (9 Jan. 1947).

42 PREM 8/1312, Telegram from Foreign Office to Permanent United Kingdom Representative to the United Nations (11 Jan. 1947).

43 *Ibid.*

44 But a document in the file contends that he may not have. "It will be seen that the telegram, although addressed to 'New York (to Permanent UK Representative to the United Nations)'," was merely passed to the Communications Department of the Foreign Office. Thus, "it can be argued that telegrams which other Departments send to their own representatives abroad through Foreign Office channels cannot be regarded as having been formally communicated to the Foreign Office unless

Office who may have been in the loop, informed the Law Officers while matters were unfolding in New York.

As for the Admiralty, it did not share key information with the lawyers.[45] After the pleadings had been submitted to the Court, Shawcross took it upon himself to gather all the relevant documents. His "insistence . . . brought to light certain documents which we ought to but cannot disclose" – namely, XCU and XCU1.[46] XCU (and its complement XCU1) was a naval operation order issued from the Commander-in-Chief Mediterranean detailing the procedures for the October 22 passage. XCU contained material which some felt conflicted with the representations the British Agent had made at the Security Council and to the International Court. In particular, XCU showed, according to Sir Hartley:

(a) that passage through the North Corfu Channel was not part of the autumn cruise;
(b) that Leander was not even due to go to Corfu at all but was sent there to reinforce the squadron;
(c) that all four ships, on reaching the end of the Medri route through the straits, were to turn about at once and to proceed due south to Argostoli for regattas;
(d) that the object of the "exercise Corfu" . . . was to trail our coats and to see whether the Albanians "had been taught a lesson";
(e) that hostilities were expected and that, if they occurred as a result of attack by the Albanians, they were not to be limited to purely defensive action on our part but punitive, retaliatory action was to be taken;
(f) that our ships were ready for a general action with Albanian batteries and were to be supported by aircraft carriers;
(g) that we had made a previous violation of Albanian sovereignty by an aerial reconnaissance, although we denied this before the Security Council.[47]

For Shawcross, XCU's revelation was distressing (even more than the realization that the voyage had been a test) because of its impact on Britain's innocent passage claim:

some additional notification to this effect is received." FO 371/72101 252042, Minute (5 Nov. 1948).

45 Initially, it seems many in the Admiralty may have been unaware of XCU. PREM 8/1312, Minute from Viscount Hall, First Lord of the Admiralty, to Clement R. Attlee, Prime Minister, para. 2 (12 Jan. 1949).

46 PREM 8/1312, Letter from Hartley Shawcross, Attorney General, to Clement R. Attlee, Prime Minister (6 Nov. 1948).

47 PREM 8/1312, Letter from Hartley Shawcross, Attorney General, to Clement R. Attlee, Prime Minister (29 Oct. 1948). "Aided" was crossed out where "made" appears.

it is not the fact that the passage was to test Albanian reactions alone which destroys its innocent character in law, but all the attendant circumstances . . . as, for instance, that use was being made of a prior aerial reconnaissance (of which I still know nothing) and that punitive rather than solely defensive action was apparently to be taken if our ships were attacked.[48]

In the fall of 1948, shortly before oral proceedings were to begin, the lawyers scrambled to decide what should be done with XCU.

After XCU's discovery, those at the highest levels of government, including the Lord Chancellor and the Prime Minister, knew mistakes had been made in the case's preparation. The lawyers had advised "in regard to the case" and crafted "statements of the facts" without knowing the content of these documents.[49] Concerned, Shawcross asked Beckett for his assessment of the document's materiality to the case. Beckett's answer was candid:

In short, while not inconsistent with the accounts which we have hitherto given of the matter before the Security Council and in our pleadings in this case, these documents may well give the impression that the primary purpose of the cruise through the Channel was to see if the Albanians would fire at us again and to give them a plastering if they did, and that the ordinary operational cruise was probably secondary, if not a camouflage. The impression which these documents give is in fact the truth.[50]

The Law Officers (or at least Shawcross) thought the document was material to the innocent passage issue.[51] But they felt that circumstances required that the document be withheld. Shawcross wrote to the Prime Minister "that [they] were faced with the disagreeable necessity of suppressing evidence" because the disclosure of the facts in XCU would likely disentitle the UK to damages and potentially "result in a judgment very adverse to ourselves."[52]

48 ADM 1/22504, Minute from Hartley Shawcross, Attorney General, to Clement R. Attlee, Prime Minister (6 Nov. 1948).

49 ADM 1/22504, Minute from William Jowitt, Lord Chancellor, to Clement R. Attlee, Prime Minister (5 Nov. 1948) (commenting on 2 Nov. note from the First Lord and a 3 Nov. Minute from the Attorney General).

50 FO 371/72100 R11937/G, Letter from Sir Eric Beckett, Legal Advisor, to Ernest Bevin, Foreign Secretary (14 Oct. 1948).

51 Indeed, initially, Shawcross was of the view that "the less unpleasant horn of the dilemma will be to disclose the documents as the implications arising from a refusal so to do might be even more sinister than those which would be justified by the documents themselves." FCO 371/72100, Minute from Sir Hartley Shawcross to Right Hon. Ernest Bevin (15 Oct. 1948).

52 PREM 8/1312, Letter from Hartley Shawcross, Attorney General, to Clement R. Attlee, Prime Minister (29 Oct. 1948).

Shawcross demanded to know why the Admiralty had not brought these key documents to the Legal Officers immediately after the incident. The Admiralty defended its delay on several grounds. In its view, XCU was irrelevant because it was the legality of laying mines and not the question of innocent passage that was under review. Moreover, the actual *manner* of the passage, it argued, and not the wording of the order, determined innocence; on October 22, the ships' actual conduct satisfied the requisite standards of innocence.[53] And, practically speaking, the Admiralty considered operational documents proprietary:

> probably 999 out of every 1,000 cases of Maritime International Law, whether in war or peace, are dealt with by the Admiralty/Foreign Office without going to any international court. In such cases the production of internal documents does not arise and it is not desirable that in the odd case which does go before a court, a totally different rule should prevail.[54]

Because disclosing XCU was thought irrelevant to Britain's case, the Admiralty thought the document should be withheld. Shawcross disagreed in principle. Writing to the Prime Minister, he declared:

> It is essential to the proper discharge of their duties that [the Law Officers] themselves should see all internal documents relevant (as EXCU orders relating to "Exercise Corfu" obviously were in the present case) to any litigation that they may have to conduct on behalf of the Crown. It is again exclusively for them to decide whether particular documents must be disclosed to the Court . . . It is not a ground for claiming privilege . . . that disclosure would lead to the Crown losing the case in connection with which the document was disclosed.[55]

In the Legal Officers' view, the Admiralty had not followed the proper procedure for preparing and proceeding with a case for HMG.

Shawcross expressed regret for authorizing the case at all. In his words, had the Law Officers been privy to XCU, they surely would "have hesitated

[53] ADM 1/22504, Note by the First Lord of the Admiralty to the Prime Minister (2 Nov. 1948). Paragraph 4 of the Note stated: "We have already said that in our opinion the proof of innocent passage lies in the character of the action taken by the ships themselves, not in the phraseology used by individuals. It was for this reason we considered it was unnecessary and undesirable to table XCU before the Court."

[54] ADM 1/22504, Admiralty, Notes on the Attorney General's Memorandum of the 3rd November, para. 1 (5 Nov. 1948).

[55] ADM 1/22504, Minute from Hartley Shawcross, Attorney General, to Clement R. Attlee, Prime Minister, p. 1 (3 Nov. 1948).

very much before becoming involved in the present proceedings."[56] He minced no words in underscoring his position on the matter:

I must make it clear that neither the Solicitor-General, nor myself, nor, I am sure, any of the other members of the Bar who are assisting us in this matter, would for a moment contemplate being parties to the course of conduct now forced upon us by the Admiralty's failure to procure and produce those documents earlier had our country's international position not been so gravely involved. As it is, we retain great misgivings about the propriety of what is being done.[57]

Shawcross was actually correct that the Law Officers, and not the Admiralty, were competent to assess all documents for relevancy to a legal action to be undertaken by the Crown. In a minute to the Prime Minister, the Lord Chancellor expressed "no doubt that an unfortunate mistake has been made in this case, in that steps were not taken to obtain the Operation Orders and put them before the Law Officers."[58] Jowitt implored the Prime Minister to "take steps to see that such a mistake never happens again."[59] Focusing on future procedures implied that nothing was to be done to repair the XCU lapse.

Shawcross, too, accepted that nothing could be done, given the stage to which the case had advanced. "[I]t goes very much against the grain for a lawyer," he said, "to have to take a course such as this."[60] He wrote:

I would certainly not become a party to the suppression of evidence in this way were not such serious international issues at stake . . . As it is, there appears to be no escape from the dilemma in which we are placed and we must go on with the risk of grave criticism and in the hope that the Albanians themselves have not succeeded, through some Communist source, in obtaining information about the contents of the documents which we are with-holding.[61]

[56] PREM 8/1312, Letter from Hartley Shawcross, Attorney General, to Clement R. Attlee, Prime Minister (29 Oct. 1948).
[57] ADM 1/22504, Minute from Hartley Shawcross, Attorney General, to Clement R. Attlee, Prime Minister, p. 3, para. 6 (3 Nov. 1948).
[58] ADM 1/22504, Minute from William Jowitt, Lord Chancellor, to Clement R. Attlee, Prime Minister, p. 2, para. 5 (5 Nov. 1948).
[59] ADM 1/22504, Minute from William Jowitt, Lord Chancellor, to Clement R. Attlee, Prime Minister, p. 3, para. 9 (5 Nov. 1948).
[60] PREM 8/1312, Letter from Hartley Shawcross, Attorney General, to Clement R. Attlee, Prime Minister (29 Oct. 1948).
[61] *Ibid.*

He made clear that, though disclosure would be "fatal," suppression "is bound to produce grave suspicion and may probably lead to severe criticism."[62]

The Admiralty maintained that there was nothing irregular in not having come forward with XCU earlier. After all, it had "regarded the issue of innocent passage as irrelevant to the charge of laying mines" and moreover, "[u]p to April of [1948] . . . were still hoping that the case before the Court might be confined to our own charge, and up to that time, therefore, there was no necessity to scrutinize the detail of all the Mediterranean documents."[63] This suggests an unfortunate lapse in communication, as the Law Officers had always considered innocent passage integral to Britain's case, irrespective of whether Albania formally challenged it.

The Foreign Office was also opposed to disclosure. The Permanent Under-Secretary conceded that the affair had been botched but saw the problem as one of finessing language rather than one of legal ethics. He acknowledged a lack of foresight in failing to warn the Admiralty to word its orders more delicately, just in case an international incident should arise.[64] The Foreign Office accepted that it had too readily assumed that the Admiralty had taken all necessary steps to obtain the relevant documents from the Commander-in-Chief.[65] Notwithstanding, like Shawcross, the Foreign Office felt that XCU should not now, at this late stage, be disclosed: "nothing can be gained in the case now before the International Court at The Hague by further investigation of this matter at this stage. It is important for the conduct of the case there that everybody concerned should work together with the greatest possible harmony."[66] In the Foreign Office's view, it was best to press on with the case and to let the XCU matter rest.

At oral proceedings in November, the Albanians forced the issue by questioning why Britain had not produced XCU. In Beckett's words, the lawyers were "of course in some dilemma over this document."[67] The lawyers first

[62] PREM 8/1312, Letter from Hartley Shawcross, Attorney General, to Clement R. Attlee, Prime Minister (29 Oct. 1948).

[63] PREM 8/1312, Note by the First Lord of the Admiralty to the Prime Minister, p. 2, para. 8 (2 Nov. 1948).

[64] PREM 8/1312, P.M./O.S./48/90, Minute from Sir Orme Sargent, Permanent Under-Secretary at the Foreign Office, to Clement R. Attlee, Prime Minister, para. 2 (9 Nov. 1948).

[65] *Ibid.* [66] *Ibid.*, para. 5.

[67] ADM 116/5758 Telegram No. 429 from Eric Beckett, Legal Advisor to the Foreign Office, to Mr. Dodds, Admiralty Official, para. 2 (19 Nov. 1948). However, it appears

"propose[d] to refuse the proposal and to make the best of it, though this refusal will be in any case damaging on the issue of innocent passage."[68] That option became more difficult when the Court formally requested the document on December 14, 1948, and asked that it be produced before the resumption of proceedings on January 17, 1949. Initially, Britain objected on ostensible national security grounds, claiming that XCU had technical information that should not be made public. The Court was receptive to this concern and assured Britain that XCU would be solely "for the use of the Court"[69]; in other words, examined privately by the judges but kept from the public record.

Soon after the Court's request, Beckett took steps to assemble the relevant decisionmakers to consider whether the UK would comply.[70] Open-mindedness and flexibility was desired, especially with respect to the Admiralty's views on the matter. In fact, the Admiralty representative, Under-Secretary P. N. N. Synott, explained to his superiors that the meeting

> is intended to be a general discussion, and not to reach a firm and final decision . . . Indeed, I gather they would rather prefer that the Admiralty representative should not attend [subject to] strict instructions from the Board. I therefore . . . ask your agreement to attending with an open mind but with a fairly clear idea of what we could suggest and of what we could or could not agree to.[71]

It is worth pausing to note Beckett's potential motivations for resisting XCU's disclosure. A decision that XCU should be produced would have required him to seek permission from his superior, the Foreign Secretary. But, he wrote to the Solicitor General, "[i]f the conclusion [from the January meetings] is that we should continue to refuse to disclose, then we do not need to trouble anybody else since we are simply going on as before."[72]

that the actual demand for the disclosure of the document was made around 23 October. FO 371/72101, Minute from Eric Beckett to Sir O. Sargent (3 Nov. 1948).

68 ADM 116/5758, Telegram No. 429, para. 3.

69 PREM 8/1312, Brief from Frank Soskice, Solicitor General, to the Foreign Secretary and First Lord, *Corfu Channel Case* (undated).

70 ADM 116/5758, Letter from Eric Beckett to Frank Soskice, Solicitor General (22 Dec. 1948). Attendance at the 4 January meeting included the Attorney General, Solicitor General, Beckett, Wilberforce (Legal Advisor) and P. N. N. Synott, Admiralty.

71 ADM 116/5758, Telegram No. 480, from P. N. N. Synott, USS Admiralty, to the Admiralty Secretary, paras. 4–5 (21 Dec. 1948). "Subject to" was crossed out.

72 ADM 116/5758, Letter from Eric Beckett to Frank Soskice, Solicitor General (22 Dec. 1948).

On January 4, a meeting was held to discuss the Court's request. Initially, the Law Officers were in favor of disclosure, while the Admiralty and Foreign Office were opposed. In making the Law Officers' case, the Solicitor General underscored "that we were here in the realm of pure law, and the question was whether, if XCU were not disclosed, the Court might assume the worst."[73] Soskice made geopolitical arguments for disclosure; refusal might prompt "the iron curtain judges on the Court [to] exploit the situation and influence some of the other judges."[74] The Admiralty expressed security concerns.

At a meeting on the following day, the discussion focused on XCU's details and whether its disclosure would undermine Britain's innocent passage claim. On the basis of the discussion, the Solicitor General would make a recommendation to the Foreign Secretary and the First Lord. The participants considered the following facts: (i) "*the passage was not an integral part of the autumn cruise*"; (ii) "LEANDER [was] added specially for the passage"; (iii) "Ships then go South to Argostoli"; (iv) the orders required "'excessive' countermeasures"; and (v) "'*retaliatory*' action of 1 hour's duration is excessive."[75] There was no consensus on the implications of these facts. Humphrey Waldock[76] thought that these facts did not prove the passage non-innocent; whereas the Attorney General thought they did.[77]

The early January meetings did not alter the Law Officers' assessment that XCU demonstrated that the passage was not innocent. Even so, in advance of the Defence Committee's consideration of the matter, Soskice, with Shawcross in agreement, ultimately recommended *against* disclosure,[78] "prefer[ring] to accept the risk entailed by non-disclosure to the certain harm of disclosure."[79]

73 ADM 116/5758, P. N. N. Synott, USS Admiralty, Notes of a Meeting held on Jan. 4, 1949 RE XCU, para. 2.

74 *Ibid.*

75 ADM 116/5758, P. N. N. Synott, USS Admiralty, Notes of a Meeting held on Jan. 5, 1949 RE XCU.

76 Waldock had been an Admiralty legal advisor during World War II and was then a Professor of International Law at Oxford. Carty, "The Corfu Channel Case," 18.

77 ADM 116/5758, P. N. N. Synott, USS Admiralty, Notes of a Meeting held on Jan. 5, 1949 RE XCU.

78 The Solicitor General's brief informed a January 10 meeting between the Foreign Office and the Legal Officers. This meeting included the Law Officers, Shawcross and Soskice, as well as the Legal Advisor to the Foreign Office, Eric Beckett. Also in attendance were the Lord Chancellor, Jowitt, and First Lord, Hall.

79 PREM 8/1312, Brief from Frank Soskice, Solicitor General, to the Foreign Secretary and First Lord, *Corfu Channel Case* (undated).

But the Solicitor General's recommendation betrayed no small ambivalence about balancing concerns about the effect disclosing would have on Britain's case with fulfilling his ethical duty to press for disclosure. Soskice warned of the downside: "if by any chance the contents of XCU should ever become discovered in any hostile quarter, it may be alleged that the British claim, if it succeeds, was enabled to do so by what is virtually a fraud in the Court."[80] Indeed, quite "[a]part from the purely legal aspect . . . the reputation that the British came to the Court ready to 'lay their cards on the table' would suffer if XCU were not disclosed."[81] Yet, he also stressed the effect on public confidence that a disclosure of XCU would cause. If the contents were revealed, they "would profoundly shock public opinion abroad and also in many quarters at home."[82]

The Lord Chancellor remained in favor of disclosure: "from the point of view of pure honesty the Court should have [the document]."[83] Jowitt regretted "that the Government of the United Kingdom, of all Governments, should in such an event be the Government which refused to disclose a document."[84]

Members of the Admiralty urged a different set of priorities. Writing to the First Lord, the Permanent Secretary to the Board of Admiralty, John G. Lang, complained of the Solicitor General's "silen[ce] about the reflection on the good name of the Royal Navy which might ensue from a disclosure of XCU to the Court."[85] The First Lord urged the Admiralty's considerations on the Prime Minister:

> our approach to the problem must be on the lines of expediency rather than of legal principles. In short we must satisfy ourselves which course – production or non-production of XCU – will be the more helpful in gaining a judgment favourable to ourselves on the two claims before the Court.[86]

An important consideration, he argued, should be "to protect the reputation of the Navy," which the First Lord's "colleagues will agree . . . [was] in the national interest."[87]

80 *Ibid.* 81 *Ibid.* 82 *Ibid.*
83 PREM 8/1312, Sir Eric Beckett's Record of Jan. 10, 1949 Meeting. This minute was sent to the Prime Minister along with a copy of the Solicitor General's Memorandum to the Foreign Secretary.
84 *Ibid.*
85 Minutes from John G. Lang, Permanent Secretary to the Board of Admiralty, to Viscount Hall, First Lord of the Admiralty (8 Jan. 1949).
86 PREM 8/1312, Minute from Viscount Hall, First Lord of the Admiralty, to Clement R. Attlee, Prime Minister (12 Jan. 1949).
87 *Ibid.*

On January 12, Prime Minister Attlee decided that XCU should not be disclosed to the Court.[88] In a further exchange, the Attorney General requested that the Prime Minister afford some real-time discretion to the Solicitor General, in case the Court asked him "to state, on his responsibility as Counsel, that there is nothing in the document which could possibly affect any issue in the case."[89] The Prime Minister rejected such a broad grant of discretion to the Solicitor General; he was to refer back for instruction should such contingencies arise.[90] So ended the XCU dilemma, a source of contention in London but generally unknown to the public.

Albania's conduct was, itself, no model of professional ethics. It had sought to discredit the UK's evidence and bolster its own case in a variety of questionable ways. The UK had adduced mine clearance charts to show that the Germans had never laid a minefield in the Bay of Saranda or in any area east of the channel and adjacent to the bay prior to 1944.[91] The charts, together with the fact that the British swept the area in October 1944 and January and February 1945, showed that a swept channel had existed since July of 1940. Logically, this led to the conclusion that the mines encountered on October 22 were newly laid.

In an attempt to disprove the charts' accuracy, Albania offered several examples in which mines were discovered in areas not marked by the German charts. By extension, this was supposed to show that the mines encountered on October 22 were also products of German chart-makers' (seemingly common) oversight. The UK contended that Albania's examples were "wholly misleading."[92] For instance, to create the perception that the location of mines discovered in the Farezina Channel was inconsistent with their location as charted, the Albanians "wrongly plotted . . . a dotted line representing part of this minefield . . . on one of the sketches attached to Annex 14."[93] To compound the misrepresentation, Albania omitted the words "scattered probably further to northward" in another sketch it submitted.[94] This proviso was a critical piece of information since this was exactly where the mines – allegedly "missing" from the charts – were actually found.

[88] Minute from Clement R. Attlee, Prime Minister, to Viscount Hall, First Lord of Admiralty (12 Jan. 1949).

[89] PREM 8/1312, Minute from Hartley Shawcross to Clement R. Attlee, Prime Minister (13 Jan. 1949).

[90] Minute from Clement R. Attlee, Prime Minister, to Hartley Shawcross, Attorney General (14 Jan. 1949).

[91] "Reply of the United Kingdom," para. 8.

[92] *Ibid.*, paras. 9, 13. [93] *Ibid.*, para. 12. [94] *Ibid.*

Britain also accused Albania of exaggerating the tension that existed between itself and Greece around the time of the May shootings by changing a secret report from General Hodgson, Chief of the British Military Mission in Albania. To create this "clumsy but deliberate piece of forgery in the documentation of its own case,"[95] Albanian agents had taken the real report and cut and pasted together five separate pieces. Read in full, the actual report discussed the skirmishes on the border. But the report went on to discount these incidents as "largely exaggerated and had been put out to counter Greek Government statements of the Albanian maltreatment of the Greek minority."[96] In other words, while the report did relay that the Greek National Guards had violated the Albanian Southern Frontier in several instances, it went on to explain that these incidents were largely overblown.[97]

To "completely invert[] . . . the sense of the report," the Albanian government was alleged to have cobbled together the heading, the last sentence of the second page, the first three lines of the third page, and then several lines from the third page, while omitting eleven lines that described the border incidents as exaggerated.[98] Presumably, the Albanian agents intended this forgery to suggest that Albanian guards, primed to defend against the Greeks, had understandably fired at the British ships that had ensigns that did not clearly identify them.[99] Upon discovering Albania's forgeries, Britain accused it of "a deliberate attempt to mislead the Court."[100] As in other cases, Britain's accusations of fraud and bad faith are unmentioned in the Court's opinion and appear not to have influenced its analysis and conclusions.

The Court's decision on April 9, 1949 addressed the three points of the Special Agreement: (1) whether Albania laid, connived in the laying, or

95 "Verbatim Record" in *Corfu Channel (United Kingdom* v. *Albania)*, ICJ Doc. 1949/1, p. 204 (11 Nov. 1949, morning) (statement by Sir Hartley Shawcross), available at: www.icj-cij.org/docket/files/1/10905.pdf.

96 "Reply of the United Kingdom," para. 32.

97 "Verbatim Record," p. 205 (11 Nov. 1949, morning) (statement by Sir Hartley Shawcross).

98 "Reply of United Kingdom," para. 32.

99 The British did not concede this point. Rather, they pointed out the incredulity of such an accusation – underscoring it highly unlikely that a cruiser squadron under the command of a Rear-Admiral would behave directly contrary to standing orders in this way and not fly ensigns. Second, given the direction from which the ships were coming, it would have been impossible for them to be Greek, not to mention the fact that Greece did not have any ships of this type. These facts would have surely be known to Albania given "its preoccupations over Greek activities." "Verbatim Record," p. 284 (11 Nov. 1949, morning) (statement by Sir Eric Beckett).

100 "Reply of United Kingdom," para. 32.

was aware of the laying of the mines; (2) whether the Royal Navy violated Albanian sovereignty on October 22; and (3) whether the Royal Navy violated Albanian sovereignty on November 12 and 13.

Since there was no direct evidence of Albanian knowledge, the Court turned to circumstantial evidence.[101] It noted that the Albanian government "constantly kept a close watch" over the channel,[102] as evidenced by the May firings on the British ships. The Albanian notes provided "evidence of its intention to keep a jealous watch on its territorial waters,"[103] as did the testimony of an Albanian Coastal Defence Commander that prior to the October 22 events he had orders "'[t]hat the look-out posts must inform [the commander] of every movement [in the Corfu Channel].'"[104] This evidence persuaded the Court that Albania was liable on the theory that "whoever the authors of the minelaying were, it could not have been done without the Albanian Government's knowledge."[105]

With respect to Albania's claim that its sovereignty had been violated, the Court laid down a general rule: "in time of peace [States] have a right to send their warships through straits used for international navigation between two parts of the high seas without the previous authorization of a coastal State, provided that the passage is *innocent*."[106] And, in the Court's view, the passage was innocent. The Court dismissed Albania's complaints about provocation; Britain's test of Albanian intentions was an unobjectionable effect of an otherwise innocent passage. That the passage was intended both "to test Albania's attitude" as well as "to demonstrate such force that she would abstain from firing again on passing ships," was consistent with innocent passage.[107] "The 'mission,'" it held, "was designed to affirm a right which had been unjustly denied. The Government of the United Kingdom was not bound to abstain from exercising its right of passage, which the Albanian Government had illegally denied."[108]

But Operation Retail did violate Albanian sovereignty. The Court rejected the UK's justification of self-defense: "The Court can only regard the alleged right of intervention as the manifestation of a policy of force, such as has, in the past, given rise to most serious abuses and such as cannot, whatever be the present defects in international organization, find a place

[101] *Corfu Channel*, 1949 *ICJ Rep.*, p. 18.
[102] *Ibid.* [103] *Ibid.*, 19. [104] *Ibid.* [105] *Ibid.*, 17.
[106] *Ibid.*, 28. The Albanian contention that the strait was not a major international highway found no favor with the Court. *Ibid.*, 29. *Cf.* Convention on the Law of the Sea, Dec. 10, 1982, 1833 UNTS 397.
[107] *Corfu Channel*, 1949 *ICJ Rep.*, p. 31. [108] *Ibid.*, 30.

in international law."[109] But this was the mildest of rebukes, even further tempered by "the Albanian Government's complete failure to carry out its duties after the explosions, and the dilatory nature of its diplomatic notes," which the Court described as "extenuating circumstances for the action of the United Kingdom Government."[110]

In the next phase of the case, the Court calculated damages and entered them against the Albanian government.

For all of their apprehensions, in the end, the Law Officers' decision to withhold XCU appears to have had little influence on the judgment. The Court drew no negative inferences:

> Those documents were not produced, the Agent pleading naval secrecy; and the United Kingdom witnesses declined to answer questions relating to them. It is not therefore possible to know the real content of these naval orders. The Court cannot, however, draw from this refusal to produce the orders any conclusions differing from those to which the actual events gave rise.[111]

Nor did the Court comment on the UK's allegations of Albanian misrepresentations.

In a post-mortem report on the case, Beckett remarked: "As [innocent passage] was a point on which we were extremely anxious about our position, involving *inter alia* as it did the document XCU which we did not disclose, it can be stated that the result surpasses our most sanguine expectations."[112] The Court's refusal to adjudge the propriety of the UK's suppression presaged its attitude toward litigants' questionable evidentiary behavior in other cases. Here, as in future cases studied, the Court quickly (and without value judgments attached) noted the controversy and moved on to settle the dispute.

Conclusion

The *Corfu Channel* case presents two "production issues" which are relevant to our analysis of fraud and counsel's ethical obligations. The first is the internal production issue, that is, the fact that the Admiralty, in a sense the client, did not produce XCU to the legal officers until late in the day. The second issue is the client's refusal to produce XCU to the Court when requested, and the comportment of the UK's lawyers.

[109] *Ibid.*, 35. [110] *Ibid.* [111] *Ibid.*, 32.
[112] W. E. Beckett, "Report by the Agent on the Corfu Case," p. 1, para. 2.

With respect to the internal production issue, the Law Officers criticized the Admiralty for having failed to turn over the documents before the lawyers even recommended that a case be brought. Interestingly, however, there was almost no discussion of whether the legal officers bore any responsibility. Their failure to procure the relevant documents seems to have been ignored. The legal officers assumed that the Admiralty should, and had, taken the initiative to produce all documents pertaining to the operation. Indeed, they proceeded to the Security Council and then prepared their pleadings for the International Court confident of this assumption.

From our review of the documents, it is not clear exactly when the Legal Officers took notice of XCU and XCU1 and fully appreciated their contents and their implication for the case. But based on the memoranda and the timing of Albania's request for the document, this realization must have dawned on them no later than the fall of 1948, shortly before the oral proceedings commenced.[113] After XCU came to light, it was the Admiralty that bore the brunt of the criticism for the internal production failure. The Lord Chancellor wrote to the Prime Minister that:

> [t]here is no doubt that an unfortunate mistake has been made in this case, in that steps were not taken to obtain the Operation Orders and put them before the Law Officers. It should have been known to the Admiralty authorities that Operation Orders might have been issued, and it must have been obvious that if such Operation Orders were issued they might have some bearing on the elucidation of the material facts.[114]

Fault here may indeed lie with the Admiralty, but we are principally interested in the question of legal counsel's obligations. Here, fulfillment of those obligations seems to have fallen short.

Ideally, the Admiralty should have volunteered all the related operational orders and communications. Yet should the lawyers have outsourced this task to a department less familiar with the requirements and procedures of litigation at the International Court? Not only was the Admiralty less accustomed to preparing cases for litigation, but also it could have had reasons for withholding documents that could damage its own reputation and morale, which could have loomed larger than the success of the case. So there are many reasons why the Legal Officers should have assumed responsibility for procuring the relevant Admiralty documents. After all,

[113] See, for example, Carty, "The Corfu Channel Case," 4.

[114] ADM 1/22504, Minute by the Lord Chancellor to the Prime Minister, p. 2, para. 5 (5 Nov. 1948).

it was the lawyers who could have best avoided "the mistake" the Lord Chancellor attributed to "the Admiralty Authorities using their judgment as to what issues were involved and what documents should be disclosed instead of making all the material available to the Law Officers so that they could decide the issue."[115]

This lapse on the part of the lawyers may indicate what Beckett referred to as some "disorder in the house,"[116] but that is not to say that the Legal Officers violated ethical obligations in failing to obtain XCU from the outset. It would have been unethical to make representations to the Court the officers *knew* to be untrue. Britain's lawyers did not construct their pleadings to get around directly contrary evidence. Nor was it analogous to the criminal law equivalent of willful blindness, where one seeks to sanitize what one suspects to be illegal behavior by intentionally taking insufficient steps to ascertain one's legal obligations. The Legal Officers, it would appear, assumed too much of the Admiralty and investigated too little on their own accord.

The more wrenching issue was the decision not to produce XCU to the Court and the adverse party. This is a more complex question in public international litigation, involving, as it does, the legal and ethical tensions of the government lawyer, especially when evidence which should be discovered under ordinary circumstances bears on current foreign policy, defense, and national security concerns. As is often the case in government–client relationships, the government legal advisors' sphere of influence was limited. Ultimately, the decision to produce XCU was not the Legal Officers' to make. In this situation, and in light of the Legal Officers' conclusion that XCU materially altered the accuracy of their claims, what were the counselors' ethical obligations and did they fulfill them?

Frank Soskice, the Solicitor General, wrote to the Foreign Secretary and First Lord on January 10 that the Legal Officers, together with the Admiralty, had considered "very carefully" whether "we ought as lawyers, advising from the purely legal standpoint, to recommend that the decision to withhold production of XCU should be reviewed."[117] Soskice gave some reasons for disclosure: the reputational risks to the British government, the negative impact on public opinion should the document be withheld, and

115 ADM 1/22504, Minute from William Jowitt, Lord Chancellor, to Viscount Hall, First Lord (5 Nov. 1948).

116 Carty, "The Corfu Channel Case," 13 (citing FO 371/72101, Minute from W. E. Beckett to Sir Orme Sargent (3 Nov. 1948)).

117 PREM 8/1312, Brief from Frank Soskice, Solicitor General, to the Foreign Secretary and First Lord, *Corfu Channel Case* (undated).

even the potential of dismissal for failure to produce a vital document. But the "legal standpoint" was tactical rather than ethical: how disclosure would impact the Court's view of the case. In terms of these strategic considerations, they recommended against disclosure.

Reasonable minds had disagreed over whether the document did in fact undermine the passage's innocence, for international law scholars have long debated the legal definition and characteristics of the right of innocent passage. The lawyers may have thus found it difficult to argue more forcefully that failing to disclose XCU was unethical.

As it developed, neither of the production issues appears to have significantly impacted the case. The failure to produce the document internally did not materially influence the way the case was processed. In the midst of the XCU debate, the Permanent Under-Secretary at the Foreign Office, Sir Orme Sargent, estimated that even if all departments had known of XCU from the start, the decision to go to the Security Council and then the International Court would have been no different. In Sargent's assessment:

> the knowledge of the facts that the passage through the Channel had been badly arranged and that the orders were unfortunately worded would [not] have prevented our bringing the mining of our ships before the Security Council because there was, in the circumstances, virtually nothing else we could do. Moreover, when the Russians vetoed the first resolution in the Security Council there was really no other course open to us than to propose that the case should go to the International Court, unless we were prepared to accept a stalemate resulting from the Russian veto. I am advised that, if we had known of the facts which have now come to light, the result, at most, would have been that we might have worded somewhat differently, some of the remarks which Sir Alexander Cadogan made in the Security Council and one or two sentences of the written pleadings we have put in before the International Court.[118]

And had the Court examined XCU, it seems likely that it would still have found the passage innocent. Recall that in its opinion, the Court specifically stated that a test passage could also be innocent. In making this determination, the Court had seen telegrams that were exchanged between the Admiralty and the Commander-in-Chief Mediterranean, on September 21 and October 26, that revealed Britain's intention to test Albanian reactions with a voyage.[119]

[118] PREM 8/1312, Minute from Sir Orme Sargent, Permanent Under-Secretary at the Foreign Office, to Clement R. Attlee, Prime Minister, para. 3 (9 Nov. 1948).

[119] *Corfu Channel*, 1949 *ICJ Rep.*, pp. 30, 31.

In a minute to the Lord Chancellor, Shawcross revealed an acute appreciation of his professional dilemma. As he questioned whether the non-disclosure of XCU was the proper course, he acknowledged the complexity of proceeding before an international tribunal when ethical obligations conflict with political and security concerns. "If the case were before an English Court, there could, of course, be no possible question. How far one is entitled to adopt a different code of ethics in regard to the International Court I do not know. Does the maxim 'My country . . . right or wrong, my country' relieve one from the professional consequences which would otherwise arise?"[120] Shawcross' question is one that government lawyers will continue to face when public policy decisions, made by different "client" departments, are contrary to how the lawyer would otherwise proceed.[121]

[120] LCO 2/4515, Minute from Hartley Shawcross, Attorney General, to William Jowitt, Lord Chancellor (1 Nov. 1948).

[121] For discussion, see W. M. Reisman, *The Quest for World Order and Human Dignity in the Twenty-first Century: Constitutive Process and Individual Commitment: General Course on Public International Law* (Leiden/Boston: Martinus Nijhoff, 2012), pp. 363–81.

4

Tunisia/Libya: strategic omissions

In 1982, the International Court of Justice handed down its judgment in a maritime boundary dispute between Libya and Tunisia.[1] The Special Agreement by which the case was submitted had requested the Court to identify the "principles and rules of international law" for the delimitation of the continental shelf appurtenant to the two states, taking account of "equitable principles, and the relevant circumstances which characterize the area." The Court was then

> to clarify the practical method for the application of these principles and rules in this specific situation, so as to enable the experts of the two countries to delimit these areas without any difficulties.[2]

The pleadings in the case were voluminous, even by the standards of maritime boundary disputes before the International Court. That was hardly surprising. The stakes were high: oil in the continental shelf area was in dispute.

In its 1969 case, *North Sea Continental Shelf*,[3] the Court had invented an "equitable principles" doctrine for determining maritime boundaries, which invited consulting a wide range of factors. Indeed, in the Court's view, "there is no legal limit to the considerations which States may take account of for the purpose of making sure that they apply equitable procedures."[4]

[1] *Continental Shelf Case (Tunisia/Libya)*, 1982 *ICJ Rep*. 18 (24 Feb.), 67 *ILR* 4.

[2] "Special Agreement" in *Continental Shelf Case (Tunisia/Libya)*, 1982 *ICJ Pleadings* 3, p. 26 (10 June 1977).

[3] *North Sea Continental Shelf (Germany* v. *Denmark/Germany* v. *The Netherlands)*, 1969 *ICJ Rep*. 3, para. 85 (20 Feb.), 41 *ILR* 29.

[4] *Ibid*., para. 93.

In the *Tunisia/Libya* dispute, the Special Agreement's term "relevant circumstances" hardly reined in that range.

One of the many possible "considerations" or "relevant circumstances" that was at issue in the written submissions and oral arguments was the location of the various petroleum concessions that each state had granted.

In its Memorial, Libya "call[ed]" "the Court['s] . . . attention to some of the highlights of the discussions"[5] the parties had had prior to litigation. In particular, pursuant to Libya's 1955 Petroleum Law and Regulation:

> It was entirely within the competence of the Libya authorities . . . to grant concessions to explore for and exploit petroleum resources within the area . . . However, the Libyan authorities had not granted an offshore concession prior to the time Tunisia granted . . . a concession to a French company . . . within an area to the west of a stepped (or zigzag) line which ran in a direction north/northeast at about 26 degrees from Ras Ajdir. Subsequently . . . the Libyan authorities granted Concession No. 137 to that company.[6]

The Libyan Petroleum Law No. 25 and the Petroleum Regulation No. 1 were published in the official gazette at the time of their enactment. "So it was made absolutely clear in 1955 that Libya was claiming a maritime boundary continuing northward from Ras Ajdir." "There can be no doubt about the general direction of the maritime boundary on Map No. 1," "[i]t runs north parallel to the meridian 12°E." "It is not conceivable," stated Libya, "that this legislation was unknown to Tunisia." Libya then, in effect, made an estoppel or waiver claim: "Yet Tunisia has made no protest or reservation at any time regarding either the Law or the Regulation."[7]

Libya rehearsed both parties' concession-granting history to paint a picture of convergence around the 26° line. Libya underscored that one of "[t]he most significant points in this history of the Tunisian concessions" was "the use of the due north line in 1964" and "the use of the 26° line from 1966 onwards."[8] Moreover, "notwithstanding a firm belief in the possession of sovereign rights up to the line shown in Map No. 1 attached to the Petroleum Regulation of 1955, Libya has exercised considerable self-restraint in never going west of the original 26° concession line in the grant

[5] "Memorial of the Libyan Arab Jamahiriya" in *Continental Shelf Case (Tunisia/Libya)*, 1982 *ICJ Pleadings* 455, para. 30 (30 May 1980), available at: www.icj-cij.org/docket/files/63/9517.pdf.

[6] *Ibid.*, para. 36.

[7] "Counter-Memorial of the Libyan Arab Jamahiriya" in *Continental Shelf Case (Tunisia/Libya)*, 1982 *ICJ Pleadings* 147, paras. 28–30 (2 Feb. 1981), available at: www.icj-cij.org/docket/files/63/9523.pdf.

[8] *Ibid.*, para. 35.

of further concessions."[9] Libya concluded its discussion of the concession history by

> not[ing] that the expression "26° line" is a notional one used for convenience. It represents the direction of the eastern boundary of a concession granted by Tunisia and the western boundary of a concession granted by Libya. It was at no time accepted by Libya as the legal line of delimitation of the areas of continental shelf appertaining *de jure* to Libya . . . However, the 26° line . . . do[es] suggest the kind of line that, in the context of negotiations, might have been put forward for discussion.[10]

In oral argument, the location of the oil concessions came up a number of times. In his opening presentation to the Court, the Libyan Agent, Ambassador Kamel El Maghur, referred to it almost immediately.[11] In commenting on a concession that Tunisia awarded in 1966, whose eastern extremity followed a line of 26° from a meridian intersecting Ras Ajdir, the land boundary of the two countries at the coast, the Agent said:

> Libya's first concession in 1968, instead of adopting as its western boundary a due north line from Ras Ajdir – as its 1955 Petroleum Law and Regulations would have warranted – avoided the possibility of conflict by adopting the same line. Libya has never granted a concession to the west of this 26° line, not because it saw its sovereign rights as ending at that line – and in this regard Libya agrees with Tunisia that a concession boundary is not a line of delimitation . . . – but because its whole policy was linked to the aim of unity and joint exploration and exploitation. Within the context of efforts to agree on the terms of joint exploration and exploitation of the area, the 26° line was a purely provisional accommodation to avoid disputes.[12]

Though it was a purely provisional accommodation, the Agent, two paragraphs beyond, criticized Tunisia for granting a concession in 1972 "that lunged to the east of the 26° line."[13] The thrust of the Agent's remarks in this regard were not so much that the 26° line had become, by agreement, a provisional line, but more so that Tunisia had used the line when it served its purposes, only to make much greater claims at a later stage.

The Agent was followed by Sir Francis Vallat, who, among other things, examined the trend of oil concessions with the help of maps and overlays. Sir Francis said:

[9] *Ibid.*, para. 37. [10] *Ibid.*, para. 43.

[11] "Verbatim Record" in *Continental Shelf Case (Tunisia/Libya)*, pp. 3–4 (29 Sept. 1981, 10 a.m.), available at: www.icj-cij.org/docket/files/63/9543.pdf.

[12] *Ibid.*, p. 8. [13] *Ibid.*, 8–9.

Early in 1968, I think it was in April, Libya granted Concession No. 137. The area of this concession is shown in yellow on the overlay. This is the area which now appears to run generally parallel on the western side with its western boundary generally at 26° from Ras Ajdir. One thus had the situation in which there were two concessions granted respectively by Tunisia and by Libya with virtually a common boundary. Theoretically there were little gaps, of course, but virtually a common boundary.[14]

The coincidence of the lines of Libya and Tunisia up until 1968 was used to underline the profligacy of Tunisian concessions beyond 26° in 1972 and thereafter[15]: the "eastward thrust" of Tunisia was compared with the "self restraint of Libya in following the 26° line from Ras Ajdir."[16]

Libya's conciliatory behavior and self-restraint was, as it were, an indication of good faith, implicit in the equitable principles doctrine and, accordingly, a "relevant circumstance." The Court was, after all, seeking a "method of delimitation [that] would ensure an equitable result."[17] In this endeavor,

it is evident that the Court must take into account *whatever indicia* are available of the line or lines which the Parties themselves may have considered equitable or acted upon as such – if only as an interim solution affecting part only of the area to be delimited.[18]

Clearly, the Court was impressed with the fact that, though Libya argued that it had never accepted that line as the "legal line of delimitation," that these lines were "the kinds of lines that, in the context of negotiations, might have been put forward for discussion."[19] The Court interpreted these words as meaning that such lines were viewed by Libya as a common basis for an agreed delimitation. The Court was also impressed by the fact that an essentially 26° line was used in the *modus vivendi* between France and Italy, the respective colonial powers, to delimit *pro tem* fisheries jurisdiction between Libya and Tunisia.[20] But, of course, that was for fishing. The

14 *Ibid.*, 45.

15 After some unsuccessful discussions in 1968 "[t]here were no further steps until Tunisia granted . . . Concessions Nos. 8 and 9. I think that this was in 1972 . . . The whole area, and it's a large one, is shown by the overlay in olive green. The area of these concessions . . . speaks for itself. It must be obvious that with such an extension eastward, even north of Tripoli, Libya could not possibly sit back and do nothing about the grant of a Tunisian concession extending, as this one did, so far south and so far east." *Ibid.*

16 *Ibid.*, 46. 17 *Continental Shelf Case (Tunisia/Libya)*, 1982 *ICJ Rep.*, p. 84, para. 118.

18 *Ibid.* (emphasis added). 19 *Ibid.* 20 *Ibid.*, para. 119.

Court was plainly giving greater weight to the de facto congruence of the petroleum claims, "the heart of the dispute."[21]

As a practical matter, the Court directed that the initial segment of delimitation, from the outer limits of the territorial sea, follow a line common to the eastern and western limits of the respective Tunisian and Libyan oil concessions. The Court stated that:

> [o]n the information available to the Court, that angle appears to be 26°; it will, however, be for the experts of the Parties to determine it with exactness.[22]

In assessing the relevant conduct of the parties, the Court found the de facto common petroleum line that emerged from the parties' respective practice to be important affirmative evidence[23] against which the Court found no compelling evidence to the contrary. Hence, the Court concluded that "[t]he 26° line therefore reflects all appropriate factors."[24]

In the dispositif, the 26° line was confirmed as the first segment of the delimitation by a vote of ten to four.[25] But, in fact, only eight of the judges arrived at that conclusion for the reasons expressed by the majority. Judge Ago concurred in the result, but explained in a separate opinion that in his view there had long been a maritime boundary in the first segment, as the colonial authorities had acquiesced in it, and that the independent states of Libya and Tunisia succeeded to it according to general international law principles and regional rules enunciated by the Organization of African Unity. Judge Ago emphasized:

> I do not in any way intend to minimize the importance of the fact that, in granting licenses and concessions for the exploration and exploitation of the hydrocarbon resources of the subsoil of the sea-bed, the Parties, up to a certain date and as far as a certain latitude, both kept to the same perpendicular to the coastline. All I wish to say is that it is this second fact which strikes me as supplementing and, above all, confirming the first, rather than the reverse.[26]

Similarly, Judge Jiménez de Aréchaga concluded, in a separate opinion, that the colonial powers had established a maritime boundary which had

[21] *Ibid.*, para. 118. [22] *Ibid.*, para. 121. [23] *Ibid.*, para. 117. [24] *Ibid.*, para. 121.

[25] *Ibid.*, 93.

> The relevant circumstances . . . include the following . . .
> (4) the land frontier between the Parties, and their conduct prior to 1974 in the grant of petroleum concessions, resulting in the employment of a line seawards from Ras Ajdir at an angle of approximately 26° east of the meridian, which line corresponds to the line perpendicular to the coast at the frontier point which had in the past been observed as a de facto maritime limit.

[26] *Ibid.*, p. 98 (separate opinion of Judge Ago).

to be respected.[27] Hence the spatial coincidence of the limits of the two countries' petroleum concessions was not decisive for either of these judges. But except for the alternative grounds for concurrence of Judges Ago and Jiménez de Aréchaga, the opinion of eight of the fifteen judges sitting in the case was based on the de facto convergence of the petroleum concessions granted by each state on the 26° line.[28]

Two years after judgment, Tunisia applied to the Court for a revision of the judgment, its interpretation, and its correction.[29] Essentially, Tunisia argued that the Court had been led, by Libyan misrepresentation, to conclude that there had been a de facto convergence between the two states with regard to petroleum concessions. Tunisia submitted the text of a Resolution of the Libyan Council of Ministers of March 28, 1968, which determined the real course of Libyan Petroleum Concession No. 137. According to Tunisia, it diverged from the various descriptions Libya had given in its pleading to the Court before the 1982 judgment. Tunisia argued that the real course of the northwestern boundary of Libya's Concession No. 137 was a fact which

> was of such a nature as to be a decisive factor in the Court's Judgment, given that the Court relied upon certain statements by Libya which prove to be contradicted by the document in question and that the actual operative provisions of the Judgment define the delimitation line to be drawn in accordance with criteria derived from those statements.[30]

Libya's de facto line was not 26° but 24°, 57′ 03″. In short, the actual situation, in contrast to the one the Court had constructed and was relying on, was that there was no de facto line common to the parties with regard to the "heart of the dispute." While this would have been immaterial for Judges Ago and Jiménez de Aréchaga, it did undermine a critical premise of the rest of the majority.

27 *Ibid.*, 131 (separate opinion of Judge Jiménez de Aréchaga).

28 In dissent, ad hoc Judge Gros rejected the majority's reliance on unilaterally granted concessions, for, in his view, such unilateral acts are not opposable to another state. *Ibid.*, para. 22 (dissenting opinion of Judge Gros). Judge Gros roundly rejected the majority's reliance on the congruence of unilateral acts by each state. Judge Oda, in dissent, did not address the majority's primary ground for adopting the 26° line for the first segment of the boundary, but rejected it in its entirety, suggesting instead quite a different line. *Ibid.*, 272 (dissenting opinion of Judge Oda).

29 *Continental Shelf Case, Application for Revision and Interpretation of the Judgment of 24 February 1982 in the Case Concerning the Continental Shelf (Tunisia/Libya)*, 1985 *ICJ Rep.* 192 (10 Dec.), 81 *ILR* 419 (Tunisia's Application, 27 July 1984).

30 *Ibid.*, para. 34.

In the revision phase of the case, the Court confirmed that Libya had not presented the correct course of the westward limit of its concessions in its pleadings. This inaccuracy was not the result of a single misstatement, but was repeated in different phases. Paraphrasing Tunisia, the Court said:

For this purpose the Court relied on the information as to the boundaries of the concessions mentioned, particularly Concession No. 137, supplied by the Government of Libya, which had granted them. In its Memorial, Libya stated that the area covered by that Concession lay "to the eastward of a line running south/southwest from the point 33° 55′N, 12°E to a point about one nautical mile offshore", adding that "The point of origin viewed from Ras Ajdir is at an angle of 26 degrees". In its Counter-Memorial, Libya mentioned the "stepped eastern boundary" of the Tunisian concession described in the 1982 Judgment as the "Permis complémentaire offshore du Golfe de Gabs" (hereafter referred to as "the Tunisian permit") and stated: "This is the Concession boundary that runs in a direction northward at an angle of 26° from Ras Ajdir." Further on in the same pleading, Libya indicated that

"on 30 April 1968, the Libyan authorities granted Concession No. 137 to Aquitaine and Exwarb . . . The western boundary of that Concession followed the direction of the Tunisian Concessions granted in 1967 to SNPA/RAP [i.e., the Tunisian permit]."

Referring to later concessions further from the coast, Libya mentioned that "The western boundary of both these Concessions followed the 26° line . . . in the grant of further concessions". At the hearings in 1981 the Agent of Libya referred to the Tunisian permit as having "moved eastward from the due north line from Ras Ajdir . . . to a line of 26° from Ras Ajdir", and went on to say that "Libya's first concession in 1968 . . . avoided the possibility of conflict by adopting the same line".[31]

Concession No. 137 had been submitted to the Court, but an annex to the Concession, "setting forth the area covered by the Concession in square kilometres as well as the co-ordinates of the boundaries of the Concession," apparently was not.[32] Though Libya argued in the revision phase that the correct course of the line could have been deduced from some of the other maps that were submitted,[33] the Court observed that:

[31] *Ibid.*, para. 14 (Judgment of 10 Dec. 1985).

[32] *Ibid.*, para. 20. In its application, Tunisia appended this "Description of Concession No. 137" to the copy of the Resolution of the Council of Ministers as if it were part of that Resolution. Libya contended that this mistake was "enough to render the Application inadmissible." The Court rejected that motion as based on "an over-formalistic approach." *Ibid.* It did not, however, comment in that connection on the fact that the same annex had not been adduced by Libya.

[33] *Ibid.*, para. 22.

while Libya emphasizes that the information it supplied to the Court in the proceedings leading up to the 1982 Judgment was accurate as far as it went, it does not in fact deny that the exact co-ordinates of Concession No. 137 were not supplied to the Court by either Party, so that Tunisia would not have been able to ascertain the exact location of the Libyan concession from the pleadings and other material then before the Court.[34]

Judge Oda was kinder to Libya and Tunisia than to the Court. Neither of the parties, he noted, assumed that the boundaries of the concessions would be an important or even relevant factor in the Court's decision:

[N]either Tunisia nor Libya can fairly be blamed for what now might in retrospect appear to be omissions. Solely the Court, which in 1982 by its own initiative lent great significance to the concessions previously granted by the Parties, was at fault in an omission, namely, of referring to the Tunisian and Libyan concessions without adequate knowledge and without any verification of their respective positions.[35]

The majority made no comment whatsoever on whether Libya or the Libyan Agent and counsel behaved improperly – whether unlawfully, unprofessionally, or negligently – in presenting a picture of events that was not entirely accurate. The Court's statutory framework enabled it to skirt the issue. Article 61(1) of the Statute, on the basis of which Tunisia had made its application for revision, provides:

An application for revision of a judgment may be made only when it is based upon the discovery of some fact of such a nature as to be a decisive factor, which fact was, when the judgment was given, unknown to the Court and also to the party claiming revision, always provided that such ignorance was not due to negligence.

Revision, under Article 61, cannot proceed unless three cumulative conditions are met. The first two conditions are objective. First, the newly discovered fact must have been central to the prior decision: "a decisive factor." Often more facts might have been discovered by each party if there had been more time. Article 61 avoids, by its first condition, creating an incentive to resume digging for facts after an unfavorable judgment. This first condition – essentially that the new fact must neutralize the force of a factual assumption that was decisive in the previous judgment – refers to the text of the judgment and the record of the pleadings.

Second, the newly discovered fact must have been "unknown" to the Court when it made its decision. On its face, this seems to be the predicate

[34] *Ibid.*, para. 23. [35] *Ibid.*, 239, para. 8 (separate opinion of Judge Oda).

of a revision application. In so wording this condition, its drafters may have anticipated circumstances in which the allegedly newly discovered fact, though not pleaded, was known by the tribunal yet deemed unnecessary for the judgment. By implication, it would certainly not have been central to the tribunal's reasoning. This condition, too, is essentially factual but, by contrast to the first condition, the facts here will not be in the record, but in the "mind" of the tribunal.

Article 61's third condition shifts from factual to legal questions: ignorance, theretofore, of the critical fact must not have been due to the complaining party's negligence. This legal question turns on the standards of due diligence of international law in these matters and might seem to implicate the fraud of the counter-party. After all, a fact that is discovered after judgment, in spite of the other party's diligence, may have been unavailable because of the fraudulent behavior of its adversary. Yet neither in text nor in penumbra does Article 61 make this relevant to revision. Even an extreme case of intentional fraud practiced on the Court (which we are not considering here) is not, per se, grounds for revising a judgment, unless all the other conditions of Article 61 are met. And if they are, fraud – or the absence of fraud – is irrelevant.[36]

Thus, in the context of Article 61, the question for the Court was not Libya's behavior but Tunisia's, namely,

> whether the circumstances were such that means were available to Tunisia to ascertain the details of the co-ordinates of the concession from other sources; and indeed whether it was in Tunisia's own interest to do so. If such be the case, it does not appear to the Court that it is open to Tunisia to rely on those co-ordinates as a fact which was "unknown" to it for the purposes of Article 61.[37]

If we analyze what the Court felt were the minima required of Tunisia, we can extrapolate what sorts of behavior on the part of a litigant before the Court are, if not laudable or even permissible, nevertheless subject to neither sanction nor opprobrium.

Tunisia contended that it was not negligent within the meaning of Article 61 because it had asked Libya for the maps. In the Court's view, that did not meet the due diligence standards of the Statute:

[36] See also *Application for Revision of the Judgment of 11 September 1992 in the Case Concerning the Land, Island and Maritime Frontier Dispute (El Salvador/Honduras: Nicaragua Intervening) (El Salvador* v. *Honduras)*, paras. 15–22 (18 Dec. 2003) (discussing these criterion), 97 *ILR* 112.

[37] *Continental Shelf Case (Tunisia/Libya), Application for Revision*, 1985 *ICJ Rep.* para. 23.

While it was no doubt correct as a matter of diplomatic practice for Tunisia to invite the Libyan Government to supply the relevant information, there was no reason why Tunisia, particularly if it was not receiving from the Libyan Government the co-operation which it apparently expected, should not employ other, perfectly lawful and proper, means to obtain it.[38]

In more detail, the Court explained:

Normal diligence would require that, when sending a delegation to negotiate a continental shelf delimitation, following the grant by each side of neighbouring or conflicting concessions, a State should first try to learn the exact co-ordinates of the other party's concession. Furthermore, it is to be expected that a State would not assert that such concession extended to its own area of continental shelf without knowing, or making efforts to discover, the exact limits of the concession. It is also to be expected that, in litigation the ultimate purpose of which is the establishment of a continental shelf delimitation, and in the course of which a petroleum concession in the relevant area is described by one party without precision, the other party will not limit itself to commenting on the matter in its pleading, but itself seek out the information.[39]

In short:

the fact that the concession boundary co-ordinates were obtainable by Tunisia, and the fact that it was in its own interests to ascertain them, together signify that one of the essential conditions of admissibility of a request for revision . . . namely ignorance of a new fact not due to negligence, is lacking.[40]

Tunisia thus failed to establish the third condition of Article 61. On this ground alone, and proceeding no further, its application for revision could be rejected.

With regard to the first objective condition, the decisive character of the newly discovered fact, the Court interpreted its 1982 judgment as relying on other factors and not on the 26° line, "its reasoning wholly unaffected by the evidence now produced."[41] It acknowledged that "[t]his is not of course to say that if the co-ordinates of Concession No. 137 had been clearly indicated to the Court, the 1982 Judgment would nevertheless have been identically worded."[42] But "[t]he details of the correct co-ordinates of Concession No. 137 would not have changed the decision of the Court as to the first sector of the delimitation."[43]

[38] *Ibid.*, para. 26. [39] *Ibid.*, para. 27. [40] *Ibid.*, para. 28. [41] *Ibid.*, para. 38.
[42] *Ibid.*, para. 39. [43] *Ibid.*

This is not completely persuasive. The language of the 1982 judgment is a *res ipsa loquitur* and the two concurring opinions provide a useful window into the deliberations of the Court. At the very least, one must say, as Judge Oda did in a separate opinion in the revision phase, that:

[i]t has become evident through the present proceedings that in giving judgment in 1982 the Court had no exact idea of the boundaries of the concessions granted by the respective Parties prior to the signing of the Special Agreement.[44]

Conclusion

The Court's interpretation of its Statute illustrates another approach to fraudulent evidence, one that, in effect, endorses a materiality standard. In the *Tunisia/Libya* case, the emphasis shifted from deciding allegations that one party may have misled the tribunal – a factual question, which depends only on whether the tribunal was, in fact, misled – to certain preliminary questions, affirmative responses to which are prerequisite to an applicant's ability to complain of fraud. In making this shift, the Court presented a relational view of materiality and fraud. The Court stated: "Any 'new fact' . . . is . . . not necessarily to be regarded as a decisive factor."[45] In other words, there must be a nexus between the new fact and the decision. Here, such nexus was absent, as "the Court's reasoning [was] wholly unaffected by the evidence [later] produced."[46] This language, although in *obiter*, suggests that the Court must first be persuaded of a fact's materiality to the judgment before it will consider the merits of an underlying fraud claim.

Yet the fact that the Court did not comment on Libya's omission need not be taken as evidence of a laissez faire policy. Arguably, the Court had not needed to reach that question if the only issue was Tunisian due diligence in seeking to secure the information in a timely fashion. It is, nonetheless, difficult to escape the implication that there is, in effect, no sanction for negligent or intentional misrepresentation. This approach stands in contrast to one which would have held Libya accountable for failing to disclose affirmatively that which would undoubtedly be a central factual tenet of its adversary's legal theory.

Finally, it is worth reflecting briefly on the legal problem that was raised in this case. A fair reading of the Court's judgment in 1982 is that the dispositive "circumstance" for the majority's decision was its conviction that there was a common de facto line for petroleum activities in a critical

[44] *Ibid.*, 236, para. 2 (separate opinion of Judge Oda). [45] *Ibid.*, para. 35 (merits).
[46] *Ibid.*, para. 38.

period of the dispute and this could be taken as reflecting the parties' notion of an "equitable" delimitation, in the special sense in which the Court was then using "equitable" in maritime boundary delimitations. Subsequent information indicated that the Court's conviction was incorrect.

The Court was in error with regard to a critical if not fundamental strand of its judgment. Of that we can have little doubt. The question left unanswered, however, was whether the Court was led into that error by one of the parties. Regardless of how we label such conduct, the question indicates the more difficult problem as it arises in international law: how shall international law deal with litigants who select, design, and present information so that the court or tribunal will misperceive the information in ways that discriminate in favor of the party presenting it?

5

Nicaragua v. *United States*: false witnesses

A critical question in the *Military and Paramilitary Activities* case, which Nicaragua brought against the United States, was whether the Sandinista Government of Nicaragua was supplying arms to insurgents in El Salvador. The United States acknowledged its support of the contras but claimed that its actions were being undertaken in collective self-defense of El Salvador, against whom Nicaragua, it alleged, was aggressing. If Nicaraguan aggression had been established, the United States' actions in and against Nicaragua could have been lawful; even then, however, particular actions would still have had to meet the various requirements of the *jus in bello* of the international law of armed conflict.

The Government of El Salvador, in its unsuccessful attempt to intervene in the case, had submitted accounts of the shipments of arms from Nicaragua to insurgents in El Salvador. El Salvador had also alleged that the insurgents had their general headquarters near Managua and used training sites in Nicaragua, which the Nicaraguan government had made available to them.[1] Without granting it a hearing, the Court rejected El Salvador's request to intervene.

Nicaragua did not oppose the intervention "in principle"[2] but it flatly denied El Salvador's charges on the critical issue that was at the heart of the United States' essential defense. In a sworn affidavit submitted to

[1] Declaration of Intervention of the Republic of El Salvador, *Military and Paramilitary Activities in and Against Nicaragua* (*Nicaragua* v. *United States*) (15 Aug. 1984), available at: www.icj-cij.org/docket/files/70/9625.pdf; see also J. Sztucki, "Intervention Under Article 63 of the ICJ Statute in the Phase of Preliminary Proceedings: The 'Salvadoran Incident,'" *Am. J. Int'l L.*, 79 (1985), 1005 (discussing the attempted intervention).

[2] "Written Observations on the Declaration of Intervention" (10 Sept. 1984), available at: www.icj-cij.org/docket/files/70/9623.pdf.

the Court, the then Sandinista Foreign Minister, Father Miguel d'Escoto, said:

In truth, my Government is not engaged, and has not been engaged, in the provision of arms or other supplies to either of the factions engaged in the civil war in El Salvador.[3]

In response to a question posed by Judge Schwebel, the Nicaraguan Agent stated:

it has not been the policy of the Nicaraguan Government to support insurgencies anywhere.[4]

Other Sandinista witnesses did not deny that some arms might have gone from Nicaragua to El Salvador. Rather they contended that if such arms had gone, they were in very small numbers and, in any case, provision of arms had never been an official policy of the Sandinista government. The essential structure of this position was neatly expressed by Commander Luis Carrión, whom Nicaragua produced as a witness in the Merits phase of the case. In response to a question posed by Judge Schwebel on September 13, 1985, Commander Carrin replied:

My Government has never had a policy of sending arms to opposition forces in Central America. That does not mean that this did not happen, especially in the first years after the revolution, in 1979 and 1980, weapons might have been carried through Nicaraguan territory, weapons that might have [*sic*] the Savadoran insurgents, as you said, as their final recipient. As a matter of fact in those first years there were several Nicaraguan citizens who went by themselves to El Salvador to join the Savadoran revolutionaries there because they felt it was a fight like ours. Our fight was very recent and many people were willing to go down to El Salvador and help in their fight. But this was never an official policy and many of them could [not] have been stopped before they left Nicaragua because most of the time they did this illegally. At one time we caught a "tica bus" which is a commercial passenger bus line which travels through Central America. We caught this bus which had a double bottom and that double bottom contained arms, weapons,

3 "Verbatim Record" in *Military and Paramilitary Activities in and Against Nicaragua (Nicaragua* v. *United States)*, Ex. II, para. 2, p. 141 (Affidavit of Miguel d' Escoto Brockmanm, 21 Apr. 1984), available at: www.icj-cij.org/docket/files/70/9639.pdf (hereinafter "Verbatim Record, Provisional Measures").

4 "Verbatim Record" in *Military and Paramilitary Activities in and Against Nicaragua (Nicaragua* v. *United States)*, p. 146 (19 Sept. 1985, 10 a.m.) (statement by Mr. Argüello Gómez, Agent for the Government of Nicaragua), available at: www.icj-cij.org/docket/files/70/9641.pdf (hereinafter "Verbatim Record, Merits").

and those were going to El Salvador. So we suppose that there might have been other loads of arms going through Nicaragua that we did not catch.[5]

Nicaragua also produced Dr. David MacMichael, a US national who had worked for the CIA on western hemisphere affairs and testified that he had been privy to US plans for covert action in Nicaragua.[6] MacMichael stated that he had seen no documents supporting the assertion that arms were flowing from Nicaragua into El Salvador.[7] He was questioned by counsel for Nicaragua, Professor Abram Chayes:

Q.: All right. I want to direct your attention now to the period of your employment with the Agency; was there any credible evidence that during that period, March 1981 to April 1983, the Government of Nicaragua was sending arms to rebels in El Salvador?
A.: No.

Q.: Was there any substantial evidence that during this period arms were sent from or across Nicaraguan territory to rebels in El Salvador with the approval, authorization, condonation or ratification of the Nicaraguan Government?
A.: No, there is no evidence that would show that.

Q.: Was there any substantial evidence that during the same period, any significant shipments of arms were sent with the advance knowledge of the Government of Nicaragua from or across its territory to rebels in El Salvador?
A.: There is no substantial evidence, no.

[5] *Ibid.*, 31 (13 Sept. 1985, 10 a.m.).

[6] *Ibid.*, 43–45. David MacMichael ran the Association of National Security Alumni. In a study of the fusion between left-wing and right-wing paranoia, "fusion paranoia," a journalist for *The New Yorker* in the United States wrote:

> MacMichael is also a member of the Covert Operations Working Group, a small band of conspiracists, aging sixties radicals and representatives of the religious left, which meets every three weeks or so in a sunny front room in an old mansion across the street from the Supreme Court to discuss what evils the United States Government – especially the C.I.A. – has been up to lately. At these meetings, Louis Wolf, the director of research for *CovertAction Quarterly*, is a regular, and so are MacMichael and Ralph McGehee, another former C.I.A. employee turned whistle-blower and watchdog. A guiding spirit of the Covert Operations Working Group is Pat Tatum, who is by profession a cabdriver. Tatum chairs the meetings, and maintains the group's mailing list, working in the early mornings and at night in the house where he rents a basement room cheap from a friend.

M. Kelly, "The Road to Paranoia," *The New Yorker* (19 June 1995), 60, 69–70.

[7] "Verbatim Record, Merits," p. 50 (16 Sept. 1985, 3 p.m.).

Q.: Was there any substantial evidence that during that period significant quantities of arms went to El Salvador from Nicaragua?
A.: From Nicaragua, that is originating in Nicaragua, no.[8]

Dr. MacMichael proceeded to state that the United States used a wide range of sophisticated means of gathering intelligence.

Q.: In your opinion, if the Government of Nicaragua was sending arms to rebels in El Salvador, could it do so without detection by United States intelligence-gathering capabilities?
A.: In any significant manner over this long period of time I do not believe they could have done so.[9]

The witness testified that there was evidence of shipments from Nicaragua in 1980 and early 1981 and that based on the evidence he had seen he "could not rule . . . out" the possible involvement of the Nicaraguan government during this time.[10]

Under questioning from the bench, Dr. MacMichael acknowledged that the probability was that he would actually rule it in.[11] But during direct examination, he had tried to cast serious doubt on the evidence that had been released by the United States regarding the period after his employment at the CIA, implying that some of it was based on disinformation the United States itself had disseminated and suggesting that defector testimony was inherently unreliable.[12] Dr. MacMichael acknowledged that political and military leaders of the Salvadoran insurgency "from time to time" operated from Nicaragua.[13]

In a long and careful examination from the bench, Judge Schwebel introduced reports from reliable newspapers in the United States of considerable arms shipments in the 1981 to 1983 period and quoted published interviews with Nicaraguan leaders.[14] MacMichael questioned some of the accounts.

In this fashion, the evidence was brought before the Court.

In its judgment, the Court reviewed the evidence and concluded:

> the Court is satisfied that, between July 1979, the date of the fall of the Somoza régime in Nicaragua, and the early months of 1981, an intermittent flow of arms was routed via the territory of Nicaragua to the armed opposition in El Salvador. On the other hand, the evidence is insufficient to satisfy the Court that, since the early months of 1981, assistance has continued to reach the Salvadorian

[8] *Ibid.*, 51–52. [9] *Ibid.*, 55. [10] *Ibid.* [11] *Ibid.*, 60. [12] *Ibid.*, 56–57. [13] *Ibid.*, 62. [14] *Ibid.*, 60–68.

armed opposition from the territory of Nicaragua on any significant scale, or that the Government of Nicaragua was responsible for any flow of arms at either period.[15]

But, given the legal theory the Court developed, the factual issue of whether Nicaragua was supplying arms and, if so, how much, shrank to the point of irrelevance:

Even assuming that the supply of arms to the opposition in El Salvador could be treated as imputable to the Government of Nicaragua, to justify invocation of the right of collective self-defence in customary international law, it would have to be equated with an armed attack by Nicaragua on El Salvador . . . [T]he Court is unable to consider that, in customary international law, the provision of arms to the opposition in another State constitutes an armed attack on that State. Even at a time when the arms flow was at its peak, and again assuming the participation of the Nicaraguan Government, that would not constitute such armed attack.[16]

"[T]he Court does not believe that the concept of 'armed attack' includes not only acts by armed bands where such acts occur on a significant scale but also assistance to rebels in the form of the provision of weapons or logistical or other support."[17] Moreover, the Court concluded that, regardless of whether there had been an "armed attack," it was beyond the United States' prerogative to exercise collective self-defense in the absence of a declaration by the victim state:

There is no rule in customary international law permitting another State to exercise the right of collective self-defence on the basis of its own assessment of the situation. Where collective self-defence is invoked, it is to be expected that the State for whose benefit this right is used will have declared itself to be the victim of an armed attack.[18]

In his dissenting opinion, Judge Schwebel concluded that the statements made by and on behalf of Nicaragua with regard to supplies of arms to the insurgents in El Salvador were "demonstrably false."[19] He attached a long factual appendix to his dissent detailing the reasons for his conclusion. With regard to the issue of submission of false evidence, he developed a high standard, to which we have referred earlier and which bears repeating,

[15] *Military and Paramilitary Activities in and Against Nicaragua (Nicaragua* v. *United States)*, 1986 *ICJ Rep.* 14, para. 160 (27 June), 76 *ILR* 1, 74.

[16] *Ibid.*, para. 230. [17] *Ibid.*, para. 195. [18] *Ibid.*

[19] *Ibid.*, para. 25 (dissenting opinion of Judge Schwebel).

given the clarity of its policy preference in a sector of international law in which policy is far from clear:

It is of course a commonplace that government officials dissemble. Reasons of State are often thought to justify statements which are incomplete, misleading or contrary to fact. Covert operations, by their nature, are intended to provide cover, to lend credibility to "deniability". In this very case, certain statements of representatives of the United States in the United Nations Security Council have been less than candid and have been shown to be inconsistent with other statements of the most senior representatives of the United States. Moreover, the Government of the United States has made some allegations against the Government of Nicaragua which appear to be erroneous or exaggerated or in any event unsubstantiated by evidence made public.

Nevertheless, there can be no equation between governmental statements made in this Court and governmental statements made outside of it. The foundation of judicial decision is the establishment of the truth. Deliberate misrepresentations by the representatives of a government party to a case before this Court cannot be accepted because they undermine the essence of the judicial function. This is particularly true where, as here, such misrepresentations are of facts that arguably are essential, and incontestably are material, to the Court's judgment.[20]

Judge Schwebel criticized the Court in that:

[i]t has excluded, discounted and excused the unanswerable evidence of Nicaragua's major and maintained intervention in the Salvadoran insurgency.[21]

In fact, the Court's legal theory rendered irrelevant the evidence that Judge Schwebel perceived as decisive. But Judge Schwebel was operating with a conception of the problem that went beyond the question of whether the misrepresented evidence was material. The Court, he said, "has chosen . . . to appear to lend its good name to Nicaragua's misrepresentation of the facts."[22] Even for Judge Schwebel, however, the act of intentional misrepresentation, in itself, does not have judicial consequences, wholly aside from whether the evidence so submitted proves to be relevant. In Judge Schwebel's view, the appropriate response to Nicaragua's indirect aggression should be an international "[u]nclean [h]ands"[23] doctrine which would deny the claimant *locus standi* to bring its claim in the Court. But apparently, the fact of presentation of false evidence is not the basis for a deprivation of *locus standi* under an unclean hands theory. It certainly could be, but it is not in the *Nicaragua* case, perhaps because, as Judge

[20] *Ibid.*, paras. 26–27. [21] *Ibid.*, para. 16. [22] *Ibid.* [23] *Ibid.*, para. 268.

Schwebel acknowledged, both parties presented some evidence that was questionable.

The post-adjudicative phase of *Nicaragua* seems to have lent support to Judge Schwebel's view of the facts. Early in the morning of May 23, 1993, an extensive arms cache exploded in the suburb of Santa Rosa in eastern Managua. An automotive-repair shop that had sheltered an underground storage bin containing rifles, grenades, and nineteen anti-aircraft missiles was destroyed in the blast that also left at least two people dead. It was reported that:

> Investigation revealed a cache of rifles, explosives and 19 anti-aircraft missiles in a cellar below the premises. The weapons were found to belong to a Salvadorean guerrilla group, the People's Liberation Forces. The discovery, proving a breach of last year's UN-brokered peace agreement in El Salvador, has humiliated guerrilla leaders eager to win respectability as politicians. They have apologised to the Nicaraguan government and have revealed other caches.
>
> . . .
>
> The affair is now being investigated by a Nicaraguan judge, as speculation mounts that the group must have had some tacit approval from the Sandinist officials. Critics of President Chamorro are now demanding an end to the power-sharing agreement that she made with the Sandinists, in the name of national unity, after her election victory in February 1990.[24]

The article continued that both Mrs. Chamorro and the Spanish government, which had allegedly ignored its ambassador's warnings about Sandinista terrorist affiliations, "risk[] embarrassment."[25]

The *Washington Post* reported:

> Explosions that ripped through a car repair shop on the outskirts of Managua at dawn May 23 [1993] sent shock waves far beyond Nicaragua. From the debris have emerged a guerilla arsenal threatening the Salvadoran peace process, documents detailing a Marxist kidnapping ring directed against Latin American millionaires, and hundreds of false passports and identity papers. The three blasts . . . killed two people, damaged 16 houses and exposed a sophisticated bunker beneath the shop containing tons of weapons, including 19 surface-to-air missiles.
>
> . . .
>
> Few familiar with the case believe such an operation could have been set up without at least the Sandinista Front acting as a willing host. Following the triumph of their revolution in 1979, the Sandinistas developed, with the help of Soviet Bloc and Cuban advisers, the most sophisticated intelligence operation in Central America.

[24] "Nicaragua; Suspicious Sandinistas," *Economist* (10 July 1993), 60–62. [25] *Ibid.*, 62.

The Sandinista Front also hosted groups from the PLO, Italian Red Brigades, ETA and Libya.[26]

Several weeks later, Salvador Sanchez Ceren, former Salvadoran guerilla commander, admitted to Boutros-Ghali, the UN Secretary General, that the weapons found in the debris and much more secreted elsewhere in the vicinity of Managua belonged to the FMLN.[27] Boutros-Ghali wrote an indignant letter over the FMLN's "deliberate attempt to mislead me" in which he expressed his "distress[ ]" upon learning "that, contrary to your [the FMLN's] assurances which I had accepted in good faith, the inventory presented to [the UN Mission in El Salvador] by the FMLN was grossly inaccurate."[28] The *Post* concluded that:

> For most of the 1980s, the FMLN received substantial arms support from Nicaragua's Marxist oriented Sandinista government, and the weapons caches are believed to date from that period. That cooperation reportedly lessened after the Sandinistas lost power in Nicaragua's 1990 elections.[29]

In September 1993, another large cache of arms was found, this one belonging to Guatemalan guerrillas.[30] For the *Times*, this demonstrated that "the Sandinistas provided extensive support for leftist rebel groups" during their regime.[31] Shabtai Rosenne concluded that:

> [t]o a very large extent these rev[e]lations brought to light a situation closely resembling that which had been described by the State Department . . . and confirmed facts elucidated by Judge Schwebel in his questioning from the Bench.[32]

Robert Turner, who reviewed this evidence, wrote that "[t]he Sandinistas deceived most of the judges on the World Court and a lot of other people

26 D. Farah, "Managua Blasts Rip Lid Off Secrets," *Wash. Post* (14 July 1993), A1, A16.

27 *Ibid.*

28 Letter from the Secretary-Gen. to the Coordinator-Gen. of the Frente Farabundo Martí para la Liberación Nacional (FMLN) (12 June 1993) in Further Report of the Secretary-General on the United Nations Observer Mission in El Salvador (ONUSAL), annex I, UN Doc. S/26005 (29 June 1993); see also J. Goshko, "Salvadorans Accused of Hiding Arms: Guerrilla Cache Said to Be in Nicaragua," *Wash. Post* (17 June 1993), A37.

29 Goshko, "Salvadorans Accused of Hiding Arms," A37.

30 T. Golden, "New Arms Scandal Adds to Nicaragua's Woes," *NY Times* (5 Sept. 1993), A20; see also S. M. Schwebel, "Celebrating a Fraud on the Court," *Am. J. Int'l L.*, 106 (2012), 102, 103; see P. S. Reichler, "The Nicaragua Case: A Response to Judge Schwebel," *Am. J. Int'l L.*, 106 (2012), 316; S. M. Schwebel, "The Nicaragua Case: A Response to Paul Reichler," *Am. J. Int'l L.*, 106 (2012), 582, 583.

31 Golden, "New Arms Scandal Adds to Nicaragua's Woes."

32 S. Rosenne, *The World Court: What It Is and How It Works*, 5th rev. edn. (Boston: Martinus Nijhoff, 1995), p. 153.

as well."[33] An interpretation less charitable to the judges is that others on the Court ignored the Sandinista actions out of sympathy with what they may have taken as a "war of national liberation." In any event, the Court could not acknowledge that the Sandinistas were in fact involved in substantial actions against the Government of El Salvador, for it might have justified United States participation in collective self-defense against Nicaragua. The Court defused this potentially explosive issue by redefining significant arms transfers to insurgents as not amounting to an armed attack.

Passions over the case and disagreements over its facts have not subsided. In a letter to the *American Journal of International Law* in 2011, entitled "Celebrating a Fraud on the Court," Judge Schwebel reflected on the case, writing that "the Court essentially accepted the truth of the affidavit of the Nicaraguan foreign minister" which had denied the Nicaraguan government's involvement in supplying arms to the Salvadoran insurgency.[34] Judge Schwebel commented: "To what should have been the profound embarrassment of the Court, it subsequently was proved that the affidavit of the Nicaraguan foreign minister was false and that the Sandinista Government of Nicaragua grossly misled the Court."[35] Then, recounting events subsequent to the case (including the 1993 discovery of the FMLN weapons caches in Managua and elsewhere), he questioned whether Nicaragua would seek payment of its $17 billion judgment against the United States, concluding that "a wider recognition of Nicaragua's fraud on the Court – and the consequent question of whether the 1986 judgment is valid in law at all – may provide [a] . . . dispositive answer."[36]

Paul Reichler, counsel for Nicaragua in the case, responded in the pages of the *American Journal of International Law*. There, he contested Judge Schwebel's assessment of fraud on the Court and rejected any suggestion that counsel's conduct had been ethically questionable.[37] He wrote, "Judge Schwebel's editorial raises concerns not only for Nicaragua, but also for its counsel. As officers of the Court, we have an ethical obligation not to submit, or to allow a client to submit, false evidence."[38] He complained that "Judge Schwebel's editorial is susceptible of being read as implying that Nicaragua's counsel failed properly to exercise this obligation."[39] With respect to the 1993 discovery of various weapons caches, Reichler noted that "[t]he presence of arms in Nicaragua in 1993 does not constitute evidence that the Government of Nicaragua was trafficking them to El

[33] R. F. Turner, "Coercive Covert Action and the Law," *Yale J. Int'l L.*, 20 (1995), 427, 439.
[34] See Schwebel, "Celebrating a Fraud on the Court," 103.
[35] *Ibid.* [36] *Ibid.* [37] Reichler, "The Nicaragua Case," 316. [38] *Ibid.* [39] *Ibid.*

Salvador seven or more years earlier."[40] "In sum," he wrote, "the evidence on which Judge Schwebel relies is only to the effect that arms were *present* in Nicaragua some years after the judgment. It is not proof that Nicaragua trafficked in arms, let alone during the period when Nicaragua told the Court it was not engaged in such activities."[41]

In his rejoinder, Judge Schwebel clarified that his "editorial was directed to the fraud on the Court perpetrated by Nicaragua" and that "[n]othing in it refers to any knowledge or action of counsel of Nicaragua" or "implies ethical lapses on the part of the counsel of Nicaragua."[42] Rather, his "central thesis is that Nicaragua misled the Court in maintaining not only that it was not engaged, but that it *never* had been engaged, in the trafficking of arms to Salvadoran rebels."[43] What troubled Judge Schwebel was that the Court had "accepted – not literally, but essentially – the truth of the false affidavit of the Nicaraguan foreign minister" in forming its "crucial conclusion . . . that the evidence regarding the flow of arms from Nicaragua to the armed opposition in El Salvador before and after the early months of 1981 was insufficient to [demonstrate] 'that the Government of Nicaragua was responsible for any flow of arms at either period.'"[44]

Conclusion

The Court's approach to resolving the issues in the *Nicaragua* case may reflect its diminished capacity as a fact-finding organ. In *Nicaragua*, the Court faced a complicated factual thicket indeed. As it noted at the outset of its opinion, "One of the Court's chief difficulties in the present case has been the determination of the facts relevant to the dispute."[45] At bottom, the issue of whether or not the Sandinistas were, in fact, supplying arms to Salvadoran insurgents boiled down to the parties' conflicting assertions. The degree to which the United States' version of events could be credited and subjected to rigorous examination was sharply limited by its decision not to participate at the merits phase. Without two fully opposed and actively engaged parties vigorously constructing the factual record through assertion and challenge, and with few formal mechanisms of its own to do so, "[t]he Court's task was therefore necessarily more difficult."[46] Rosenne pinpointed this limitation: "The International Court . . . [is] at the same

[40] *Ibid.*, 319. [41] *Ibid.*, 320. [42] Schwebel, "The Nicaragua Case," 582. [43] *Ibid.*
[44] *Ibid.*, 583; but see Reichler, "The Nicaragua Case," 317 (contending that the Court "*gave no weight at all* to this affidavit") (emphasis in original).
[45] *Nicaragua* v. *United States*, 1986 *ICJ Rep.*, para. 57. [46] *Ibid.*

time a court of first instance and a Supreme Court. It is rare for supreme courts to determine facts themselves, and even more rare for them to hear witnesses. Trial experience is not a qualification required of the Members of the International Court under either Article 2 or Article 9 of the Statute."[47]

Perhaps to compensate for these shortcomings, the Court in *Nicaragua* leaned heavily on legal theories of armed attack and collective self-defense that allowed some circumvention of the factual differences. Using such methods, the Court is quite unlikely to detect a fraud; it leaves such revelations, presumably, to the parties themselves. Then again, Judge Schwebel seemed unconvinced that the problem was one of institutional inability to distinguish truth from misrepresentation, but rather the Court's unwillingness to confront what to him was an obvious instance of the latter. On this interpretation, even if the Court does suspect a fraud in a case, its collegium may not only lack the capacity but even more troubling the desire to corroborate its suspicion. Routing its legal analysis around the putative fraud becomes the more manageable course, which poses no risks for a party submitting fraudulent evidence.

The Court's difficulty detecting fraud may be compounded by the reality that international counsel might not know (or even suspect) that its client is lying. Counsel Reichler's commentary makes plain, if there was, indeed, a fraud on the Court in this case, at least foreign counsel for Nicaragua had not been aware of it and therefore could not have brought the matter to light. We revisit the question of how and to what extent international counsel is obligated to dig for fraud or investigate the client's representations in the case of *Qatar* v. *Bahrain.*

[47] S. Rosenne, Address to the United Nations Conference on Public International Law (15 Mar. 1995) (on file with authors).

6

The Iran–United States Claims Tribunal: burdens of proof

In an interactive world, domestic social upheavals will always have some international consequences. They can be especially disruptive when the upheavals occur in states that are tightly integrated in the global economy. The Iranian Revolution of 1979 is a prime example. From the time the Pahlavi Dynasty succeeded the Qajars, the political leadership of Iran was bent on rapid and comprehensive modernization. In this venture, Iran aggressively courted many public and private actors from the science-based and technological civilization of the West. The oil wealth of the country permitted successive governments to conclude many contracts with foreign governments and foreign businesses in order to build an infrastructure for the country that would enable it to expand its own industrial and scientific base. After the nationalization of the Anglo-Iranian oil company by the Mossadegh government, the United States replaced the United Kingdom as the major foreign power, for purposes of both military supplies and economic and cultural contacts. The increasing revenues from oil permitted the successive governments of the ambitious young Shah to conclude even more international agreements.[1]

In 1979, the Pahlavi government was overthrown and Iran was transformed into an Islamic Republic under the leadership of the Ayatollah Khomeini. The myriad relationships between the United States and Iran deteriorated so rapidly they seemed to evaporate. In November 1979, Iranian "student militants" seized the United States Embassy in Tehran and Consulates in other parts of the country and held the diplomats hostage for

[1] For an overview of these events, see C. N. Brower and J. D. Brueschke, *The Iran-United States Claims Tribunal* (The Hague: Martinus Nijhoff, 1998), pp. 2–6.

more than a year.[2] The US government froze Iranian assets in the United States.[3]

To increase pressure on Iran to release the hostages, the Carter Administration issued licenses to American claimants against Iran permitting them to sue Iran in United States courts with the expectation that final judgments could be satisfied from the $12 billion in Iranian assets that had been frozen.[4] Many suits were commenced. After an abortive attempt at a rescue mission, the United States found itself with few options and confined itself to economic actions against the Islamic Republic.

In the waning hours of the Carter Administration, the deadlock between the two governments was broken by agreements negotiated in Algiers through the good offices of the Algerian government. The Declaration of the Government of the Democratic and Popular Republic of Algeria, or the "Algiers Accords," as they are popularly known, provided for the return to Iran of a substantial amount of the frozen assets after payment of some outstanding debts to American banks and, most important for this discussion, the transfer of $1 billion to a security account in the NV Settlement Bank of the Netherlands in the name of the Bank of Algiers Paris Branch. The Algiers Accords also established a claims settlement tribunal, to "conduct its business in accordance with the arbitration rules of the United Nations Commission on International Trade Law (UNCITRAL) except to the extent modified by the Parties or by the Tribunal."[5] The Tribunal was to issue awards with respect to claims by US nationals against Iran, Iranian nationals against the United States, and the two governments against each other. The awards were to be paid from the escrow account. If and when the funds in the bank were exhausted, Iran was to replenish them as required.[6]

Three chambers were established; each composed of two judges appointed by the governments of Iran and the United States respectively, the third, a neutral, selected jointly or by a contingent appointment mechanism. The Iran–US Claims Tribunal has operated since 1981. Almost all

[2] See generally, S. Moody, *444 Days: The American Hostage Story* (New York: Routledge, 1981).

[3] Exec. Order No. 12170, 44 Fed. Reg. 65,279 (14 Nov. 1979).

[4] See Iranian Assets Control Regulations, 31 CFR pt. 535 (1979); see also W. Mapp, *The Iran-United States Claims Tribunal: The First Ten Years*, 1981–1991 (Manchester University Press, 1993), pp. 6–7.

[5] Declaration of the Government of the Democratic and Popular Republic of Algeria concerning the Settlement of Claims by the Government of the United States of America and the Government of the Islamic Republic of Iran, Article III(2).

[6] For a general overview, see Brower and Brueschke, *The Iran-United States Claims Tribunal*, pp. 7–10 and nn. 19–23.

of the 4,700 private claims have been resolved, which has resulted in over $2.5 billion in awards to United States nationals and companies.[7]

As we saw in our discussion of the *La Abra* and *Weil* claims in the nineteenth century and the *Sabotage Cases* in the first half of the twentieth, claims tribunals, as public international institutions, have certain features that make them more susceptible to unscrupulous actions. In contrast to ad hoc governmental arbitrations, in which counsel on each side are government lawyers subject to diverse bureaucratic controls but lacking private counsels' economic incentives to win a case, claims tribunals must depend upon private claimants and their lawyers for the gathering and presentation of evidence. Yet the tribunals do not have (or, at least, in the case of the Iran–US Claims Tribunal, have elected not to develop) some parts of the arsenal of sanctions that domestic legal systems use to restrain and control moral hazard. Thus, the temptation to tamper with evidence to which dishonorable, weak, or morally corrupt people are always prone is not tempered by the credible threat of the application of significant punishment.

Ad hoc tribunals, by their nature, dissolve after award, and hence are structurally incapable of reopening awards unless the parties renovate or recreate the tribunals themselves. By contrast, the Iran–US Claims Tribunal, as a standing tribunal, is a member of a class that has the common institutional possibility of reopening awards secured by fraud. But that institutional capacity does not address the policy question: is reopening desirable or should the policy of finality prevail. The holding of the German–US Mixed Claims Commission in the *Sabotage Cases* did not speak to policy, but effected its preference for finality by reasoning that no discrete award was final until all of the claims subject to the Commission's jurisdiction had been decided; under this theory, it was only at this point that its jurisdiction over any specific case terminated. But the Commission had already ruled that newly discovered evidence that had not been previously suppressed fraudulently did not warrant reopening an award. An intentional fraud that had succeeded in misleading the Tribunal seemed to be the critical factor.

In addition, the *Sabotage Cases* raised the sensitive issue of denouncing a government for manufacturing and submitting fraudulent evidence, an element that makes the holding unique. Most of the claimants in the Iran–US Claims Tribunal have been private parties. Article III(3) limited the

[7] US Dep't of State, Iran–US Claims Tribunal, available at: www.state.gov/s/l/3199.htm. For background information on Iran–United States Claims Tribunal, see www.iusct.org/background-english.html.

governments' representative role to claims of less than $250,000. Hence, the sensitive political dimension of publicly characterizing a government as a fraudfeasor, especially when that government's cooperation continued to be an important part of the tribunal's effectiveness, was less likely to arise in the Iran–US setting in cases of claimant-induced fraud. For all of these reasons, one might think that the cases before the Iran–US Claims Tribunal would have provided a good deal of what students of the field of emergency medicine call "clinical data" on the problem of fraudulent evidence, both pre- and post-award.

Burdens of authenticity and forgery

Our study begins with an examination of the Tribunal's prima facie authenticity rule: the mechanism it has used for evaluating the authenticity of evidence before it finalizes an award. The Tribunal affords a strong presumption of authenticity for official government documents. In the nature of things, much of the evidence that claimants had to rely on was based on official documents of the former imperial government. Given the revolutionary changes and the continuing turmoil and the severely limited contacts between Iran and the United States, it was often not feasible to validate adduced documents by checking in the ministries or departments in which they appeared to have originated. In an early case, *Ultrasystems Inc.* v. *Iran*,[8] the American arbitrator, Judge Mosk, commented on the evidentiary difficulties presented to parties and the Tribunal:

> The parties and the Tribunal operated under difficult circumstances. Of two key witnesses, one is deceased and the other is incarcerated in Iran. Other witnesses were unavailable. Claimant did not have access to certain documents and witnesses. There were various discrepancies among those documents produced. Restrictions on travel between Iran and the United States, the lack of relations between the two countries, the age of the claim and language differences exacerbated proof problems.[9]

But Judge Mosk did not feel that this empowered the Tribunal to undertake its "own investigation of the facts." Rather he assumed that these difficulties and uncertainties were simply part of the task that falls to an international tribunal. He did, however, turn to Iranian law to justify drawing "adverse

[8] *Ultrasystems Inc.* v. *Iran*, 2 *Iran-US Cl. Trib. Rep.* 100 (1983).
[9] *Ibid.*, 115 (concurring opinion of Richard M. Mosk).

inferences from the failure of that party to produce such evidence" within its possession, a position he confirmed in another concurring opinion in a later case.[10]

Judge Mosk's approach has a certain moral attraction, for it seems to impose a sanction on a party that is not cooperating, by creating a prima facie presumption of validity for documents submitted by claimants: if the respondent, presumptively in possession of the potential rebuttal documents, did not adduce them, it was appropriate to draw negative inferences. But its apparent moral attraction is misleading, for this approach may recreate the problem Mexico encountered in *Weil* and *La Abra*.[11] Under the best of circumstances, it is difficult to disprove fraudulent documents by adducing documents that do not exist, a challenge that only magnifies when the state archives are in disarray and especially when a coordinate assumption holds that the party purportedly responsible for the disarray may not benefit from it. Judge Mosk's approach could create an incentive for the unscrupulous claimant to submit fraudulent evidence in circumstances like these, especially if there is no "clean hands" doctrine according to which a party submitting fraudulent documents surrenders its *locus standi in judicio*.

In *Bank Sepah* v. *City Bank NA*,[12] the claimants relied on the authority of Iran to submit documents on its behalf. In one phase of the case, the Tribunal asked for confirmation of the Iranian Deputy Agent's authority to withdraw a claim that was duplicative, as it had already been filed under a different file number.[13] At face value, the issue was whether Iranian officials had presumptive authority to engage in actions before the Tribunal; but the language was broader and seemed to assign a general validating function to Iranian officials for Iranian documents. The American arbitrator on the panel, Judge Holtzmann, disagreed with the delay respondents caused by demanding "further evidence of the authority of the officials who signed [the documents]."[14] He opined that the "Tribunal should be able, without such inquiry, to rely and act on documents signed by the Agent or Deputy Agent of the Islamic Republic of Iran on behalf of that Government or any of its agencies, instrumentalities or controlled entities."[15] On more general grounds, Judge Holtzmann noted that the Tribunal had not

[10] *Ibid.* (quoting Articles 300–02, Civil Procedure Code of Iran); *Cal-Maine Foods, Inc.* v. *Iran*, 6 *Iran-US Cl. Trib. Rep.* 52, pp. 65–66 (1984).

[11] See Chapter 1 this volume.

[12] 2 *Iran-US Cl. Trib. Rep.* 30 (1983).

[13] *Ibid.*

[14] *Ibid.*, 35 (Howard M. Holtzmann, dissenting from Orders Requiring Iranian Officials to Submit Further Proof that they are Authorized Representatives of the Entities for Which they Acted, January 24, 1983).

[15] *Ibid.*

previously endorsed this rather squeamish approach to authenticity and drew attention to its consequences:

Hundreds, perhaps thousands, of documents have been filed with the Tribunal on behalf of Iranian parties. There has been little consistency with respect to the form of the Iranian signatures on such documents. Often the documents are signed by the Agent or Deputy Agent; indeed requests by Iranian entities for extensions of time and various motions are typically so signed, and have been acted upon even though the Statement of Claim or the Statement of Defense may have been signed by a different Iranian official and may have designated another representative. In a number of Cases, Iranian parties have ignored the requirements of Article 4 and Article 19, paragraph 2 of the Tribunal Rules which require a party to give written notice of the names of its representative . . . nevertheless, subsequent documents signed by various officials have been received and acted upon. The title or authority of Iranian signatories is not always clear. However, despite these inconsistencies, the Tribunal has not previously, on its own motion, ordered further proof that a document was signed by an authorized Iranian representative.[16]

In Judge Holtzmann's view, to insist on more than the prima facie approach had traditionally required, "impose[d] a new and time-consuming burden on the Tribunal which further complicates . . . procedures and delays action on cases before us."[17]

In *Cal-Maine Foods, Inc.* v. *Iran*,[18] the majority reached its decision on the merits by relying on a variety of documents, no one of which was by itself conclusive. The concurring and dissenting opinion of the Iranian arbitrator, Judge Ansari Moin, questioned the Tribunal's decision to find authentic a handwritten letter, which "b[ore] neither a number nor a letterhead." Although the letter was dated December 1, 1979, and apparently signed by one Ahmad Gerami, Judge Moin felt that its validity and authenticity were "highly questionable," as it "could have been written at any time." Moreover, the letter was inconsistent with numerous other valid documents submitted by both of the parties.[19] It is interesting that the Judge did not infer a "clean hands" doctrine that would have justified non-suiting the claimant if the document were fraudulent (which seemed to have been the implication of his objection). Instead, he seemed to assume that the only sanction for submitting a potentially false document would be the rejection of that document with no other effect on the remaining submissions of the claimant.

[16] *Ibid.*, 36 (internal citations omitted). [17] *Ibid.* [18] 6 *Iran-US Cl. Trib. Rep.* 52 (1984).
[19] *Ibid.*, 71 (opinion of Parviz Ansari Moin, concurring in part and dissenting in part).

The dissent in *Cal-Maine Foods* and several later cases suggest that certain characteristics of documentary evidence, including signatures,[20] use of letterhead[21] or government paper,[22] consistency with other valid papers,[23] filing the original with the Tribunal registry,[24] and corporate documentation[25] are relevant to the prima facie authenticity analysis. However, it was only in *Golshani* v. *Iran*[26] that the Tribunal articulated a test for burdens of proof and authenticity and suggested the way that a Tribunal should react to fraud or forgery in a pending case. *Golshani* is a puzzling case, as the Chamber's holdings are not entirely consistent with what the Chamber was actually doing. The standard it announced seemed to reflect the same sort of virtually "gravitational" judicial respect for documents *qua* documents which had been expressed in *Cal-Maine*; that approach creates a heavier burden on the party seeking to impeach a document for fraud. Upon closer examination, however, the majority and separate opinions reveal a more complex methodology.

The claimant, Golshani, was a dual Iran–United States national[27] who claimed that the Government of Iran had expropriated "his ownership interest in the Tehran Redevelopment Corporation [TRC] and other corporate shareholdings and properties."[28] Golshani contended he was the owner of these properties pursuant to a deed of conveyance executed by their former owner, Rahman Golzar Shabestari, a relative.[29] Iran contended that the deed was a forgery, created several years after the purported

[20] *Ibid.* [21] *Ibid.*

[22] *Golshani* v. *Iran*, 29 *Iran-US Cl. Trib. Rep.* 78, para. 61 (1993) (noting that use of government-issued paper and signatures of the transacting parties were considered to be "[i]ndicia of [a]uthenticity").

[23] 6 *Iran-US Cl. Trib. Rep.* 52, p. 71 (opinion of Parviz Ansari Moin, concurring in part and dissenting in part).

[24] *Riahi* v. *Iran*, 39 *Iran-US Cl. Trib. Rep.* 158, para. 101 (2003) (concurring and dissenting opinion of Assadollah Noori) (referring to Iranian contract law, "[w]ith respect to shares, the Claimant could have satisfied the 'delivery' and 'possession' requirement [of the underlying law] if she could have filed the original share certificates with the Tribunal . . . In the absence of such proof, the allegation of transfer by donation must fail").

[25] *Gulf Associates, Inc.* v. *Iran*, 35 *Iran-US Cl. Trib. Rep.* 45, para. 27 (1999) (finding that the share certificates "on their face" show that the children in question became owners of the Gulf Association's capital stock).

[26] 29 *Iran-US Cl. Trib. Rep.*

[27] In an interlocutory award issued on 30 June 1989, by Chamber Three, the Chamber held by majority that Golshani's effective nationality was United States. Abrahim Rahman Golshani and Government of the Islamic Republic of Iran, Interlocutory Award No. ITL 72–812–3 (30 June 1989).

[28] 29 *Iran-US Cl. Trib. Rep.*, para. 1. [29] *Ibid.*

conveyance for the purpose of pursuing the case, because Golshani, as an American, would have standing while Golzar, an Iranian, would not.[30]

Early in the proceeding, the Tribunal decided to treat the question of the validity or forgery of the deed as a preliminary issue. Two rounds of pleadings were exchanged on this issue, experts for each side examined the originals submitted by the other, and three days of hearings were held.[31] As a matter of law, the Tribunal held that the party offering the document in question has the initial – prima facie – burden of proving that the document is authentic. After doing so, the burden of proving that the document is a forgery shifts to the other party.[32] The Tribunal seemed to derive this burden-shifting standard from an analysis of Article 24(1) of the Tribunal's Rules: "[e]ach party shall have the burden of proving the facts relied on to support his claim or defence."[33] This reflects the well-known maxim *actori incumbit probatio*, which, on its face, seems completely even-handed in assigning burdens of proof. But, in applying the doctrine, the Tribunal actually created an asymmetrical regime:

> the Respondent has contended that the Deed, dated 15 August 1978, was in fact fabricated in 1982. Having made that factual allegation, *the Respondent has the burden of proving it.* However, the Tribunal need only concern itself with the question whether the *Respondent has met that burden if the Claimant has submitted a document inspiring a minimally sufficient degree of confidence in its authenticity.* It is therefore up to the Claimant first to demonstrate *prima facie* that the Deed is authentic.[34]

Because many documents have a certain per se or inherent credibility, all a party submitting the document need do to establish prima facie that it is authentic is to produce it. Once that is done, the party seeking to impeach the document must "prove" it is a forgery, which, as a more searching standard, entails a heavier burden of proof. In *Golshani*, this meant that the claimant, who had asserted a claim against the Government of Iran based on expropriation of his property, essentially established the prima facie authenticity of the document proving such ownership by the document itself. The respondent, who raised the defense of forgery, then had to *prove* his forgery claim. In his separate opinion, Judge Aghahosseini objected that:

> [t]he Rule that the burden of proof lies on him who affirms a fact and not on him who denies it (*ei qui affirmat, non ei qui negat incumbit probatio*) admits of no exception – none whatsoever.[35]

[30] *Ibid.*, para. 23. [31] *Ibid.*, 124 (separate opinion of Mohsen Aghahosseini)
[32] See *ibid.*, para. 47 (majority opinion). [33] *Ibid.*, para. 49. [34] *Ibid.* (emphasis added).
[35] *Ibid.*, 123 (separate opinion of Mohsen Aghahosseini).

Plainly there is a tilt toward the party submitting the document. But is that not dictated by the official reality with which an international tribunal must contend? The transaction costs of examining every document would be prohibitive while the presumption of validity of "official" documents, which is in part designed to deal with the cost factor of particularized verification, is plausible. Hence the presumption relies on certain *extrinsic* features of the document, as prescribed by its governing law. Without stating it explicitly, the Tribunal assumed that *locus regit actum* and applied the standards of the *lex instrumenti* by means of a *renvoi* to the law under which the document had been created.

The Tribunal quoted and relied upon the claimant's expert, Dr. Motazed-Baheri, former Minister of Justice of Iran and former Professor of Law at Tehran University.[36] He had testified that an official document is entitled to a presumption of authenticity insofar as it is "a document which is prepared by a government official (a Notary Public) in accordance with that government official's legal authority as well as the applicable laws and regulations and which represents a legal agreement signed by the parties thereto."[37] As Dr. Motazed-Baheri put it:

> Certain transactions – in particular, those involving real property – must be capable of being relied upon by anyone. It can be said that the most important foundation for a civilized nation is confidence and security in transactions and contracts . . . The precautionary measures taken by the Iranian legislature in formulating the laws for preparation of official documents are purely for the purpose of enhancing the confidence and security of the public in transactions represented by an official document and for safeguarding the rights of third parties who are affected by the statements made in an official document.[38]

As such, the Tribunal did not set an especially high standard for prima facie authenticity. While not every official-looking document would warrant a presumption of authenticity, a document that bears a "minimum of indicia" can meet Dr. Motazed-Baheri's definition.[39] The Tribunal was careful to note, however, that it was not necessary for the document to comply with all applicable regulations – for example, the payment of registration fees – in order to be presumed authentic. But if the omissions and irregularities were of "a nature or number that the document on its face does not inspire the 'confidence and security' normally associated with an instrument of that kind," it may not be eligible for a presumption of authenticity.[40] The

[36] *Ibid.*, para. 52 (majority opinion). [37] *Ibid.*, para. 54. [38] *Ibid.*, para. 65.
[39] *Ibid.*, para. 54. [40] *Ibid.*, para. 55.

document must be shown to serve the purpose of official documents that is, "enhancing the confidence and security of the public in transactions represented by an official document and for safeguarding the rights of third parties who are affected by the statements made in an official document."[41]

With this sort of methodology, the Tribunal's actual examination of the extrinsic features of the deed was, by its nature, limited. The Tribunal noted several of these characteristics: it was written on government-issued paper whose vintage was consistent with the stated date of registration; it contained the signatures of the contracting parties, of the Notary Public and his assistant; and it had a notary seal.[42] In terms of the method the Tribunal had propounded, those extrinsic indicators should, one would have thought, have been sufficient to establish the prima facie validity of the deed.

Yet, its formal theory notwithstanding, the Tribunal drew no conclusion from the examination of the deed's extrinsic features. Rather, it immediately launched into an examination of *intrinsic* factors that were incompatible with the approach it had just enunciated. The Tribunal quoted, in its entirety, a clause in the deed that deferred the apparent transfer of authority for fifteen solar months, which would have been a useful explanation if the conveyance had actually taken place (if at all) considerably later.[43] It also remarked on the magnitude of the transaction, noting its "monumental nature."[44] But that was only the prelude to an even more searching examination of the internal content of the deed. The Tribunal found a number of inconsistencies in the text of the deed itself. For example, it noted that the deed purported to transfer shares in TRC which, according to the seller's statements made at the hearing, were actually registered in the name of his wife and children.[45] Second, the deed mixed TRC's assets and the personal holdings of Golzar, the seller, an inconsistency apparent from Golzar's affidavit submitted with his Amended Statement of Claim.[46] Third, the deed described the transferred assets only briefly, and referred to a second document, the *Procès-Verbal*, which allegedly contained more detailed descriptions of the properties transferred by the deed.[47] Yet the claimant did not produce the *Procès-Verbal*; in fact, he could not recall its existence when questioned at the hearing.[48]

[41] *Ibid.*, para. 65. It is interesting to note that concurring Judge Aghahosseini agreed that "official documents notarized by government officials are entitled to a strong presumption of authenticity and validity that can only be overcome with substantial and uncontroverted evidence to the contrary." *Ibid.*, 131 (separate opinion).

[42] *Ibid.*, para. 61 (majority opinion). [43] *Ibid.*, para. 59. [44] *Ibid.*, para. 60.

[45] *Ibid.*, para. 62. [46] *Ibid.*, para. 63. [47] See *ibid.*, paras. 67, 68, 99.

[48] See *ibid.*, para. 71.

The Tribunal ultimately found that although the deed contained several indicia of (extrinsic) authenticity, these irregularities prevented a finding of prima facie authenticity.[49] While the word "fraudulent" was not used, several statements in this part of the award implied as much. For example:

> [i]t is questionable, in the Tribunal's opinion, whether a deed with such characteristics . . . is a document that may be considered to have passed genuinely through the regular Iranian notarial process.[50]

Now, it is apparent from this part of the *Golshani* opinion that the Tribunal was applying an operational method that went beyond the extrinsic tests it had facially opted for in its statement of the law on the matter. If one were to codify what was done in this part of *Golshani*, and not what was said, the test for prima facie validity required, in addition to extrinsic features of the instrument in question, a substantial demonstration based on its intrinsic features. The Tribunal's reluctance to articulate a theory which expressed what it was actually doing may have derived from a desire to avoid the significant transaction costs inherent in opening all documents to such a searching test.

If there were any place for application of a clean hands doctrine, it would have been here. Instead, the Tribunal held that the claimant "still has the opportunity to prove that the Deed is *prima facie* authentic through corroborating evidence."[51] Such a generous option might make sense if the party proffering the fraudulent document was itself a victim of fraud (e.g., had been given the fraudulent document), for it should not be punished for the acts of another. But Golshani, who averred that he had participated in the drafting of the deed and had vouched for its authenticity, could hardly claim a presumption of innocence. When the Tribunal concluded that it was questionable whether the document had "passed genuinely through the regular Iranian notarial process,"[52] it was necessarily saying something about Golshani's testimony.

But the claimant had an opportunity to resuscitate the document. He had submitted two "corroborating" affidavits: one from the claimant himself and one from Golzar. After examining those affidavits, the Tribunal found striking inconsistencies among many of the elements of the submissions: the date of the transfer of assets from Golzar to the claimant;[53] the motivation

[49] See *ibid.*, para. 74. [50] *Ibid.*, para. 72. [51] *Ibid.*, para. 75.
[52] *Ibid.*, para. 72. [53] *Ibid.*, paras. 78–83.

behind the transfer;[54] the timing of the transfer;[55] the consideration for the transfer;[56] and the percentage of shares allegedly transferred.[57] The majority concluded:

In sum, the Tribunal, having been unable to conclude on the basis of the Deed alone that it is an official document entitled to a presumption of authenticity, has considered the Claimant's corroborating evidence and found many disturbing inconsistencies.[58]

Because the Tribunal found that the claimant had not met the burden of making out a prima facie case of authenticity, it declined to address the question of whether the respondent had met the burden of proving that the deed was a forgery.[59]

The *Golshani* Tribunal's decision does not provide a coherent theory for examining documents whose authenticity has been challenged. The *Golshani* Tribunal purported to begin its evaluation of the claimant's prima facie case of authenticity with an analysis of the "[d]eed alone,"[60] suggesting a relatively simple and efficient test for determining prima facie validity – reference to certain extrinsic features of a document. But the Tribunal quickly moved beyond an extrinsic evaluation to inquire into various inconsistencies between the deed and the affidavits of the claimant and the seller, and even the content of the deed itself. It remains to be seen how future tribunals will apply that test.

In his separate opinion, Judge Aghahosseini, the Iranian arbitrator, referred to expert testimony indicating that the document appeared false on its face: the seal was not genuine – a key word was repeated in a manner wholly inconsistent with an authentic notary seal – and the notary signature was forged.[61] In his view, if the seals were, in fact, defective, these manifest defects could disqualify the document without need for an intrinsic analysis. Thus, even if the Tribunal had adopted an express policy of examining only the face of the document in the first stage of its prima facie authenticity analysis, the document could still have been rejected facially. Judge Aghahosseini was, in our view, correct.

Less persuasive was Judge Aghahosseini's dissent from the majority's conclusion that the claimant need only make out a prima facie case of authenticity in order to shift the burden of proving forgery onto the respondent. Judge Aghahosseini reasoned: "Throughout the case and at the end

[54] See *ibid.*, paras. 84–93. [55] See *ibid.*, paras. 94–99.
[56] See *ibid.*, paras. 100–02. [57] See *ibid.*, paras. 103–09. [58] *Ibid.*, para. 121.
[59] See *ibid.*, para. 122. [60] *Ibid.*, para. 121.
[61] *Ibid.*, 152–57 (separate opinion of Mohsen Aghahosseini).

of the day, the duty to prove an asserted fact remains with him who makes it."[62] This would impose heavy transaction costs on the arbitral process. (Hence, the standard of proof is merely the preponderance of the evidence.) When the claimant provides proof of the authenticity of a document and that evidence is not contradicted by the respondent, the claimant prevails not because he has proved authenticity and the respondent has failed to prove a forgery but because the claimant's document has not been effectively impeached or, as Judge Aghahosseini put it, "preponderates."[63] By contrast, Judge Aghahosseini would use a single-phase test to evaluate evidence; rather than first determining whether the claimant has made out a prima facie case for the authenticity of the deed, he would examine all the evidence and conclude that the respondent's assertion of forgery prevails.

Golshani is important because it paved a way around the use of the label "fraud": if a document's authenticity appears suspicious for non-extrinsic reasons, the prima facie test can be adjusted to reject the document as evidence, without using "fraud" as the stated rationale. In Judge Aghahosseini's separate opinion, he undertook to demonstrate that the document was a forgery and that the refusal to pronounce explicitly on this matter "violates not only the facts of the Case and the Tribunal's earlier directives, but the dictates of good policy considerations."[64]

> A broader study of the Tribunal's case-law will readily reveal that the course of action here adopted, far from being an isolated one, is just another application of this Tribunal's reluctance to call a forged document by its proper name, when it comes to realize its true character. The only factor distinguishing the within Case from other relevant precedents of the Tribunal is perhaps the fact that this time, in order not to touch on the taboo of forgery, the Tribunal has additionally had to go back on its own promises.[65]

Most striking was Judge Aghahosseini's policy analysis. The issue for the Tribunal, in his view, was

> the growing problem of the abuse of its process by a considerable number of unscrupulous parties who, in Case after Case, relied upon altered or wholly forged documents to support their utterly unfounded claims – a practice which not only wasted much of the Tribunal's time and resources, but threatened the very integrity of its process.[66]

62 *Ibid.*, 124. 63 *Ibid.* 64 *Ibid.*, 123. 65 *Ibid.* 66 *Ibid.*, 183, para. 2.2.

However, without the capacity to impose penal sanctions, the only deterrent to arresting the abuses was "to be *forthright* in exposing the instances of abuse and in censuring the perpetrators."[67]

The alternative – the Tribunal's failure to employ this only available means – not only will be interpreted by unconscientious parties as a sign of the Tribunal's indifference to the misuse of its process, but will in fact act to encourage further use of fabricated evidence; evidence which, in the measured view of the prospective perpetrators, will be either accepted by the Tribunal as genuine or, at the worst, simply set aside as unauthentic, with no adverse consequences.[68]

The Tribunal awarded Iran costs of $50,000, which might be taken as the imposition of a sanction. Judge Allison, who concurred in the opinion, dissented on this point, contending that Iran's own arguments were "so convoluted, contradictory and incomprehensible" that the Tribunal's time and effort was unnecessarily consumed in resolving the forgery issue.[69] But because this falls short of the conspicuous condemnation – the shaming sanction – that Judge Aghahosseini demanded, he concluded his dissent with a blistering condemnation:

In Case after Case, where the evidence would admit of no conclusion other than the forgery of the submitted documents, the Tribunal refuses not only to address the perpetrators' conduct, but to even characterize the documents as forged. Indeed, it inevitably tries to employ formulae under which the rejection of the documents by the Tribunal would not affect the perpetrators' good character![70]

Judge Aghahosseini's opinion asks whether the majority, by removing the stigma of a finding of fraud, encourages it.

Not long after *Golshani*, the Tribunal in *Dadras International and Per-Am Construction Corp.* v. *Iran*[71] elaborated on the relative burdens of proof for authenticity and fraud. It confirmed that the party alleging fraud bears a substantially heavier burden than the party claiming a document's authenticity. The claimants, Dadras International and Per-Am, produced, inter alia, the contract and pre-contractual communications in support of their claim for payment of services rendered and lost profits arising from an alleged construction contract concluded with TRC.[72] The respondent claimed the documents were forgeries.[73] The Tribunal seemed to confirm that the claimant bore the burden of showing that contractual

[67] *Ibid.* [68] *Ibid.*
[69] *Ibid.*, paras. 10, 14 (concurring and dissenting opinion of Richard C. Allison).
[70] *Ibid.*, 183, para. 2.2 (separate opinion of Mohsen Aghahosseini).
[71] 31 *Iran-US Cl. Trib. Rep.* 127 (1995). [72] *Ibid.*, paras. 1–5. [73] *Ibid.*, paras. 113–18.

documents were prima facie authentic.[74] But, in a seeming departure from earlier cases, the Tribunal ratcheted the burden of proving allegations of fraud or forgery. In this case, the party claiming fraud faced an "enhanced standard of proof," one that required a showing of "clear and convincing evidence."[75] Applying this enhanced standard, the respondents' direct and circumstantial evidence of forgery failed and the contract was found valid and enforceable.[76]

In dissent, Judge Aghahosseini again urged a theory based on a single-phase test, asserting that the majority had not "understood or respected" "the elementary rules on the burden of proof."[77] Under a proper application of the burden-shifting rules,

> where a *prima facie* case . . . is made out, the opponent must offer evidence pointing to some reasons "for doubting". If he does so, then, and this is most important, the evidence before the tribunal, *whether adduced by the proponent in support of his contention or by the opponent in support of his denial*, must be considered together in order to determine whether or not the proponent's burden of proof is met.[78]

After claimants had adduced evidence that the documents were authentic, the respondents could adduce evidence to the contrary whereupon the Tribunal should have considered "the whole of it" together to determine whether the claimants had carried their burden of proof.[79]

Judge Aghahosseini argued that the Tribunal had incorrectly mischaracterized the respondent's evidence, which was intended to challenge authenticity in the first instance, as an affirmative defense of fraud and only then to be considered subsequent to a finding of authenticity. The Tribunal had thus "fail[ed] to distinguish between the two distinct defenses of

[74] *Ibid.*, para. 132 (finding the contract "contains all of the elements necessary to create a binding agreement between the parties and therefore appears, on its face, to constitute a valid and binding contract"). Though, as Judge Aghahosseini points out, the majority never explicitly equated facial validity and prima facie authentic – one is left to infer that. *Ibid.*, 249 (dissenting opinion of Mohsen Agahosseini).

[75] *Ibid.*, para. 124 (majority opinion).

[76] *Ibid.*, para. 241. Another interesting point in this case is that an affidavit of the same Mr. Golzar who had been disbelieved in *Golshani* was adduced as evidence of the fraud; Golzar here testified that he had never signed the contract, which bore his signature. In finding Golzar incredible, the Tribunal placed weight on his previous behavior in *Golshani*, "agree[ing] that a 'deserved stigma' does indeed follow Mr. Golzar." The Tribunal felt it could not "but justifiably fear that a man who has once presented highly suspect documentation and testimony under oath to an international arbitration tribunal may have few scruples in repeating the act." *Ibid.*, para. 158.

[77] *Ibid.*, 285 (dissenting opinion of Mohsen Aghahosseini).

[78] *Ibid.*, 252. [79] *Ibid.*, 253.

denying the authenticity of a given document and an affirmative allegation of forgery."[80] The effect of the majority's approach, he insisted, was to afford claimants "the easy way of showing the authenticity of their documents in isolation, and unchallenged by the Respondents' rebutting evidence."[81] Whether or not the unitary model would produce a more accurate – or more manageable – result, the majority's clear and convincing standard does make it easier for tribunals to reject evidence of fraud if couched as a defensive claim of forgery rather than as evidence rebutting authenticity.

Despite some disagreement on this point, the Iran–US Claims Tribunal appears to have adopted a clear and convincing standard. As later cases confirmed, "forgery must be proved with a higher degree of probability than other allegations in these Cases."[82] Subsequent cases have applied the standard in other contexts. For example, the Tribunal's application of the clear and convincing standard in *Aryeh* v. *Iran*[83] dealt with a knowledge element in reference to criminal-fraud-related allegations under Iranian law. *Aryeh* concerned alleged expropriation of shares and interest in several corporations.[84] The respondent claimed that the memoranda of association and the registrations for four of these corporations were forged, and no valid corporations existed under Iranian law.[85] The Tribunal was not persuaded that the documents were proven forged, and in any event declined to find a crime of fraud had occurred because the respondent had not proven the elements of forgery under Iranian law.[86]

In a counterfactual analysis, the Tribunal reasoned that even if the respondent had proven that the documents were forgeries, the crime of using forged documents would still not have been committed because the claimant did not have the requisite intent under Iranian law. The respondent had not adduced evidence to prove the claimant had knowingly submitted forged evidence in her case before the Tribunal.[87] The Tribunal seems to have been persuaded by the claimant's contention that, even if she had intentionally forged the corporate documents, that forgery would still be immaterial to her claim because it was not intended to deceive the Tribunal specifically – the forgery would have transpired before "anybody could have contemplated the 1979 Revolution."[88]

[80] *Ibid.*, 248. [81] *Ibid.*, 283.
[82] *Aryeh* v. *Iran*, 33 *Iran-US Cl. Trib. Rep.* 272, para. 159 (1997).
[83] *Ibid.* [84] *Ibid.*, para. 1. [85] *Ibid.*, paras. 121–33.
[86] *Ibid.*, para. 164. It was thought plausible that the signor of the registrations had had a power of authority and that the signature on the memoranda was hers. *Ibid.*, paras. 161–62.
[87] *Ibid.*, para. 165. [88] *Ibid.*, para. 154.

Ultimately, the fraud claims were found time-barred. This is an odd addition to the trend of the Tribunal's analyses of fraud.

Fraud and the inherent power to reopen

The next part of our inquiry considers the Iran–US Claims Tribunal's stance on reopening decided cases that prove to have been previously tainted by fraud. This takes us back to the dilemma of *Weil* and *La Abra* and the *Sabotage Cases* which we considered in Chapters 1 and 2.

In the early cases in which the issue was raised, the Iran–US Claims Tribunal reserved the question of whether it possessed the inherent power to reopen awards which had been secured by fraud or forgery. In *Dames and Moore* v. *Iran*,[89] the respondent requested that the award be reopened in light of post-hearing allegations that the claimant's proffered affidavit testimony and invoices were false.[90] The respondent proposed four provisions in the Tribunal's rules as authority to reopen the case: Article 15(1) and (2) (dealing with equal treatment of parties); Article 29(2) (providing for reopening of a hearing before a final award is issued); Article 35 (providing for requested interpretations of awards); and Article 37 (providing for the making of an additional award as to claims presented but omitted from the award).[91]

The Tribunal prefaced its analysis with a general policy manifesto against reopening:

> As a matter of principle the Claims Settlement Declaration and the Tribunal Rules militate against the reopening and reconsideration of awards once rendered.[92]

The Tribunal concluded that none of the cited provisions provided authority for reopening the award.

> To the contrary, rather than providing even limited exceptions to finality, they prescribe the methods for achieving it in various circumstances.[93]

On the issue of whether there was an inherent power to reconsider awards alleged to have been based on fraud, the Tribunal stated:

> The implied or inherent power of an international claims tribunal in this area is an issue which has been subjected to learned analysis and limited judicial scrutiny, with wholly inconsistent results.[94]

[89] 8 *Iran-US Cl. Trib. Rep.* 107 (1985). [90] *Ibid.*, 113–14. [91] *Ibid.*, 114.
[92] *Ibid.* [93] *Ibid.*, 115. [94] *Ibid.*, 117.

But the Tribunal did not have to rule on the general question as it concluded that the new exhibits unearthed by the respondents "do not raise justified concern that the processes of the Tribunal have been subverted."[95] The exhibits showed only that a part of the money claimed by the claimant had been paid, that the new invoices produced by the respondent were "identical in all material respects" to those of the claimant, and that the statement of a witness for the claimant that the invoices remained unpaid as of early 1979 was "not inconsistent with [the respondent's] implied allegation . . . that the payment was made 7 May 1979."[96] Thus,

[t]he instant request for reopening and reconsideration, however, falls well short of justifying any such effort to ascertain the precise balance struck between finality of Tribunal dispositions, on the one hand, and the integrity of its processes on the other.[97]

In *Henry Morris* v. *Iran*,[98] the Tribunal was petitioned to reopen an award because of procedural due process violations in the prior phase: certain exhibits had been presented and arguments made for the first time at the hearing. Once again, the Tribunal averted the question:

[w]hether a Chamber or the Full Tribunal, despite the absence of any express provision, has inherent power to review and revise an Award under exceptional circumstances – e.g., when an Award was based on forged documents or perjury – is a question which the Tribunal does not need to reach in this decision.[99]

Yet, here again, practice trumped theory. The Tribunal did cursorily review and, in effect, reject the applicant's grounds for reconsideration.[100] So the question remained open as to whether the Iran–US Claims Tribunal believed that this was a power inherent in all international tribunals, but effectively unavailable to ad hoc tribunals after they had dissolved, or whether it was a special property of claims tribunals, which were, as in the *Sabotage Cases*, *functus officio* only upon the conclusion of their final decision.

In a later case, *Ram International Industries* v. *Air Force of Iran*, the Tribunal moved grudgingly away from its earlier position, conceding that "it might possibly be concluded that a tribunal, like the present one, which is to adjudicate a large group of cases and for a protracted period of time would by implication, until the adjournment and dissolution of the tribunal, have the authority to revise decisions induced by fraud."[101]

[95] *Ibid.*, 118. [96] See *ibid.* [97] *Ibid.*, 117.
[98] 3 *Iran-US Cl. Trib. Rep.* 364 (1983).
[99] *Ibid.*, 365. [100] *Ibid.*
[101] *Ram Int'l Indus.* v. *Air Force of Iran*, 29 *Iran-US Cl. Trib. Rep.* 383, p. 390, para. 20 (1993).

> [F]or the purpose of a revision the new fact has to be decisive, in the sense that when placed alongside the other facts of the case, earlier assessed, it seriously upsets the balance, and consequently the conclusions drawn by the tribunal.[102]

This is a pragmatic and consequentialist rather than formalistic test. Whatever the new fact, the Tribunal will not proceed to consider the alleged evidence of fraud, if, assuming its accuracy, and in the light most favorable to the complaining party, it would still not disturb the legal basis of the award. It is certainly not a "clean hands" doctrine, which would penalize the party that had engaged in fraud, even if the fraud had no effect on the outcome of the arbitration. Nor is it at all certain that it represents a consensus of the judges on the Tribunal. Judge Aldrich, in his study of the Tribunal's jurisprudence, describes the pre-*Ram* jurisprudence as a "consistent, prudent approach," while characterizing the *Ram* Tribunal as "gratuitously engaged in speculation."[103] Judge Aldrich does not seem persuaded that there were many cases of fraud.

In *Ram*, the Tribunal concluded that neither of the alleged instances of fraud would have affected the outcome and that therefore there was no need to reopen the case.[104] Whether or not the Colonel's signature was forged, it was evidence only of the timeliness, not the fact, of delivery, so it would not have affected the legal basis of the award.[105] As for the allegation that the evidence of delivery of the goods had to be false because an inventory list did not show the presence of the goods in the warehouse, the Tribunal discovered that the list included only those goods that were in the warehouse at the time it was compiled, some six years after the alleged delivery of the goods. Hence the list could not prove whether the goods were actually delivered.[106] In sum, while the new evidence the respondent adduced may have cast some doubt on some of the evidence originally submitted by the claimants, as it did not affect the substance of the award, it did not justify reconsideration.[107]

In later cases, the Tribunal did not take advantage of the possibility which *Ram* had created. In *Riahi* v. *Iran*,[108] in considering whether to reopen a case on the basis of alleged procedural defects, the Tribunal invoked the

102 *Ibid.* This standard was later quoted and applied in *Birnbaum* v. *Iran*, 33 *Iran-US Cl. Trib. Rep.* 286, para. 3 (1995).

103 G. H. Aldrich, *The Jurisprudence of the Iran-United States Claims Tribunal* (Oxford University Press, 1996), p. 456.

104 *Ram*, 29 *Iran-US Cl. Trib. Rep.*, paras. 21–22. 105 *Ibid.*, para. 21. 106 *Ibid.*, para. 22.

107 See *ibid.*, para. 23.

108 *Riahi* v. *Iran*, 2004 WL 2812132, *Iran-US Cl. Trib.* (17 Nov. 2004), para. 45.

Harold Birnbaum decision's "firm view" on the absence of an inherent power to reopen:

There is not much room for reading implied powers into a contemporary bilateral arrangement; for its authors are aware of past experience. It is to be expected that today, two States that intended to allow the revision of awards rendered by a tribunal established pursuant to a treaty between them would do so by an unequivocal expression of their common will. Clearly Iran and the United States did not so provide in the Algiers Declarations . . . But the existence of express rules providing that the award is "final and binding," coupled with the silence of the contracting Parties concerning the possibility of revision, makes it difficult to conclude that any inherent power to revise a final award exists.[109]

Even if the Tribunal theoretically had inherent powers to reopen, the *Riahi* Tribunal seemed skeptical that any set of facts could, in fact, trigger the power in practice. The Tribunal commented that "[e]ven in that context [fraud], the Tribunal has not reached a single decision confirming the existence and need to apply its 'inherent power,' whatever that may be."[110]

Judge Brower dissented from this narrow, formalistic understanding of the inherent power. In his view, the inherent power to reopen a case, especially for reasons of fraud, derived from the Tribunal's unstated obligation to maintain the integrity of the process.[111] Judge Brower cited *Dames and Moore* to demonstrate that the Tribunal had authority to exercise its inherent power in order to restore the balance between "the finality of Tribunal disposition, on the one hand, and the *integrity of its processes* on the other."[112] He reasoned that the balance "tilt[ed] . . . away from the rule respecting the finality of judgments" when something has occurred to create a "justified concern that the processes of the Tribunal have been subverted."[113] Judge Brower's interpretation was certainly spacious enough to cover instances of fraud.

As to the general question of the Tribunal's authority to reconsider an award,[114] Judge Brower held that authority to reopen exists notwithstanding any "final and binding" rule "particularly . . . if the relevant tribunal, like this Tribunal, sits in judgment on a large number of cases for an extended period of time."[115] He supported this proposition with a citation to the *Sabotage Cases*.[116]

Aside from the question of whether a tribunal has the power to reopen a case affected by fraud is the question of whether a tribunal will sanction a

[109] *Ibid.*, para. 42 (quoting the 1995 *Birnbaum* decision). [110] *Ibid.*, para. 43.
[111] *Ibid.*, para. 45 (dissenting opinion of Judge Charles N. Brower). [112] *Ibid.* [113] *Ibid.*
[114] *Ibid.*, para. 40. [115] *Ibid.*, para. 43. [116] *Ibid.*, n. 86.

party responsible for fraud. Here, several cases are instructive and suggest that the Iran–US Claims Tribunal, like several others in our study, are reluctant to do so. In *Uiterwyk Corp.* v. *Iran*,[117] for example, Iran sought late in the proceeding to produce a witness and documents intended to impeach the credibility of various members of the Uiterwyk family. The majority of Chamber One refused to admit the witness and his documents, on the ground that the motion was insufficiently noticed and out of time. Though the decision was taken for "procedural reasons,"[118] the Chamber proceeded to elaborate on the consequential test propounded in *Ram*:

> [G]iven the nature of the issue and the conflicting evidence of the Parties with respect to it, it is far from certain that the matter would be clarified by further briefing or an additional hearing. Moreover, even if the evidence sought to be offered by Mr. Paksima were admitted and believed, its principal consequence would be to reflect adversely upon the credibility of various members of the Uiterwyk family. The Tribunal need not resolve this thorny issue because, as shown below, it has adequate evidence upon which to determine the issues in this Case without relying upon the affidavits or testimony of the members of the Uiterwyk family.[119]

Judge Mostafavi dissented from the procedural decision and withdrew from the deliberations, on the ground that in light of the alleged bribery, "it was the Tribunal's duty to question the veracity of the statements made by the other witnesses in this Case" and the accuracy of the figures provided by the Claimant's accountants.[120]

We are not concerned, in this discussion, with the impact that withdrawal of a member of a Tribunal has on its competence, but rather on the substantive legal view that was implicit in Judge Mostafavi's dissent. Judge Aghahosseini had argued for use of the "F" word as a punitive sanction against fraudfeasors. Judge Mostafavi, by contrast, seemed to be more concerned with the consequences of a fraud *within* the case in which it was perpetrated.[121] The fraudfeasor did not lose its *locus standi in judicio* outright under some sort of "clean hands" doctrine. Rather, the burden of proof

117 19 *Iran-US Cl. Trib. Rep.* 107 (1988). 118 *Ibid.*, para. 28. 119 *Ibid.*

120 See *ibid.*, 166 (letter from Mr. Mostafavi to Mr. Böckstiegel, 3 June 1988).

121 When the majority refused to accommodate him, Judge Mostafavi declined to take part in the deliberations in the case. He argued that after a declaration of refusal to take part in the case by one of the arbitrators, further proceedings could take place only if the arbitrator were replaced. *Ibid.*, 167. He also asserted that since he had not participated in the deliberations and had not seen any of the draft awards, he could not be named as an arbitrator in the draft award. *Ibid.*, 168–69. Nevertheless, Judge Mostafavi's name appears in the Partial Award, *ibid.*, 107, although without a signature.

shifted against him, as if the Tribunal were saying, "because we have already established that you are a liar, we are no longer inclined to believe anything you say unless you prove it conclusively." The majority in *Uiterwyk* implicitly rejected this rather sensible and practicable proposal in relying on other evidence adduced by the claimants, apparently under the usual standard of proof. That is an approach that could encourage fraudulent behavior, as Judge Aghahosseini warned. Similarly opposed to the Tribunal's reticence to wrestle with sticky issues of fraud, the Iranian arbitrator in *Lischem Corp. Gifted, Inc.* v. *Atomic Energy Organization of Iran* protested, in a note appended to his signature, the majority's refusal to investigate allegations of fraud and bribery.[122]

Other cases reveal the Tribunal's reluctance to attach real sanctions to the failure to authenticate evidence. At most, it might signal some disapproval through the awarding of costs, though that motivation is far from clear. In *Ultrasystems*, for instance, the Tribunal refused to give effect to a critical letter in the case:

> The first question to resolve is thus whether the letter represents a valid approval of the final billing, binding on [respondent]. The Claimant [Ultrasystems] has presented evidence in support of the authenticity of Mr. Motazed's signature on the letter. On the other hand a number of circumstances surrounding the signing of the letter cast serious doubt on whether the letter can be considered as an approval of the final billing binding on [respondent]. There are, moreover, certain admitted inaccuracies in the final billing which render it in our view an unreliable basis for any decision as to the amount of [respondent's] liability. Our conclusion is therefore that the final billing is not binding on [respondent].[123]

Despite the implication that the letter was inauthentic, the Tribunal allowed Ultrasystems to establish its case by other means, and the focus shifted to how much the respondent owed on the bill.[124]

The respondent argued that it had paid some of the amount claimed by two checks and that one of the checks bore a handwritten text in Farsi indicating that it had been cashed.[125] The respondent also submitted a statement from the claimant's bank indicating that the amounts represented by the checks were credited to its account and that its principal agent in Iran had written checks drawing on the additional funds.[126] On this basis, the Tribunal found that payment had been made and that the claimant was

[122] 7 *Iran-US Cl. Trib. Rep.* 18, p. 25 (1984).
[123] 2 *Iran-US Cl. Trib. Rep.*, p. 106 (partial award). [124] See *ibid.*, 106–07.
[125] *Ultrasystems, Inc.* v. *Iran*, 4 *Iran-US Cl. Trib. Rep.* 77, p. 78 (1983) (final award).
[126] See *ibid.*

not entitled to that amount in the final award.[127] The question – if any – of the authenticity of the letter-bill was avoided.

The American arbitrator, Judge Richard M. Mosk, dissenting, considered the proof of payment differently. He noted that the Tribunal had granted the respondent "an opportunity to submit *evidence* to support the genuineness of certain checks" it had introduced as proof of payment.[128] But the respondent had produced only unauthenticated documents and statements with several inconsistencies: the cashed checks and withdrawal records were for only a portion of the disputed amounts and a statement of bank transactions indicated that after September 9, 1978, the respondent's account was increasingly in the red.[129] Judge Mosk insisted that once the authenticity of evidence is challenged and an opportunity to prove it is afforded, failure to do so should affect the weight given to such evidence.[130] Hence, he argued that there was no direct evidence to support the proposition that the claimant was paid.[131]

But Judge Mosk seemed to agree that the Tribunal lacked the power to reopen an award. When it issued its Final Award, the *Ultrasystems* Tribunal, in addition to finding the checks proper evidence of payment, also adjusted the costs of arbitration, awarding them to the respondent. Judge Mosk protested:

> Since there is no justification for the award of costs to Isiran and since there is absolutely no basis for the majority's determination of these costs, it is apparent that in its award of costs, the Tribunal is adjusting the costs already awarded to the Claimant in the Partial Award. This it cannot do. There is no provision in Tribunal Rules or elsewhere for a modification of an award, except in the case of any "clerical or typographical errors, or errors of similar nature."[132]

We can only speculate that the implicit justification for these costs bore some relation to the quality of the claimant's proof. The tribunal has yet to address squarely the question of what sanctions, if any, to impose upon parties who fail to make out a prima facie case of authenticity.

Overall, the Tribunal has shown itself to be strikingly reluctant to consider the consequences of submitting false evidence. The majority in *Golshani* concluded that the claimant had not made a prima facie case of authenticity so it did not reach the question of whether the respondent had met its burden of proving that the deed was a forgery. The claim was dismissed for lack of proof of ownership and the respondent was awarded

[127] See *ibid.*, 78–79. [128] See *ibid.*, 80 (dissenting opinion of Richard M. Mosk).
[129] See *ibid.* [130] *Ibid.* [131] See *ibid.* [132] *Ibid.*, 81 (citations omitted).

costs.[133] Yet the Tribunal refrained from accusing the claimant of submitting forged documents. It did not even censure the claimant for presenting evidence for which he could not make out a prima facie case of authenticity.

While it was clear that the questionable authenticity of a document as essential as the deed in the *Golshani* case had to lead to dismissal of the case, the Tribunal has not clearly indicated whether the falsity of more peripheral documents would require any sanction at all. As for evidence whose prima facie authenticity had not been established, would the Tribunal disregard such evidence altogether? Or would it, as Judge Mosk urged in *Ultrasystems*, merely discount the weight accorded such submissions?

Judge Aghahosseini's dissenting opinion conceded that the Tribunal has no penal sanctions at its disposal and that all it could do to counter the introduction of false evidence was "to be *forthright* in exposing the instances of abuse and in censuring the perpetrators."[134] Would such censure carry any adverse consequences in arbitration? Shame sanctions have proved of limited utility in international settings. Judge Aghahosseini warned that the Tribunal's reluctance to label forged evidence as such would encourage further use of fabricated evidence; "evidence which, in the measured view of the prospective perpetrators, will be either accepted by the Tribunal as genuine or, at the worst, simply set aside as unauthentic, with no adverse consequences."[135] In one of the starkest examples, in *Uiterwyk*, evidence of the claimant's bribery triggered no sanctions. Despite the uncontroverted evidence that the claimants had offered a witness half of the award if he would testify in their favor, the majority did not require an investigation into the other evidence submitted by the claimants.[136]

In general, rather than the forthright acknowledgment that Judge Aghahosseini urged, the Tribunal's more favored tack, it appears, has been to short-circuit a finding of fraud in the first instance. This preference appears in several forms in *Dadras* and *Aryeh*: in couching fraud claims as affirmative defenses rather than evidence rebutting authenticity, and in requiring "clear and convincing" proof to prove a fraud. Similarly, the Tribunal averted an explicit finding of fraud in *Davidson* v. *Iran*.[137] There, Judge Noori's dissent criticized the majority for excluding apparently fraudulent evidence on an unrelated technicality:

133 *Golshani*, 29 *Iran-US Cl. Trib. Rep.*, paras. 122–23.

134 See *ibid.*, 183 (separate opinion of Mohsen Aghahosseini). 135 *Ibid.*

136 See *Uiterwyk*, 19 *Iran-US Cl. Trib. Rep.*, pp. 116, 162.

137 *Davidson (Homayounjah)* v. *Iran*, 36 *Iran-US Cl. Tr.* 43 (2000) (dissenting opinion of Assahollah Noori).

Cognizant of the fact that such malicious and fraudulent behaviour undermines the expropriation/deprivation claim and any decision upholding it, the Majority closes its eyes to that group of evidence by qualifying it as evidence falling after the relevant period. I agree that the documents were all related to the period after 19 January 1981, but the fact remains that they were tampered with, distorted, and mistranslated to make it appear as if certain deprivative measures were taken against the Claimant's property prior to the closing date of the relevant period (on or about 20 June 1980) and that those measures were not ephemeral. By ignoring this group of evidence, the Majority appears to have felt at liberty to accept contentions not supported by any contemporary evidence.[138]

The Tribunal's decision to exclude on technical grounds four witnesses' testimonies, which had denied the existence of the contract between the *Dadras* claimants and TRC, was to the same effect.[139]

Conclusion

This survey of the Tribunal's encounters with fraudulent evidence reveals its marked disinclination to call a spade a spade. Instead, the Tribunal has devised a test for adjudicating allegations of fraud that averts pejorative terminology, not to speak of more meaningful sanctions. The prima facie authenticity test reduces the likelihood that the Tribunal will *label* any evidence fraudulent, even if the outcome of application of the test is rejection of the evidence. If the proponent of the evidence fails to establish its prima facie authenticity, the Tribunal will simply label it inauthentic, as in the *Golshani* case, and refuse to consider it in deciding the claim.

If, however, the party adducing the evidence establishes prima facie its authenticity, the burden shifts to the other party to prove that it is fraudulent. Theoretically, the Tribunal could consider the proof of forgery

138 *Ibid.*, para. 82.

139 In the *Dadras* case, the Chamber allowed the parties to submit post-hearing pleadings to comment on the "relevance, materiality and weight" of the Golzar affidavit, which had been filed late. In their comments, respondents submitted affidavits from four officials who had apparently been involved in the negotiation of the contract. The Tribunal excluded those statements as "an impermissible attempt to introduce further new, late and unauthorized evidence into the record contrary to the express terms of the Tribunal's Order." 31 *Iran-US Cl. Trib. Rep.*, paras. 37–43. Interestingly, however, their testimony had claimed that the contract never existed. See *ibid.* (dissenting opinion of Mohsen Aghahosseini) ("In a most surprising reaction to these highly significant revelations, the Majority in the Chamber hastily issued the Order of 27 April 1994, under which all affidavits submitted in relation to Mr. Golzar's testimony by those with intimate knowledge of the pertinent facts were simply excluded from the evidence. This, as I stated in a Dissent to the said Order, was utterly unjustified.").

or fraud adduced by the opposing party and declare the original evidence fraudulent, but the practical application of the test as applied in *Golshani* suggests that such a finding is quite unlikely. The Tribunal's test for prima facie authenticity examines conflicts between the face value of the evidence and other corroborative proof that the proponent of the evidence supplies. A false document which does not survive this phase of the examination will be declared not prima facie authentic; it will not be declared fraudulent. If it does survive, it has little to fear from the clear and convincing standard required to prove it false.

In the practice of the Iran–US Claims Tribunal, there are no sanctions for the use of fraudulent evidence. Although the claimant's case in *Golshani* was dismissed and the claimant himself was assessed costs of arbitration, it is far from clear that these actions were intended as punishment for having proffered fraudulent evidence. The Tribunal dismissed the case because the deed was the sole proof of ownership. If a piece of evidence of marginal importance had failed the prima facie authenticity test, the Tribunal would have presumably responded with a less drastic measure. Nor is it clear that the Tribunal's dismissal of a case for lack of proof because of failure to establish prima facie the authenticity of a key document is with prejudice; the Tribunal's jurisprudence seems to suggest that the proponent of the evidence is free to file another claim. At most, the *Ram* case demonstrated a grudging willingness to come to grips with the problem of fraudulent evidence, yet the will to actually address it still seemed lacking.

7

The *Taba* arbitration: duties of disclosure in the pre-arbitral phase

The *Taba* case may be an exception to Sir Hersh Lauterpacht's historical assumption: "with one or two insignificant exceptions, there are no historical instances of fraud or error in the conclusion of treaties."[1]

> The elaborate manner in which negotiations are conducted, and the time which lapses between the signature of a treaty and its ratification, exclude any reasonable possibility of fraud and error.[2]

In *Taba*, one of the parties made an error in the Compromis by which the dispute was submitted to arbitration. Judgments as to whether it was fraudulently induced will turn on an assessment of the legal and ethical responsibilities of adverse parties in the negotiations leading up to the conclusion of a compromis.

Egypt and Palestine had been parts of the Ottoman Empire. In 1841, Mohammed Ali Pasha, then ruling Egypt, secured from the Divine Porte an acknowledgment of Egyptian autonomy as a hereditary Khediviate or Pashalik within the Empire. The administrative boundaries between the Khediviate and Palestine and the Vilayet of the Hejaz, contiguous in the Sinai region, were not drawn with precision, an ambiguity not then, apparently, deemed of any concern. In 1885, a little over a decade after completing the Suez Canal, Britain concluded a treaty with the Divine Porte to formalize its status in Egypt.

By the early twentieth century, world war was on the horizon and it became urgent to remove clouds over boundaries delimiting what had until

[1] H. Lauterpacht, *Private Law Sources and Analogies of International Law: With Special Reference to International Arbitration* (Hamden, CT: Archon Books, 1970), pp. 175–76.

[2] *Ibid.*, 176.

then been a sleepy area between nominal units of the Ottoman Empire. On October 1, 1906, the Ottoman Sultanate and the Egyptian Khediviate reached agreement as to what was to be called the "administrative separating line" between Palestine, the Hejaz, and the Sinai. The separating line was described in geographical terms in Article 1 of the 1906 Agreement and, in accordance with Article 2, was also indicated by a black, broken line on duplicate maps that were signed and exchanged as part of the agreement. (The Khediviate's map, which the British kept, disappeared; Egypt produced an alleged copy of the Ottoman Turkish map in the arbitration, but it lacked the signatures that would have authenticated it.[3])

The 1906 Agreement also provided for demarcation. Article 3 stated:

> Boundary pillars will be erected, in the presence of the Joint Commission at intervisible points along the separating line, from the point on the Mediterranean shore to the point on the shore of the Gulf of Akaba.

In the eighteen days following the signing of the agreement, ninety-one temporary markers, telegraph poles, were erected along what the surveyors intended to be a straight line: ninety-one supposedly intervisible "sentries," posted across the desert. The two British officers assigned to the task, Mr. E. B. H. Wade, a surveyor, and Captain R. C. R. Owen, an intelligence officer, issued reports on the demarcation of the Taba area. Their accounts were not entirely consistent, perhaps owing to the generality of their descriptions. Owen reported that two poles were set on the "Taba Hills," while Wade reported that three were set on the "east cliffs of Taba."[4]

On December 31, 1906, the first of the permanent masonry boundary pillars, topped by one meter of iron, was laid in place. According to contemporaneous accounts, it was placed at Taba, replacing the telegraph pole there. The pillar was erected in the presence of the acting governor of Sinai, Captain A. C. Parker, who had been seconded from intelligence in Cairo. Parker took photographs of the first pillar and it came to be known

[3] See *Location of Boundary Markers in Taba Between Egypt and Israel*, 20 *R. Int'l Arb. Awards* 1, para. 49 (29 Sept. 1988). Israeli counsel believed that Egypt had an authentic copy of the map, which it refused to submit to the proceedings. This allegation, in addition to the allegations surrounding the (unsuccessful) destruction of Boundary Pillar 90 and the concealment of the destruction of the Parker site, is a third issue of alleged fraud in the *Taba* case. See "Verbatim Record of the Hearing" in *The Egyptian-Israel Arbitration Tribunal Established in Accordance with the Compromis Signed 11 September 1986* (14–25 Mar.; 11–15 Apr., 1986), p. 657.

[4] *Location of Boundary Markers in Taba*, 20 *R. Int'l Arb. Awards*, para. 54. The award here describes them as "pillars," as do some of the contemporaneous accounts. In fact, the pillars, at the site of each telegraph pole, were erected later.

in the arbitration as the "Parker Pillar." On February 9, 1907, the last of the ninety-one pillars was erected.

The 1906 Agreement may have resolved one dispute, but international politics and conflict swirled over the sands of Sinai for the next three-quarters of a century. In the aftermath of World War I, the Ottoman Empire disintegrated and Britain acquired control over Palestine by virtue of a Mandate. The Balfour Declaration, promising Jews a national home in Palestine, coincided with the rise of Arab nationalism. Palestine became the theater of conflict between Jews and Arabs in the 1920s and 1930s. In 1948, Britain relinquished control over the parts of Palestine it still retained and Israel brought itself into existence. Immediately, Israel had to defend itself against the armies of neighboring Arab states, purporting to act on behalf of the Palestinian people.

The first Arab–Israel war concluded in 1949. In that, as in the subsequent wars, the Egyptian–Israeli border was the scene of fighting. In 1956, Israel, in concert with France and the United Kingdom, invaded Egypt. France and the United Kingdom seized the Suez Canal and Israel advanced deep into the Sinai Peninsula. When the invading states were obliged to withdraw, a United Nations peacekeeping force was established along the Israel–Egypt border in the Sinai Peninsula,[5] but only on the Egyptian side.[6] Egypt agreed to withdraw its forces to a distance of five kilometers.[7]

Israel reentered the area in 1967, at the beginning of the Six-Day War. The conclusion of that campaign saw Israel in control of all of the Sinai Peninsula, down to the southern bank of the Suez Canal. Israel remained there, as a belligerent occupant, for the next twelve years. As the belligerent occupant, Israel introduced many topographical changes, including the removal of the cliff where the Parker Pillar had stood.

In Israel's politics, the Six-Day War ushered into ascendance "Greater Israel" factions in Israeli politics demanding the incorporation of territories that had, at one time or another, purportedly been parts of ancient Israel. Extensive developments of territories secured in the war were undertaken. Sinai was part of this Middle Eastern "manifest destiny." For some in Israel, increasing development in the area was aimed toward permanent control; for others, it was a means of increasing pressure on the Arab states to trade land for peace. The Arabs refused to negotiate. The facts on the ground thus seemed to move toward permanence.

5 GA Res. 1000, A/RES/394 (5 Nov. 1956) (establishing the peacekeeping force, UNEF).

6 See Middle East-UNEF 1, "Background," www.unorg/en/peacekeeping/missions/past/unef1backgr2.html.

7 *Location of Boundary Markers in Taba*, 20 *R. Int'l Arb. Awards*, para. 98.

The Egypt–Israel Peace Treaty of 1979 halted this process. That treaty, based on a land-for-peace swap, secured the return of Egyptian territories seized in 1967 in a phased withdrawal that would culminate in 1982. Egypt was to regain "the full exercise of Egyptian sovereignty up to the internationally recognized border between Egypt and mandated Palestine."[8] The Treaty, which defected from the "No's" of Khartoum, led to Egypt's ostracism by the Arab world. Henceforth, one thrust of Egyptian foreign policy sought to prove that the peace process was the only practical way of securing the return of all the Arab territories lost in 1967.

In 1978, an Egyptian-born Israeli businessman, Eli Papushado, received permission from the Begin government to begin construction of a luxury hotel complex in a patch of Sinai desert called Taba that had been secured by Israel in 1967. Taba huddles along a beach on the Gulf of Aqaba, near to the Israeli city of Eilat. As long as Israel appeared bent on remaining in Sinai, the exact legal location of Taba was of no moment. By 1982, when Israel withdrew from Sinai, the hotel was well advanced in construction. Egypt was later to contend that by this time, Israel was engaged in creating a fait accompli in an area which was contested.[9]

Around the same time, in 1981–82, the Joint Boundary Commission which the Peace Treaty had established commenced demarcation of the boundary between the two states. The Commission accepted the 1906 British–Ottoman agreement as having established the international boundary. To confirm this line on the ground, the Commission was to use the 1906 boundary pillars or their crumbled remnants. Where they no longer existed or were no longer identifiable, the Commission determined where they must have stood:

> What was required of the Joint Commission, was to identify the location of the boundary pillars – in other words, to identify the old boundary pillars or their remnants, or if neither the pillars nor the remnants still existed, to identify the locations where the old boundary pillars originally stood.[10]

[8] The Camp David Accords from 17 September 1978 included an agreement on "the full exercise of Egyptian sovereignty up to the internationally recognized border between Egypt and mandated Palestine."

[9] As it argued: "once Egypt was apprised of these Israeli activities it promptly lodged a series of official protests which extended to all actions involving any such *fait accompli*." "Memorial of the Arab Republic of Egypt, In the Matter of an Arbitration Between the Arab Republic of Egypt and the State of Israel," para. 2.11 (13 May 1987) (footnote omitted). Egypt's protests are found in Annex 3 of its Memorial.

[10] *Ibid.*, para. 2.18. The Israeli delegation to the Joint Commission shared this essential methodology: the work consisted of "locating the existing border stones on aerial photographs and in sections where these boundary stones are missing to locate the points of

The Joint Commission agreed on over seventy of the boundary pillars, including the locations for vanished pillars and locations for additional pillars. But in two areas, one of them Taba, the Commission was unable to reach agreement. The Commission found some pillar remnants in the Taba area, but rather far from the coast. The Egyptian officials concluded these inland remnants marked the final pillar. Israel disagreed, whereupon the provisional agreement, which had been reached on a number of other pillars, dissolved. The dispute resolution mechanism of the Peace Treaty was brought into operation.

At this point, one should note that the Commission had agreed upon an additional pillar during the process. As a result, the agreed Boundary Pillar 90 or "BP 90" may have actually been the original BP 89, meaning there were two original pillars remaining to be found, BP 90 and BP 91. For whatever reason, however, the parties agreed that only one more original pillar was needed. This decision makes the pleadings confusing because both sides presented their submissions as "BP 91." The real BP 91, the 1906 final pillar, was the Parker Pillar. As mentioned above, however, the Parker Pillar ceased to exist sometime after it was initially erected and its topographical site was significantly altered around 1970.[11] Henceforth, our references to "BP 90" are not to be confused with the original BP 89. Subsequent references to BP 90 are to the pillar (remnants) that Egypt proposed as BP 91 (or, BP 91(E)).

Among other things, the *Taba* arbitration is distinctive in the number of explicit allegations made in the course of the hearings of different forms of fraud practiced by each of the parties.[12] Some also appeared in the British and Israeli press.[13] None of these allegations is even mentioned in the award, an omission that recurs in many of the cases we have reviewed in this book. If one reads only the *Taba* award, but does not review the written pleadings and especially the transcript of oral argument, one will be unable to assess the extent to which allegations and issues of fraud may have influenced the Tribunal's decision. Hence, our inquiry must review enough of the procedure to enable us to assess provisionally the validity of the fraud allegations, so that we can try to reconstruct the Tribunal's reaction to the allegation of fraud.

the boundary according to the description in the 1906 agreement." *Location of Boundary Markers in Taba*, 20 *R. Int'l Arb. Awards*, para. 100.

11 *Location of Boundary Markers in Taba*, 20 *R. Int'l Arb. Awards*, para. 227.

12 D. W. Bowett, "The Taba Award of 29 September 1988," *Isr. L. Rev.* 23 (1989), 429, 441.

13 See, for example, *Monitin* article, in n. 18 below; *Times* article referenced in the "Verbatim Record," pp. 77–78.

The Compromis

Article VII of the Peace Treaty provided for dispute resolution by negotiation, conciliation, or arbitration. On September 11, 1986, the parties concluded a Compromis[14] whose language reflected a good deal of calculation and bargaining, some of which was rehashed in oral argument. The preamble of the Compromis stated the common postulate of the dispute:

> Recognizing that a dispute has arisen, as defined in Article II of this Compromis, on the location of fourteen boundary pillars of the recognized international boundary between Egypt and the former mandated territory of Palestine as stipulated in the accordance with the Annex [to the Compromis], which the parties wish to resolve fully and finally.

The specific question posed to the Tribunal was set out in Article II:

> The Tribunal is requested to decide the location of the boundary pillars of the recognized international boundary between Egypt and the former mandated territory of Palestine, in accordance with the Peace Treaty, the April 25, 1982 Agreement, and the Annex.

Section 5 of the Annex gave precise instructions to the Tribunal that restrained the scope of its answer:

> The Tribunal is not authorized to establish a location of a boundary pillar other than a location advanced by Egypt or by Israel and recorded in Appendix A. The Tribunal also is not authorized to address the location of boundary pillars other than those specified in paragraph 1.

The set of possible locations of the final pillar was also set forth in the Annex, which provided the opponents' respective submissions for the boundary. Section 2 stated in relevant part:

> For the final boundary pillar No. 91, which is at the point of Ras Taba on the western shore of the Gulf of Aqaba, Israel has indicated two alternative locations, at the granite knob and at Bir Taba, whereas Egypt has indicated its location, at the point where it maintains the remnants of the boundary pillar are to be found.

The two Israeli submissions placed the terminus of the boundary that, Israel averred, had been established by the 1906 Agreement, to the south of the Taba hotel complex, putting the complex in Israeli territory. The

[14] *Location of Boundary Markers in Taba Between Egypt and Israel*, 20 *R. Int'l Arb. Awards* 1, Compromis, app. A p. 107 (11 Sept. 1986).

Egyptian submission for BP 91 located the boundary further to the north, putting the Taba hotel complex in Egyptian territory.

From the pre-arbitral phase and, in particular, the design of the Compromis, the parties proposed quite different roles for the Tribunal. Israel asserted that "the task of the Tribunal is to determine what that boundary was and to express it by the location of boundary pillars."[15]

> The task of the Tribunal is to express the recognized international boundary between Egypt and the former mandated territory of Palestine in terms of the location of boundary pillars. It is not the task of the Tribunal to seek the location of boundary pillars that were on the ground during the period of the Mandate. If this were the meaning of Article II of the Compromis the word "recognized" would have had no relevance to the description of the boundary with which the Tribunal is concerned. It is obvious that "recognition" attaches to the boundary, not to its pillars, and that therefore the reference to the location of the pillars is to their location as an expression of the recognized boundary. If the boundary does not run where a pillar was located, then the pillar was wrongly located and must be relocated.[16]

By contrast, Egypt's conception of the Tribunal's task was bound to the physical site of the pillars:

> In view of the fact that these pillars are those of an already existing demarcation identified by numbers, the decision on the location of controverted pillars (which is limited by the terms of the Annex to the Compromis to a choice between the locations indicated by the Parties for each of the 14 pillars contested by Israel) can only be a decision identifying the location of these pillars.[17]

For Egypt, the fundamental notion of the arbitration was that remnants of a boundary pillar, if authoritatively identified as such, were dispositive. For Israel, the fundamental notion was that text controlled: text was to trump an actual boundary pillar location, whether intact or identified only by its remains, if it could be demonstrated that the pillar's location was not consistent with the terms of the 1906 Agreement.

These issues generated further disagreements, not simply as to what the Tribunal should do, but also as to the research methodologies of each of the parties, their respective evidentiary burdens, and, in particular, what each of the parties was obliged to submit to the Tribunal and to its opponent.

[15] "Memorial of Israel, The Egypt-Israel Arbitration Tribunal Established in Accordance with the Compromis Signed 11 September 1986," para. 3.5 (13 May 1987).

[16] *Ibid.*, para. 5.9. [17] "Egypt Memorial," para. 3.42.

Maps, pictures, and references in governmental documents had been prepared and issued over the years. Some of these, preserved in the archives of the parties, were apparently only discovered or their significance only appreciated well into the arbitration so that they were first submitted to the Tribunal (and admitted) at the oral hearing stage of the arbitration.

During the pre-arbitral phase, it was alleged that certain elements of the Israeli military establishment mounted a rogue operation. According to an article in *Monitin*, an Israeli weekly, several operatives were reportedly dispatched, by the then Minister of Defense to destroy the original BP 90. According to the account cited by Egypt:

> [A] two-man team, one of whom was "the surveyor" and the other the operator, went to that rocky hill, smashed up the frontier marker, and dumped the fragments in the sea. David Levy, Minister of Housing, was directly responsible for [one saboteur] while Ariel Sharon, Minister of Agriculture, was directly responsible for [the other saboteur].[18]

Calling the saboteurs clumsy, the author of the article that Egypt cited wrote that it transpired that the surveyor and operator had mistaken the area and had actually dumped the nearby triangulation stone into the sea. Parts of the base of the pillar remained and the shaft, which fell over a ridge, remained close by and could be identified as the remaining part of the pillar. "The affair was kept strictly secret by all concerned... out of fear for their own skins," *Monitin* reported.[19]

Whether or not the account was correct, there was debris that appeared to be the remains of a pillar. And if the operation actually took place, and its objective was to mislead Egypt by destroying a pillar that might have undermined Israel's claims to Taba and to induce Egypt to select a site for BP 91 more favorable to Israel's case, it had the opposite effect. Enough debris remained for one to see that something like a boundary pillar had been there. And, indeed, it became Egypt's submission for the ultimate boundary marker, BP 91(E). To be clear: this was never the "final" pillar but rather – if any – the penultimate pillar. But Egypt did not know that.

The Israelis knew that Egypt's submission was not the Parker Pillar and assumed that their counterparts had similar knowledge. Israeli counsel

[18] R. Edelist, "The Taba Deception Who Gave the Order? First Exposure of a Double Deception 'Exercise' and Treble Clumsy Oversight in the Affair of the Taba Border Dispute," *Monitin* (Jan. 1986) translated version reprinted in "Rejoinder of the Arab Republic of Egypt, In the Matter of an Arbitration Between the Arab Republic of Egypt and the State of Israel," Annex 3, p. 2 (1 Feb. 1988).

[19] *Ibid.*, 4.

assumed that the Egyptians knew that their selection could not be BP 91, the Parker Pillar, but were intentionally choosing it instead of Parker in order to gain slightly more territory and the site of the hotel.[20]

A certain amount of suspicion is probably useful for international political negotiators but too much suspicion can blind people to simple and obvious facts. The Israelis may have been ignoring a rather obvious possibility – that Egypt was making a mistake – and reading the Egyptians incorrectly, for, as mentioned above, a decisive refutation of the "No's" of Khartoum was one of Cairo's critical political objectives. The Egyptian team was under instructions to secure a "legal" award rather than a territorial compromise. In light of these contextual considerations, perhaps Egypt was simply making a mistake.

The pleadings

Written pleadings were exchanged simultaneously. As is often the case when this arrangement is adopted, the pleadings are confusing, as each side shifted its position regarding which number pillar was at issue. Some confusion, as mentioned earlier, derived from the fact that the Joint Commission had added a new boundary post, pillar 88. This meant that the Joint Commission's BP 90, whose position satisfied both parties, was actually the original BP 89. Since the parties were arguing over the location of BP 91, the final original pillar, they should have been proposing two pillars in their respective submissions, not one, or at least identifying the penultimate pillar even as they presented their submissions for the final one. Instead, both sides obfuscated or bungled the original numbering until late in the day, when they scrambled to explain the confusions away.[21]

[20] Israel argued at the hearing that "Egypt had knowledge that there was a further site of a pillar" but, "to put it very bluntly, apparently wished to acquire further territory." "Verbatim Record," pp. 849, 851–52.

[21] Both sides were guilty of this inconsistency. Since Israel argued that BP 91(E) was not even a penultimate pillar site, but merely a trig point, and since it also argued that there had been ninety-one original pillars, it itself had to account for both BP 90 and BP 91. Israel did suggest two sites but they were alternates for the same pillar, BP 91. In arguing that each of the two Israeli proposals for BP 91(I) was truer to the 1906 Agreement, intervisibility not historicity was its main argument. Had Israel then suggested two sites, to represent the original BP 90 and BP 91, it would have had to posit a second point intervisible with the original BP 89, one that again would have lacked historicity. It would not have been to Israel's advantage to emphasize the lack of historical grounding for its final pillar positions by proposing a second, entirely ahistorical, if intervisible, pillar.

There was a similar inconsistency on the Egyptian side. Though there were actually two original pillars to go, we find only one in Egypt's original submission. Since it argued

In its Memorial, Egypt supported its submission for BP 91(E) with cartographic and other documentary evidence, including the photographs that Captain Parker had taken. Egypt used the photograph for three ends. First, it used them to rebut the Israeli submissions. On this front, it succeeded, but only in part. The key photograph and its annotation by Parker were analyzed extensively and Egypt easily demonstrated that neither of the Israeli submissions could have been the Parker Pillar:

These photographs demonstrate conclusively that neither of the claimed Israeli locations for Boundary Pillar 91 can be correct. Both claimed Israeli locations . . . are visible features [in the photographs] . . . They both lie to the *west* of the boundary pillar, that is on the Egyptian side of the line.[22]

Yet that contention did not really join issues with Israel, for Israel had not contended that its submissions were necessarily places where the boundary pillars had actually been erected, but rather places where they could or should have been erected if there were a proper international legal application of the terms of the 1906 Agreement. It was the Egyptian approach that took the actual location of boundary pillars as controlling. Thus, as a rebuttal to the Israeli approach, the photographs were not really on point.

Second, Egypt used the photographs to support its own position, contending that the photograph proved BP 91 had been erected "on a cliff overlooking the Gulf of Akaba at the end of the eastern ridge above Wadi Taba."[23] Egypt asserted:

Then, too, we have the extremely valuable photographic evidence, in particular the photographs taken by Captain Parker showing Pillar 91 when first constructed in 1906. It would be hard to find more convincing evidence than these pictures, taken long before the dispute and just after the placing along the boundary of the permanent boundary pillars had occurred. Comparison with present-day photographs, as noted above, confirms the fact that they were indeed taken of Pillar 91.[24]

The Parker photographs purportedly confirmed (at least, in Egypt's first pleading) that BP 91 "must be at or in the immediate vicinity of the location indicated by Egypt."[25]

that that pillar, BP 91(E), was the final pillar, Egypt seemed to be operating on the assumption that the Joint Commission's BP 90 was the original BP 90. Because Egypt had only one possibility in mind for a boundary pillar, it would have been awkward for it to deal with the actual number of BP 90. See, in this regard, Bowett, "The Taba Award of 29 September 1988," 438 n. 20, where Professor Bowett admits that BP 90 was really BP 89.

[22] "Egypt Memorial," para. 6.108. [23] *Ibid.*, para. 6.103. [24] *Ibid.*, para. 8.61.
[25] *Ibid.*, para. 6.109.

Egypt also used the photographs to develop rebuttal evidence. This was necessary because the photographs actually showed that the Parker Pillar had been erected on a cliff that was not present at the site of BP 91(E), the place, in Egypt's compromissary submission, where the remains of some sort of boundary marker had been found. Egypt tried to finesse this geographical discrepancy by hypothesizing subsequent topographical changes and by expanding its submission from the location of the Pillar to include its "immediate vicinity":

The qualification "or in the immediate vicinity" is necessary because a cliff of the type shown in the photographs is no longer visible at the precise location indicated by Egypt. A charitable explanation might be that there has been a rock-fall; a less charitable explanation would suggest that there has been a deliberate attempt to remove evidence of where the boundary pillar was originally located by removing the cliff on which it was standing.[26]

This effort to explain the photographic discrepancy encountered its own difficulties. A rock-fall would have explained why the remains of the pillar were still in "the immediate vicinity." But if Israel had removed the cliff, in line with the "less charitable explanation," there would have been no pillar remains. Given the presence of the iron flange and mortar remains of some sort of pillar, which Egyptian officials found in 1981, the cliff removal hypothesis seems improbable.[27]

The Egyptian hypothesis of malintentioned removal is interesting in the context of the subsequent allegations of fraud. It indicates that from its very first pleading Egypt had calculated the possibility that topographical changes might have been artificially and maliciously induced in the area of Taba. Egypt characterized this hypothesis in its memorial as the "less charitable" explanation. Since spontaneous geographical changes, the other option Egypt tendered, are neither charitable nor uncharitable, the implication was that Israel effected topographical changes with the intention of misleading Egypt or the Tribunal. As will be seen, the implication that something concealed and underhanded had been done was ultimately important for Egypt's argument.

From the start, Israel knew about the Parker Pillar. It did not, however, discuss it in its Memorial, since it was irrelevant to its textual thesis:

[26] *Ibid.*

[27] Unless one were to hypothesize that Israel removed the cliff, but carefully collected and preserved the ruins of whatever structure had been on it and then replaced the remains at the coordinates at which they had originally been found, in such a way as to conceal the fact of the removal of the cliff itself.

regardless of whether the Parker Pillar had historically been a boundary pillar, it was incorrectly placed in terms of the 1906 Agreement. Nor did Israel's argument need to focus on the remnants of BP 90.[28] Rather, Israel mostly sought to show that BP 91(E) did not meet the linearity and intervisibility requirements of the pillars, prescribed by Article III of the 1906 Agreement and subsequent authoritative documents. It argued that either of its alternative submissions would meet these tests.[29]

Egypt's Counter-Memorial was largely devoted to refuting the arguments in Israel's Memorial, including, notably, the implication of Israel's submission: that since BP 91(E) was not the final point, the Tribunal was compelled to decide in favor of whichever of Israel's proposed boundary points met the specifications of the 1906 Agreement, since the Compromis allowed no other option than choosing one of the proposed points.[30]

Egypt objected to this reading of the Compromis and insisted that there could not be an award of *non liquet* (where a tribunal cannot decide):

> If, *arguendo*, neither of the locations advanced by the Parties is exactly borne out in the opinion of the Tribunal by the evidence made available to it, then in Egypt's submission the Tribunal would be bound to choose the location of that Party which is the more consistent with the evidence.[31]

Here again, the parties' positions stemmed from a fundamental difference in the interpretation of the Compromis. Israel demanded a return to the text and its explication regardless of the actual position of the boundary pillars. Egypt insisted on a search for the boundary markers that had been erected. This was the first mention of the possibility of a *non liquet* in the arbitration and it was raised defensively by Egypt; it claimed *non liquet* was a covert Israeli strategy.[32]

In its Counter-Memorial, Israel turned the Parker photographs against Egypt, contending that they indicated a totally different pillar from

[28] "Israel Memorial," para. 3.39. [29] See, for example, *ibid.*, para. 8.54.

[30] "These two alternatives constitute findings in favour of Israel, for even a negative finding according to (ii), that the locations of the disputed boundary pillars are not 'the locations advanced by Egypt' (though not termed positively as a finding by the Tribunal in favour of the positions advanced by Israel), would amount to an endorsement of the actual de facto situation in which Israel continues its military occupation of the locations on the terrain which are consistent with its contentions." "Counter-Memorial of the Arab Republic of Egypt, In the Matter of an Arbitration Between the Arab Republic of Egypt and the State of Israel," para. 2.43 (12 Oct. 1987).

[31] *Ibid.*, para. 2.47. [32] *Ibid.*, para. 2.43.

BP 91(E). The Parker photos showed a pillar some 284 meters to the southwest of BP 91(E) and at an altitude of 27 rather than 91 meters. In Israel's view, Egypt had thus effectively abandoned its submission of BP 91(E).[33] Since the mandate of the Tribunal, at Egypt's own insistence, required it to select one of the submissions of the parties and no other, the Tribunal had no choice but to accept one of the remaining Israeli submissions.[34] At this point in the process, Israel disclosed that it had removed the site where the Parker Pillar (and Israel was not willing to concede that it was a legitimate boundary pillar) would have stood:

> The site was removed probably in January-February 1970 during the improvement of the road to Taba and to points further south along the coast of Sinai. There was nothing secret or sinister about that operation. It was done openly in order to improve access to the area of Wadi Taba and the coast south of it.[35]

Article VIII of the Compromis prescribed Memorials and Counter-Memorials for the written phase of the arbitration, but it also allowed a subsequent exchange of "rejoinders" at the request of either party. In light of what was becoming the Parker fiasco in the Counter-Memorials, Egypt exercised that option. Acknowledging that BP 91(E) was not, after all, the celebrated Parker Pillar, Egypt developed a three-part response in its Rejoinder. First, Egypt pressed an interpretation of the Compromis that reemphasized a "critical date" of 1922. Egypt contended that by 1922, the Parker Pillar no longer existed and BP 91(E) had become the de facto final

[33] "Counter-Memorial of Israel, The Egypt-Israel Arbitration Tribunal Established in Accordance with the Compromis Signed 11 September 1986," para. 2.07 (12 Oct. 1987).

[34] *Ibid.*, paras. 2.01, 2.03.

[35] *Ibid.*, para. 2.12. Professor Bowett cleverly turned Israel's photo argument on its head. Israel had argued that since the Parker photograph site ruled out BP 91(E) and that since the Tribunal was bound to choose one of the submitted sites, the site must be one of Israel's submissions. These submissions had been submitted on a different theory than adherence to the Parker site, so the argument was cohesive. In response, Bowett said that the photo could not possibly represent the Israeli sites, which was true, so since the Tribunal was bound to choose one of the submitted sites, it must choose Egypt's. Both sides used the photo to make the negative argument that one's own submission might not be ideal, but because the photo clearly excluded the other party's submission, the only solution was to use one's own. See also "Egypt Rejoinder," para. 2.21. The problem with Bowett's rejoinder is that Egypt used the photo to support its own submission and later was forced to concede the photo failed to do so. The photo actually ruled out Egypt's submission as well. What Egypt was basically saying was that based on the photo none of the sites was the final historical pillar, which, of course, was essentially correct. While Egypt had other props for its argument, the clever rejoinder was somewhat weaker than Israel's argument.

pillar.[36] Second, crying foul, Egypt alleged that Israel had tried to destroy BP 90 (its ultimate choice for BP 91(E)). Third, crying foul, even louder to cover its own error about the location of the Parker Pillar, Egypt alleged that Israel had improperly suppressed pertinent information.

As to its critical date claim, Egypt contended that:

> The photographs do not in the least invalidate Egypt's position, because there is ample evidence that from 1906 onwards there always was a boundary pillar at BP 91(E), which was the final pillar on the critical date, 1922. What is relevant to the present dispute is that the Parties have agreed in the Compromis that, having located BP 90, there is only *one* more pillar to be located by the Tribunal before the boundary reaches the coast. In fact Egypt believes that, in view of what has been revealed in Israel's Counter-Memorial about the changes to the terrain made by Israel, the photographs in fact show a pillar at the seaward end of the eastern ridge. The location of the pillar in the photograph does not have to be decided by the Tribunal. It is irrelevant except as clear evidence that BP 91 could not have been on either of the two alternative Israeli locations. Egypt has evidence that by 1912–13 the only pillar on the eastern ridge overlooking Wadi Taba was the pillar at an altitude of 298 feet. Thus, 10 years before 1922 the only pillar that existed was at BP 91(E). Once BP 91 is located by the Tribunal, *as it stood in 1922*, the course of the boundary from BP 91(E) must continue directly down the ridge to the sea. It is absolutely impossible to interpret this so as to place any part of the hotel complex, or indeed of Ras Taba, on the Israeli side of the boundary.[37]

The non-existence of the Parker Pillar by the critical date or critical period was now an indispensable strut of the Egyptian argument that Egypt's BP 91(E) was de facto the final pillar.

[36] "Egypt believes . . . that the pillar shown in the Parker photographs . . . disappeared some time between 1907 and 1913 so that it had ceased to exist long before the 'critical date' in the present arbitration, that is to say, 1922. By the year 1922, the map and other evidence presented by Egypt demonstrates clearly that the last pillar in the 1906 boundary line was at the location identified as BP 91(E)." "Egypt Rejoinder," paras. 2.15, 2.16.

[37] *Ibid.*, para. 1.04. The Rejoinder also went out of its way to explain why Counsel had discovered the Parker photographs since they now no longer supported Egypt's submission:

> There is one further factor relevant to Egypt's disclosure of the Parker photographs. Their relevance can hardly be disputed. Would a party be justified in withholding from the Tribunal relevant evidence merely because it could not fully explain the circumstances under which, over 75 years ago, that evidence disappeared from the terrain? Egypt took the view that concealment of the evidence from the Tribunal would not be justified in those circumstances.

Ibid., para. 1.05.

The second foul Egypt cried was the "extrinsic information" it adduced that Israel had tried to destroy the pillar at BP 91(E).[38] These allegations were delivered with great indignation and may have had what trial lawyers style an "atmospheric value," but they failed to advance the substantive Egyptian case. If there was an effort to destroy the pillar, it failed to achieve its objective. Enough of the shaft and base of BP 91(E) remained for Egypt to rest its submission on it. Hence, this attempted fraud had had no consequence.

The third foul Egypt cried was that Israel had destroyed the Parker Pillar site in 1970. Egypt contended that Israel was aware of the Parker photographs "long before" signature of the Compromis and

> that Israel owed a duty to the Tribunal (and indeed to Egypt) to disclose the extent of the engineering works carried out on the eastern ridge overlooking Wadi Taba (involving the removal of "some natural obstacles") after 1967; and that Israel signally failed to make any such disclosure until forced to do so by the need to comment on the Parker photographs which Egypt had submitted in evidence.[39]

This claim was somewhat subverted by the fact that Egypt had already explicitly hypothesized in its own Memorial that there had been topographical changes in the area. Therefore, although Egypt was forced to change its argument regarding BP 91(E)'s location as a result of the new "revelatory" topographical data, its argument about the extent of its shock that there had been topographical changes was disingenuous:

> [i]t hardly lies in Israel's mouth to suggest that Egypt has "changed the location which it attributes to BP 91" when Israel had so altered the terrain on the eastern ridge overlooking Wadi Taba as to have rendered it impossible to determine with precision where the pillar shown in the Parker photographs had originally stood.[40]

In sum, Egypt charged Israel with prior knowledge. Not sharing it, Egypt argued, amounted to foul play. As Egyptian counsel argued:

> Israel knew that Parker was a different pillar; Israel knew that they had destroyed the cliffs on which Parker had been located; Israel knew that they had destroyed Boundary Pillar 91(E), and Israel had photographic evidence to prove all of these things. What did Israel say to the other Party with which it was negotiating in good faith? Nothing, Mr. President, absolutely nothing. Despite all these references to acting in good faith, establishing of procedures for a final and complete resolution, Israel said nothing.[41]

[38] *Ibid.*, para. 2.14. [39] *Ibid.* [40] *Ibid.* [41] "Verbatim Record," p. 831.

These allegations would have provided little legal traction unless Egypt could point to a cognizable duty that Israel had violated. The duty Egypt invoked was good faith:

By failing to disclose whether any such evidence was found at what it claims to be the site of the so-called "Parker pillar" prior to the removal of that site in 1970 by Israeli engineers, Israel is flouting the principles of good faith as applied in the law and practice relating to international arbitration. Good faith requires openness and co-operation from both Parties. Israel, having admitted in its Counter-Memorial that Israeli engineers had, in 1970, removed what Israel claims to be the site of the "Parker pillar," should have immediately revealed all documentary or other evidence in its possession relating to that (and indeed any other) alteration of the terrain on the eastern ridge overlooking Wadi Taba.[42]

Within this contention, Egypt made three distinct legal arguments: (1) quasi-estoppel; (2) a duty of unsolicited comprehensive discovery; and (3) an adverse inference rule. Each argument must be considered more closely.

The quasi-estoppel claim rested on the existence of a legal prohibition on secretly altering the landscape. If Israel did so, and Egypt was misled, Israel could not then claim, Egypt argued, that Egypt was precluded from amending its submission when it realized that it had assumed facts that were incorrect. The argument turned on whether, as a matter of fact, the change was carried out with the intention of distorting the legal procedure and whether, as a matter of law, Egypt had to discover the changes for itself or Israel had a duty to inform it.

Whether or not the Parker Pillar had disappeared within a decade of its erection, Israel had excavated the site on which the Parker Pillar had stood in approximately 1970 in order to expand a road that passed in its vicinity. But that fact could serve as a premise in the Egyptian syllogism only if it could be shown that in altering the landscape, Israel had violated international law. And it was far from certain that the changes undertaken about 1970 were inconsistent with the obligations of a belligerent occupant.

Second, in suggesting a duty of unsolicited comprehensive discovery, Egypt alleged that Israel, along with the notification in the Counter-Memorial about the road expansion in 1970, should have "immediately revealed" all documentary evidence relating to that and other alterations of Wadi Taba.[43] This suggestion distracted attention from the more pertinent question of why Egypt had itself not requested any and all evidence

[42] "Egypt Rejoinder," para. 2.23. [43] *Ibid.*

pertaining to topographical changes in the area. We will return to this point below.

Third, the adverse inference rule implies that as a matter of law, suppression of evidence by one party to an international arbitration brings into operation an inchoate arbitral power to draw "adverse inferences." Egypt quoted Witenberg and Sandifer[44] to this effect, but neither citation addressed a situation in which the offending party subsequently revealed the information. Nor, as noted above, did this Egyptian argument reach the question we addressed in the *Libya/Tunisia* case: whether the relevant information was accessible or reasonably accessible and whether a party would have been legally responsible for itself securing it.

In the light of these three legal arguments, one can begin to understand the importance to the Egyptian case of the link, which Egypt had to draw, between the BP 90 destruction fiasco and the obliteration of the site of the Parker Pillar in 1970. Some in the Israeli government may well have acted improperly in the BP 90 incident, but it proved to be an essentially immaterial escapade. If it occurred, it was a shoddy demolition job and, finding the remnants, Egypt proposed the site to the Tribunal as BP 91(E). In other words, Egypt correctly identified the remnants of BP 90 as an authentic boundary pillar, but misidentified it as the ultimate pillar and not as the penultimate boundary pillar (or a trig point). Egypt then locked itself to its pillar – the wrong pillar – in the Compromis. Arguably, however, the reason for Egypt's mistake was not the putatively bungled demolition of BP 90 – whatever the motivations for it may have been – but the legally innocuous demolition and removal of the site on which the Parker Pillar had been erected sometime around 1970. Thus, the critical legal issues came to revolve around the life and after-life of the Parker Pillar and the fact that Egypt had developed a legal theory in ignorance or misappreciation or both.

Apparently, Egypt had insisted on limiting the Tribunal to only two options in the Compromis by a careful formulation of the question in Article 2 and in sections 2 and 5 of the annex.[45] The Tribunal had to choose one submission rather than the other, but not to invent alternatives. With the revelation of the true location of the Parker Pillar, Egypt found its own formulation fatal, for BP 91(E) could not be the final boundary pillar.

Israel's argument was thus simple: Egypt's submission could not be correct, because BP 91(E) was actually (the original) BP 90. Since Egypt's submission was impossible, the Tribunal was left with only two options – both

[44] *Ibid.* [45] See "Verbatim Record," p. 853.

Israel's. As Israel had suggested early in oral argument, the Tribunal could follow the pattern of the Joint Commission and derive the boundary point from the text of Article 1 of the 1906 Agreement and then select whichever of the Israeli submissions was most appropriate for BP 91.[46] Again, this method precluded the Tribunal from selecting BP 91(E) because it was actually BP 90. Alternatively, Israel suggested that the Tribunal could declare itself unable to decide because none of the submissions was congruent with the position of the Parker Pillar, the authentic BP 91. Though Israel urged that the Tribunal's inability to choose one of the pillars would not be tantamount to a *non liquet*,[47] the result would have been effectively the same. This possibility would have left Israel in possession of Taba until another arbitration or a negotiated settlement. Egypt was hoist on its own petard. It had insisted on the Tribunal choosing only one of the parties' submissions; it foreordained its defeat.

By this point, Israel's argument had developed as follows: BP 91(E) had never been a pillar but rather a trig point and, moreover, even if it were taken as a pillar, it was certainly never the *final* pillar but rather the penultimate pillar.[48] Whatever may have been its state of mind during negotiations, Israel, for its part, did not admit that it had been mistaken. Nor did it concede that Egypt had been confused.[49] Why should it? Israel assumed that Egypt had assimilated and integrated information about topographical changes, but had been pursuing a different strategy. Egypt, for its part, did

[46] See *ibid.*, 397–98, 899. [47] See *ibid.*, 396.

[48] Israel argued during the oral proceedings:

> the evidence points to a first or a final pillar . . . *not* at the location of BP 91(E). And Israel's case falls into two parts there. First it says there is no terminus at BP 91(E) . . . Second, it says, in any event, there is evidence that the terminus was elsewhere, namely at the Parker Pillar . . . [I]f what the Tribunal is looking for is pillars, then the final pillar, and the only final pillar, was at the Parker location, throughout – and I emphasize it – throughout the period of the mandate.

Ibid., p. 889. Egypt criticized Israel for withholding this argument until the oral phase. See *ibid.*, 835.

[49] Israel opined:

> Egypt has . . . chosen the wrong location for the final BP 91, and it has further compounded its error. For even following the methods adopted by Egypt, which is searching only for remnants of stones . . . not only did Egypt choose a site for a pillar that is incompatible with the binding instrument defining the boundary, namely, the 1906 Agreement, but worse than this, from its point of view, it has chosen a site that Egypt itself has proven to be a penultimate pillar.

Ibid., 3, 848–49. Further, as Israel put it:

> Is Egypt now claiming that they were not aware of this language . . . put in at Egypt's insistence? Or were they not aware of the physical location of the site they claimed – . . . The language of the Compromis was not reached in haste in an overnight session. It was negotiated with Egypt word by word for over 12 long months . . . Did Egypt

not press Professor Abi-Saab's argument of *error omnium, error nullius*, which would have given the Tribunal some scope for adjustment, but instead argued that there had been conscious deception, putting fraud and bad faith at the center of the arbitration.[50]

Pursuing this tack, Egypt argued that the parties' intentions at the time of the negotiation of the Compromis should govern:

> [T]he state of mind of the Parties, what they actually knew, is important in correctly interpreting the Compromis, because what they knew, the state of their knowledge, is relevant to the correct interpretation of what they agreed to in the Compromis; it is therefore crucial to the task of this Tribunal.[51]

First, Egypt contended that Israel had concealed information during the Joint Boundary Commission period. Egypt argued that it had been continuously excluded from the area since 1956, during which time topographical changes had occurred. Because Israel had changed the terrain without informing Egypt, its experts had to rely on obsolete maps and historical data and consequently mistook the remnants of BP 90 for the location of BP 91. As counsel for Egypt said, with respect to Egypt's knowledge as of 1982:

> what they [Egypt] did *not* know is perhaps equally important. They did not know in 1981–82 of the destruction of the Parker site. They knew nothing of the extent to which Israel had removed the cliffs on which Parker had originally stood. And of course they had no reason to believe that the maps they were using were wrong.[52]

In Egypt's view, Israel's alleged concealment during this period "d[id] not look . . . like a frank genuine collaboration in good faith with the Egyptian representatives to locate this pillar."[53]

By 1986, when the Compromis was concluded, counsel for Egypt claimed that Egypt would have had only one additional datum: the photograph of the Parker Pillar.[54] Even this information could only have been misinterpreted because of the radical change of terrain, of which Egypt could have had no knowledge.[55] So, in the words of Egyptian counsel, "Egypt's knowledge was basically the same as before, i.e., a state of comparative ignorance."[56] As a consequence, Egypt argued, "Israel is legally

have any grounds on which to assume that BP91(E) was in fact BP 91, the final pillar? The answer, I believe, is they did."

Ibid., 853–54.

[50] *Ibid.*, 732–33. [51] *Ibid.*, 828. [52] *Ibid.*, 829. [53] *Ibid.*, 830. [54] *Ibid.*, 831.
[55] *Ibid.*, 834. [56] *Ibid.*, 831.

estopped from advancing its 'final pillar' argument on the interpretation of the Compromis."[57]

Israel disputed the picture of Egypt operating in "a state of comparative ignorance." The existence and location of the critical Parker Pillar was not a secret. It had been in the public domain since 1983, when it was published in a book on the history of the Sinai entitled *The Diaries of Parker Pasha.*[58] The United Kingdom had delivered a copy of the book to Egypt in 1985, one year before the Compromis was concluded. (Though the Egyptian Agent, in his opening remarks, stated that Egypt had only learned of the Parker photograph in January 1987, this was surely a misstatement or an admission that counsel had not absorbed its significance.)[59] The Israeli Agent argued that Egypt had access to all the relevant information:

> From the time that the dispute over Taba arose, that is some time in December 1981, until the signing of the Compromis in September 1986, nearly five years elapsed. During this period there were lengthy negotiations, including high-level interventions by the United States, there were meetings at the highest governmental levels, there was tremendous public debate, and intensive press coverage. And the Egyptian members of the delegations who we were negotiating with informed us of the very wide, intensive press coverage in Egypt, as well as in Israel, of the issues. The Parties held scores, if not more, of meetings attended on both sides by army officers, military and civilian cartographers, surveyors, advisers, and of course lawyers. Egypt recruited its most experienced map experts, and some, including General Mohsen, who knows Sinai like the back of his hand, and Colonel El-Shenawi, are with us here at these proceedings. Not only did these Egyptian experts attend meetings but the surveyors repeatedly visited the Taba area. From the Egyptian pleadings, the Tribunal has learnt that the Joint Commission visited the site on 3 December 1981, that the Egyptians, including General Mohsen, visited the site on 14 January 1982, and that there was a further visit on 8 March 1982, and later in August 1983.[60]

The Agent noted that "Israel ha[d] acceded to every Egyptian request to visit the sites in Taba," allowing access to surveyors and then optical equipment. Israel had dispensed with formalities, allowing direct flights in Multinational Force and Observers (MFO) helicopters. Furthermore, more than a year before the Compromis was concluded, Egypt had large-scale maps in its possession showing where the Parker Pillar would have been.[61]

[57] *Ibid.*, 844.

[58] A. C. Parker, *Parker Pasha, The Diaries of Parker Pasha: War in the Desert, 1914–18, Told from the Secret Diaries of Colonel Alfred Chevallier Parker* (London: Quartet Books, 1984).

[59] "Verbatim Record," p. 850. [60] *Ibid.*, 849. [61] *Ibid.*, 850.

Regarding the allegedly covert destruction of the hill on which the pillar had stood, the Egyptian Agent said in oral argument, "when we were negotiating the drafting of the Compromis in 1986 the destruction of the cliff was considered a very well-guarded top secret in Israel."[62] The Israeli Agent responded:

> the cliffs at the Parker site were indeed cut away but they were cut away by the Department of Public Works when widening the road some *16 years earlier*. Since then, tens of thousands – if not hundreds of thousands – of tourists have used that road. The opening of the road, this road to Sharm el Sheik, was done of course publicly and, in fact, widely reported in the press. Further, Egypt has even produced aerial photographs on which it could easily have identified these changes. If this was a top secret operation by Israel, it must have been one of the strangest ones that has ever taken place. There was clearly no secret here.[63]

Hence, the Israeli Agent argued, "at the time of the signing of the Compromis, it is abundantly clear that Egypt was fully aware of the existence of the Parker Pillar."[64] Israel argued that Egypt consciously ignored the Parker Pillar and built its case on what was, in fact, BP 90 because that terminus would have given it approximately 10 percent more of the disputed territory than would the actual location of BP 91.[65]

During the oral proceedings, counsel for Egypt and Israel attributed diabolical machinations to each other. Israel urged the Tribunal to recognize "Egypt's feigned ignorance regarding the Parker Pillar."[66] After all, Israel prodded, how could Egypt have "assumed" that the Parker Pillar did not exist after 1912–13 when Egypt was on the ground for much of the subsequent period? It was "quite extraordinary . . . there should have been either such an unawareness of the situation or such an unconcern to check the situation."[67] It was equally improbable, Israel argued, that Egypt would have casually made this assumption in 1979–81 or 1982–86. This all led to the conclusion that "Egypt could not really have been unaware of the presence of the Parker Pillar."[68] On the defensive, Professor Lauterpact opened one of his arguments with some "observations" regarding "Egypt's obsession with bad faith."[69] Indeed, Egypt's theme of bad faith and intentional concealment was repeated throughout. As the Egyptian Agent, Nabil El-Araby, averred:

[62] *Ibid.*, 700. [63] *Ibid.*, 854. [64] *Ibid.*, 851. [65] *Ibid.*, 852. [66] *Ibid.*, 914. [67] *Ibid.* [68] *Ibid.* [69] *Ibid.*, 879.

for the last eight years, Egypt has encountered a continuous policy of concealment of evidence, destruction of evidence, and a lack of good faith and frankness in explaining Israel's position.[70]

The award

As presented by the parties, the case was untidy, replete with allegations of fraud and bad faith, and punctuated with ominous statements by Egypt about the implications of an adverse decision for the peace process.[71] But for all of that, the underlying dispute was simply an international boundary dispute. Thus, the Tribunal proceeded in a very workmanlike fashion to what it styled "preliminary issues." As is often the case, preliminary issues proved to be outcome-determinative. We are, of course, interested in the issue of fraud and will comment on other aspects of the award only as they bear on it.

The first preliminary issue was methodology. By analyzing the language of the Compromis, the Tribunal rejected the approach and method Israel had proposed. As will be recalled, Israel had urged the Tribunal to rely on the text of the 1906 Agreement, assigning considerably less probative value to the location of boundary posts or their remnants in case of discrepancy between text and physical location. The Tribunal adopted the proposed Egyptian method instead:

> The Tribunal will therefore have to decide the locations of the fourteen boundary pillars on the basis of the boundary between Egypt and the former mandate territory of Palestine as it was demarcated, consolidated, and commonly understood during the period of the Mandate.[72]

[70] *Ibid.*, 703.

[71] See concluding statement of Egyptian agent:

> "[T]he interpretation of the Compromis advanced by Israel would not only require the Tribunal to violate the Compromis . . . but would also involve Israel in *three* distinct breaches of its international treating obligations towards Egypt." The third such breach was "most significantly" that "Israel would be in breach of its legal obligation in the Peace Treaty of 1979 to withdraw its forces behind the recognized international boundary . . . [I]t is the considered opinion of the Government of Egypt, without any doubt, that Israel's whole aim in securing a *non liquet* would be to stay in possession of Taba."

Ibid., 844. In all probability, an adverse award would not have disrupted the peace process, as both Egypt, Israel and powerful third parties had strong and independent reasons for its continuation. Whether the rhetoric had any influence on the Tribunal, one cannot say.

[72] *Location of Boundary Markers in Taba Between Egypt and Israel*, 20 *R. Int'l Arb. Awards*, para. 172.

For cases of doubt about the location of a boundary pillar, the Tribunal indicated that it would treat the 1906 Agreement "merely as an indice among others."[73]

Relying on extant demarcation rather than text is sound policy and rests on strong precedent. Giving evidentiary value to what was "commonly understood" as the boundary is also sound.[74] But it was, to say the least, curious for the Tribunal, in cases of doubt, to take the text of the 1906 Agreement "merely as an indice among others." What other indices, one wonders, did the Tribunal consider relevant? This preliminary decision essentially rejected both Israeli submissions, because neither of the Israeli submissions "was a regular pillar of the recognized international boundary."[75] So quite aside from whether the Agreement's criteria for boundary points – intervisibility and linearity – may have been fulfilled by Israel's submissions,[76] neither of Israel's submissions could be the basis for the award.

Egypt also proposed a way for the Tribunal to consider the location of the Parker Pillar, which was outside the trifecta of options. The parties had agreed on a preponderance of evidence rather than a conclusive evidence rule, which was logical if a *non liquet* or a finding of *terra nullius* was to be averted. In the course of the arbitration, Egypt had sought to persuade the Tribunal to give this rule a "physical distance" as well as a "relative weight" dimension.[77] In other words, wholly apart from the question of whether point A was the final boundary location, the Tribunal, in Egypt's view, could still choose point A if it were physically closer to the actual final boundary location than points submitted by the other party. This proposed evidentiary corollary was critical for Egypt's case after it became clear that the Parker Pillar had been the final pillar and not BP 91(E). BP 91(E) was the closest of the three submissions to the Parker Pillar.

On its face, the Tribunal rejected the Egyptian proposal:

> The "preponderance of evidence" rule means that the Tribunal may find for location A in the above example if the evidence for A is stronger than the evidence

[73] *Ibid.*, para. 173.

[74] But see P. Weil, "Some Observations on the Arbitral Award in the Taba Case," *Isr. L. Rev.*, 23 (1989), 1.

[75] *Location of Boundary Markers in Taba Between Egypt and Israel*, 20 *R. Int'l Arb. Awards*, para. 218.

[76] In fact, the award found that there were other difficulties with Israel's submissions. *Ibid.*, paras. 219–25.

[77] *Ibid.*, para. 176.

for B. But if there is no evidence for A, it cannot be replaced by evidence for C, even if C is physically nearer to A than to B.[78]

The Tribunal's explicit finding was compelled by arbitral theory and the restrictive language of the Compromis. Had the Tribunal said that it was deciding on point A (i.e., BP 91(E)) because of the compelling evidence for point C (i.e., the Parker Pillar), it would, in effect, have been deciding in favor of a point not submitted to it. Inasmuch as the Compromis explicitly prohibited such a decision, it would have been an *exècs de pouvoir*. Yet, its cautious language notwithstanding, the Tribunal's methodology compelled it, in practice, to consider Parker's location. To avoid an *exècs de pouvoir*, the Tribunal refrained from making other locations the basis of its decision, but not from discussing other locations.[79] "Other" locations became an element of the preponderance of evidence, if not the boundary point selected in the award itself. The location of the Parker Pillar, which was adduced and argued by the parties, was ineluctably part of the evidence.

A second preliminary question was whether Egypt had non-suited itself by asserting that the Parker Pillar was the final pillar, but submitting a different pillar, the penultimate one, in the mistaken belief that it was the Parker Pillar. Israel had argued that this amounted to a withdrawal of Egypt's submission and required an award in favor of one of the Israeli submissions. Egypt insisted it had not withdrawn its submission and the Tribunal agreed:

When it [Egypt] realized its error, however, it reiterated in the Counter-Memorial, in the Rejoinder, and at the oral proceedings its Submissions made in the Memorial. The location of BP 91(E) falls undoubtedly within the scope of all these Submissions.[80]

The Tribunal had already rejected, by necessary implication, the Israeli submissions since neither was based on a boundary pillar. Hence the "preliminary" decisions really meant that the Tribunal would decide for Egypt or render an award of *non liquet*. The Tribunal rejected a *non liquet*. The reason for this rejection was not that the parties had not allowed for the possibility of a *non liquet*, but rather that such an interpretation would have meant that one party had adopted a position in the Compromis that could not prevail. As the Tribunal put it:

[78] *Ibid.*

[79] *Ibid.*, para. 177 ("[T]he Tribunal is not precluded from discussing 'other' locations, but it may not adopt any decision on their location.").

[80] *Ibid.*, para. 181.

it cannot be assumed that a Party to the Compromis could have signed the sentence containing the words "final pillar" having the Parker pillar in mind and with the expectation that BP 91(E) would thereby be excluded beforehand as a possible choice for the location of BP 91.[81]

The reason why this cannot be "assumed" is that it would be contradictory, inconsistent with the purposes of the Compromis, and the principle of good faith:

Such conduct would have been contradictory and not consistent with the wish, affirmed by the Parties in the preamble of the Compromis, "to resolve fully and finally" the dispute between them and "to fulfill in good faith their obligations, including their obligations under this Compromis."[82]

Since the possibility of BP 91(E) qualifying as the final boundary marker had to be assumed to be part of the Compromis:

[t]he question which the Tribunal has to decide is whether BP 91(E) satisfies the test of being "the final boundary pillar . . . at the point of Ras Taba on the western shore of the Gulf of Aqaba."[83]

First, the Tribunal concluded that until about 1967 the Parker Pillar existed and also that "from around 1917 and throughout the critical period until a time after 1967 there was a boundary pillar at the location of BP 91(E) which, during this whole period, was considered to be a boundary pillar."[84] Thus, the Tribunal held, "both the Parker pillar location and the location of BP 91(E) were recognized by the States concerned as forming part of the boundary line during the critical period."[85] Then, by a rather elastic use of some of the terms in the 1906 Agreement and the Compromis, the Tribunal answered its question in the affirmative:

As BP 91(E) is situated on the ridge east of Taba its location could reasonably be understood as being in conformity with the words "at the point of Ras Taba."[86]

The words "on the shore" mean that the pillar was to be at a distance not far from the shore and visible from the shore. While the location of the Parker pillar undoubtedly fits this description better, the location of BP 91(E), which is situated on the cliffs and from where one has a large view over the Gulf, at a distance of approximately 170 metres from the shore, also could reasonably be understood as lying "at the point of Ras Taba on the western shore of the Gulf of Aqaba." The

[81] *Ibid.*, para. 242. [82] *Ibid.* [83] *Ibid.*, para. 241. [84] *Ibid.*, para. 235.
[85] *Ibid.*, para. 237. [86] *Ibid.*, para. 243.

Tribunal therefore comes to the conclusion that Israel's plea of *non licet* cannot be admitted and that Egypt is not precluded from claiming BP 91(E).[87]

The interpretations of the critical terms are very, very broad, but the conception of the case here is not implausible: the Compromis, as interpreted by the Tribunal, asked the Tribunal to determine the final boundary marker of the 1906 Agreement but restricted the Tribunal's competence to three options. Only one of these options had been an actual boundary marker – Egypt's submission, BP 91(E). True, Egypt incorrectly assumed in its Memorial that BP 91(E) was the Parker Pillar. But this was inconsequential for two reasons: first, Egypt promptly corrected itself and, second, even if it had not, the Tribunal was restricted to the definitions of "final pillar" that the parties had prescribed in the Compromis. Hence, the only question for the Tribunal was whether the description in the 1906 Agreement could embrace BP 91(E).

One may conclude that the Tribunal reached a just decision. The boundary point that had been demarcated by the parties to the 1906 Agreement was the Parker Pillar. In terms of the intervisibility and linearity criteria, it may not have been a precise execution of the language of the 1906 Agreement, but the important point was that it was the execution on the ground and, as such, supplanted the text of the treaty. Moreover, it had been accepted thereafter. The closest submission to it was BP 91(E). In this respect, whether there had been errors or improper behavior, the essential thrust of the Egypt–Israel Peace Treaty was vindicated.

Issues of fraud and bad faith

Consistent with the comportment of international tribunals that have been presented with such allegations, the Tribunal did not pass judgment on Egypt's allegation of Israel's improper behavior.

The Tribunal gave primacy to the physical location of the boundary markers during the Mandate, taking into consideration "any relevant evolution with regard to the delimited and demarcated boundary prior to the critical period."[88] This was the methodology proposed by Egypt. The value of the text of the 1906 Agreement was of secondary importance; it was only "an indice among others, as to what was the situation on the ground during the critical period."[89] With this approach, the allegations of tampering with boundary markers or the sites on which they had stood

[87] *Ibid.*, para. 244. [88] *Ibid.*, para. 173. [89] *Ibid.*

became largely irrelevant. As they related to the post-Mandate period and, most specifically, to the period 1967 to 1981, when Israel was in exclusive control of the area, they could be of relevance "only to the extent that they may reveal or illustrate the understanding of the situation as it was during the critical period."[90] In fact, the Tribunal did not consider them:

> [I]n the present case the Tribunal has felt it to be of only limited use to consider events belonging to the troublesome period after the termination of the Mandate and during which period also the nations involved were not the same as before.[91]

This approach averted the need to deal explicitly with allegations of fraudulent evidence. Yet, implicitly, a professional ethical judgment had to be made: was Egypt or Israel legally responsible for Egypt's mistaken assumption that the Parker Pillar was BP 91(E) and, by implication, if Israel was responsible, was Egypt entitled to be rescued? A subtle and indirect judgment on these points may be discerned in two sections of the award.

It will be recalled that the Tribunal had grappled with the fact that BP 91(E) was not the final boundary marker. The Tribunal reasoned that:

> it cannot be assumed that a Party to the Compromis could have signed the sentence containing the words "final pillar" having the Parker pillar in mind and with the expectation that BP 91(E) would thereby be excluded beforehand as a possible choice for the location of BP 91.[92]

The words "cannot be assumed" here meant "will not be assumed," for an international decisionmaker could certainly have assumed it. In the view of the *Taba* Tribunal, what cannot or will not be assumed, at least here, was that a party negotiating a compromis could make a mistake and agree to terms that effectively precluded it from prevailing.

The reason why the Tribunal rejected the assumption is that:

> [s]uch conduct would have been contradictory and not consistent with the wish, affirmed by the Parties in the preamble of the Compromis, "to resolve fully and finally" the dispute between them and "to fulfill in good faith their obligations, including their obligations under this Compromis."[93]

It is one thing to interpret an ambiguous text on the assumption that a party intended the interpretation favorable to it. It is quite another thing to reject explicit language because it is prejudicial to the party that insisted on it. In the traditional conception, states are deemed equal and, in arm's

[90] *Ibid.*, para. 175. [91] *Ibid.* [92] *Ibid.*, para. 242. [93] *Ibid.*

length negotiations, will be held to their agreements. The parties will be bound by their agreements even when they do not serve what an objective observer might characterize as their genuine interests. As Judge Anzilotti said, "it is only fair that a government should bear the consequences of the wording of a document for which it is responsible."[94]

Other tribunals have held that the competitive character of negotiation is not a *guerre à outrance*, but is subject to critical normative restraints. In *Lac Lanoux*,[95] the Tribunal held that where a unilateral decision was legally authorized, the decisionmaking state was obliged to take account of the genuine interests of the affected state. The International Court, in the seminal *North Sea Continental Shelf* case, held that even negotiated agreements with respect to maritime boundaries could be scrutinized for their compatibility with equitable principles.[96] *North Sea* and *Lac Lanoux* suggest that a tribunal may revise, by "interpretation," negotiated instruments that prove prejudicial to the interests of one of the parties.

The *Taba* Tribunal rejected the approach of Judge Anzilotti in favor of that of *North Sea*. To avoid a result prejudicial to Egypt, the possibility of BP 91(E) qualifying as the final boundary marker had to be made somehow compatible with the Compromis. The Tribunal simply postulated that it "could not be assumed" that Egypt's submission could be excluded.

In the final paragraphs of the Award, the Tribunal reinforced its conclusion that the penultimate boundary marker could be taken as the final marker, with a second more critical assessment. It is here that one finds a second implicit normative judgment:

> It is clear that an indication on the ground would not have been conceivable for the Parker pillar, given the disappearance of its site around 1970. The location of BP 91(E) was the last pillar location along Egypt's claimed line which in 1986 could be indicated on the ground.[97]

Now the issue here was not Egypt's ignorance of certain facts, but whether Egypt should have known the facts. The Tribunal's words here import a

[94] *Polish Agrarian Reform and the German Minority (Germany* v. *Poland)*, 1933 *PCIJ* (ser. B) No. 60, at 175, 182 (29 July) (dissenting opinion by M. Anzilotti), 7 *ILR* 497.

[95] *Lake Lanoux Arbitration (France* v. *Spain)* (Arbitral Trib. 1957), 24 *ILR* 101.

[96] *North Sea Continental Shelf Case (Germany* v. *Denmark/Germany* v. *The Netherlands)*, 1969 *ICJ Rep.* 3 (20 Feb.), 41 *ILR* 29.

[97] *Location of Boundary Markers in Taba Between Egypt and Israel*, 20 *R. Int'l Arb. Awards*, para. 242.

radical constitutional change in the conception of the role and responsibilities of counsel and tribunal in international law.

The Tribunal does not say that indication of the Parker Pillar on the ground would have been "impossible." Rather, it was not "conceivable." What does "conceivable" mean in this context? It was certainly *possible* to indicate the location of the Parker Pillar, for its disappearance around 1970 would not have made an "indication on the ground" *impossible*. In point of fact, Egypt, in its Memorial, had addressed the discrepancies between the topography of BP 91(E), descriptions in the 1906 Agreement, descriptions in other materials, and the topographical features visible in the Parker photograph. In so doing, it hypothesized "a deliberate attempt [on Israel's part] to remove evidence of where the boundary pillar was originally located by removing the cliff on which it was standing."[98] Nor was this an implausible hypothesis. Faced with the discrepancy and the time lapse, an engineer would have hypothesized major gradient and topographical changes. So Egypt was aware of the fact that there had been extensive construction in the Taba area.

In calling for a location (Article II), the Compromis demanded no more than a location in a horizontal plane. If the site where the Parker Pillar stood had been changed and Egypt was factoring this possibility into its calculations, Egypt could have inferred the pillar's location in a horizontal plane by reference to the surface changes. Thus, if Egypt had actually factored in topographical changes prior to the Compromis or the arbitration, it would have been possible for it to locate where the Parker Pillar had stood and to submit those coordinates to the Tribunal. In short, an indication on the ground was certainly possible. And if it was possible, the fact that Egypt did not select the Parker site as its candidate would have been its own responsibility, for which it would have had to bear the costs.

Perhaps the Tribunal intended the word "conceivable" to import a looser standard, one which asks merely whether a reasonable person in Egypt's situation, taking the reasonable steps expected of counsel, would have perceived a particular fact. In this sort of inquiry, the Tribunal would first consider whether Egypt could have secured the relevant information early in the preparation of the case, had it assigned a researcher the task of assembling records of any topographical changes in Taba between 1967 and 1981. Article III(2) of the Compromis facilitated such marshalling of evidence:

[98] "Egypt Memorial," para. 6.109.

> A party may, by notice in writing through the registrar, call upon the other party to make available to it any specified document or other evidence which is relevant to the question and which is, or is likely to be, in the possession or under the control of the other party.

Yet there is no indication that Egypt exercised its right and asked Israel for the information, asked to visit Israel in order to search public records, or retained an Israeli lawyer (Jewish or Arab) to search public records for indications of changes that might have occurred between 1967 and 1981. We are not aware of any factor that prevented Egypt from accessing Israeli public documents. Israel was not a closed society in which the search for such information by a lawyer or other researcher could be hazardous to health. If the standard developed by the International Court in *Continental Shelf*, which we considered in Chapter 4, were applied, *mutatis mutandis*, to the *Taba* dispute, the Court would presumably have found that responsibility for failing to discover the evidence in question was Egyptian and not Israeli.[99] Egypt could have secured the data on the leveling of the Parker site by a bit of research and analysis.

If, however, Israel had actively concealed or misrepresented information, this would have limited the universe of information that Egypt could have reasonably obtained. Did Israel misrepresent the situation by omitting mention of the photographs until its Counter-Memorial? Though there were explicit allegations of violation of a duty of good faith, there is no mention in the same pleadings of an actual withholding. Rather Egyptian counsel criticized Israel, as we saw, for first revealing the destruction of the Parker site in its Counter-Memorial.

Article VIII provided that "[w]ritten pleadings shall be filed simultaneously . . . and then be transmitted simultaneously by the registrar to each party." Thus as a practical matter, Israel could not have known how Egypt planned to use the Parker photograph until it saw its Memorial. Israel knew that Egypt had the Parker photographs, which the parties had received no later than 1985 thanks to the British government. The Parker photograph was published by a press specialized to Middle Eastern matters in 1983, so specialists working on the case could be expected to have notice of it. As the Compromis was concluded in 1986, there was ample time to digest the photograph and take it into account in drafting the Compromis.

99 See "Verbatim Record," pp. 932–36 (describing the means Egypt had at its disposal to ascertain the facts on the ground).

For Israel, the photograph was essentially irrelevant, as it rested its case on the text of the 1906 Agreement, not on the possible location of boundary posts which no longer existed. All Israel knew prior to receipt of the Egyptian Memorial was Egypt's insistence on BP 91(E) as "the final boundary pillar . . . at the point where it maintains the remnants of the boundary pillar are to be found." In oral argument, Israel stated that it had believed that Egypt rejected other potential points and adopted BP 91(E) as its submission precisely because it gave it all of Taba and more.[100] So it was natural for Israel to assume that Egypt was also uninterested in the Parker photograph precisely because it was inconsistent with its own submission. The first opportunity Israel would have had to adduce information refuting the Egyptian reliance on the Parker photograph would have been in its Counter-Memorial. Which is precisely when it adduced the explosive rebuttal information.

Could Israel have guessed that Egypt would try to rely on the Parker photographs as justification for its submission that BP 91(E) was the "final" pillar? Israeli counsel knew that the Parker Pillar's site had been demolished in the road expansion operation on or about 1970, but this was hardly recondite evidence. It was a matter of public record and simple visual confirmation. The Parker Pillar would certainly not have been a winning submission for Israel; it would have lost the hotel complex. Israel's entire theory of the case was designed to deal with this problem by proposing a pure textual orientation. The textual defense, by its nature, did not require any mention of the Parker photographs. Since the Compromis provided that each party had to make its case in chief in the Memorial and use the Counter-Memorial for its rebuttal and damage control, there would have been no reason for Israel's Memorial to mention information not relevant to its theory. So the answer to the question posed is that even though Israel omitted mention of the Parker photographs in its Memorial, the record does not sustain the contention that Israel actively misrepresented information.

[100] "Verbatim Record," p. 852. From our study of the record, we think that more likely than Israel's claim of Egyptian conscious greediness, the answer is much simpler: Egypt made a mistake. Egypt had not thoroughly researched or digested some of the critical material that was reasonably available to it and only focused on and began to understand critical issues after the procedure had commenced. At one stage, counsel for Egypt actually acknowledged that he and his colleagues had only begun to understand the issues at that point. "[F]rankly we have been trying to fit together the various pieces of this jigsaw and only now do we feel, with some confidence, that we have the true picture." *Ibid.*, 799.

Conclusion

The issue central to our inquiry is international legal ethics. When Israel allowed construction of the privately owned hotel near Eilat, there was at least some uncertainty as to whether that territory belonged to Israel or was merely under its possession as a belligerent occupant. Either way, upon the Peace Treaty, Israel was about to return the occupied territory but wished an adjustment in the boundary by negotiation or, barring that, by third-party legal procedures in order to retain the hotel. An authoritative legal application by reference to the boundary markers that had been established after 1906 would probably have produced a decision in favor of Egypt and assigned the hotel and the land on which it stood to it. Israel's lawyers were asked to design and argue a legal theory that might allow Israel to prevail. The theory, which was not implausible, was that where pillars no longer existed, decisions should be made by reference to the original criteria of the 1906 Agreement and not to the way they may have been implemented. Once embarked on such a legal strategy, were counsel for Israel obliged to assist Egypt in making the best case it could for its own theory? Put differently, was Israel under an affirmative legal obligation to correct Egypt? If Israeli counsel did not, did their behavior amount to fraud or, at least, unprofessional conduct?

Recall that in the "crying foul" argument in its Rejoinder, Egypt attributed its belated enlightenment to information that Israel had released in the course of the proceeding, when, in fact, the information had been available in Egyptian archives and records in Israel. As the arbitration progressed, the critical legal question became whether, at the time of the conclusion of the Compromis, Egypt was confusing the remnants of BP 90 with the final pillar as a direct consequence of a violation of a duty that Israel owed it or as a direct consequence of its own errors. This inquiry necessarily turns on whether Israel had such a duty.

Overall, it is difficult to escape the conclusion that Egypt's failure to take account of the Parker photograph in the compromissory process was its own error. Egypt's belated use of the Parker photograph compounded its problem. Consider: the 1906 Joint Commission had established ninety-one boundary markers. Because the 1982 Joint Commission had established "agreed BP 90" just beyond the Taba area, the dispute between the parties was by definition over the location of a single, final boundary pillar. At that time, the Israeli commissioners suggested, as Israel had since 1981, that the pillar stood near the dom palms, in the vicinity of the well, because of linearity and intervisibility with BP 90 in accordance with criteria established by the 1906 Agreement and other evidence. This would have assigned the hotel complex to Israel. The Egyptian Commissioners had insisted on going over to what became BP 91(E).

It is in the time period between the work of the Joint Commission and the conclusion of the Compromis that Egypt felt that Israel had violated an obligation of good faith. In its Rejoinder, it will be recalled, Egypt said:

> that Israel owed a duty to the Tribunal (and indeed to Egypt) to disclose the extent of the engineering works carried out on the eastern ridge overlooking Wadi Taba (involving the removal of "some natural obstacles") after 1967; and that Israel signally failed to make any such disclosure until forced to do so by the need to comment on the Parker photographs which Egypt had submitted.[101]

Egypt elaborated its argument:

> By failing to disclose whether any such evidence was found at what it claims to be the site of the so-called "Parker pillar" prior to the removal of that site in 1970 by Israeli engineers, Israel is flouting the principles of good faith as applied in the law and practice relating to international arbitration. Good faith requires openness and co-operation from both Parties. Israel, having admitted in its Counter-Memorial that Israeli engineers had, in 1970, removed what Israel claims to be the site of the "Parker pillar," should have immediately revealed all documentary or other evidence in its possession relating to that (and indeed any other) alteration of the terrain on the eastern ridge overlooking Wadi Taba.[102]

All of this, *pace* Egypt, was part of a pattern of breach of good faith:

> [F]or the last eight years, Egypt has encountered a continuous policy of concealment of evidence, destruction of evidence, and a lack of good faith and frankness in explaining Israel's position.[103]

Assuming, for the sake of argument, the facts Egypt alleged, what would Israel have had to do to discharge its duty of good faith?

Plainly, Egypt's subsequent problems would not have been avoided if Israel had said in the course of the Joint Commission's life that in the period 1967 to 1981 extensive engineering works had been carried out on the eastern ridge overlooking Wadi Taba. Egypt would have been no better off with respect to locating the Parker Pillar (with this information that may have been available in any case) than it would have been had Israel said nothing. It appears not to have been enough, in Egypt's argument, that the information was available and could have been gained by application

[101] "Egypt Rejoinder," para. 2.14. [102] *Ibid.*, para. 2.23.
[103] "Verbatim Record," p. 703.

of standard legal research techniques. It may not even have been enough if a stack of maps and charts of Israeli activity from 1967 to 1981 had been discovered by Egypt. What Egypt seems to have been insisting in its Rejoinder, as Israel's duty and Egypt's right, was to be told where the Parker Pillar was.

Perhaps Egypt believed that in the course of the ten months of negotiations over the Compromis, Israel should have explained in very explicit terms, something like the following:

Our case is based on reliance on the 1906 Agreement and not on the location of boundary markers, which, over the last 75 years, could have disappeared because of natural causes, been carried off by Bedouin or been moved by the Turks, by the British, by the UN, by you or by us, all of whom had an interest, at one time or another, in changing the boundary. We understand that your theory of the case is different and is based on the actual location of the boundary markers in 1922 and that you're going to submit a single point, BP 91(E), as that final point. We think you're using the wrong theory but if you insist on using it, we have to tell you that if you make that submission, you're going to lose. If you just look at the obvious engineering changes since 1967 and the photographs of Parker, the British intelligence agent, who was there when the pillar was put up, you know, the photographs in the book the British government sent you a year ago, you'll see that BP 91(E), which seems to give you the most territory, is actually going to lose the case for you. Maybe we all made a mistake in agreed BP 90 or maybe BP 91(E) was just a trig point that you're mistaking for a boundary pillar. We don't know. All we can tell you is, it's not the Parker Pillar and if you base your case on it, you're going to lose. So take our advice. Don't use BP 91(E). Take 10 percent less and go for the site of the old Parker Pillar.

If Israel had done something of that sort, it would, under the ethical theory Egypt appears to be advancing in its Rejoinder, have fulfilled its duty of good faith to Egypt. If Egypt had still failed to get the message, it would not have been because Israel had violated an alleged duty of discovering information to the other party.

In oral argument, Israel rejected that it had such a duty: It is "just not good sense to suggest that because Israel did not indulge in an enormous splurge of materials at the beginning of this case, there has been some act of bad faith, some lack of candour, some improper holding back."[104] Israel pointed out the implications of requiring a party to ensure one's adversary has grasped all the critical facts:

there is no rule, no rule of international law . . . which says that error or ignorance or careless oversight are elements pertinent to the interpretation of the treaty . . . If the Egyptian approach to treaty interpretation were correct, any State party to a

[104] *Ibid.*, 884.

treaty could get out of its obligations by saying "I did not intend that. I was misled, there was error, there was ignorance." . . . States . . . are responsible to exercise due care, to do quite simply their homework. To make sure they know what they are negotiating about. And they cannot come to any tribunal, after the conclusion of a treaty, and say "Please excuse us because we did not know what we were doing."[105]

On this view, whether the test was conceivability or possibility, Egypt would have failed because it was certainly possible to secure the information and reasonable to assume that the opposite party would.

One cannot help but conclude that when the Tribunal says that it "was not conceivable" that Egypt could have known about the Parker Pillar site, it is actually adopting Egypt's conception of what constitutes good faith in pleading and negotiation. Between 1981 and 1986, at some point between the Joint Commission operations and the conclusion of the Compromis, the duty of good faith implicit in the Tribunal's approach required Israel to think through Egypt's case and not simply make information that might be of use to Egypt available to it, but to actually give it the information and make very clear that it was understood. The implications of the Tribunal's conceivability test certainly differ from the test that the International Court used in *Continental Shelf*. If one were to hypothesize the *Taba* case proceeding to the International Court, under the Statute, as a "new fact" claim (which is, of course, far fetched for many reasons) and also hypothesize that the Court would then follow its own jurisprudence, the Court would have shifted the burden of discovering the critical fact to Egypt.

One might also wonder whether the Tribunal's conceivability test rested in part on an assumption that Israel had a duty as occupant, separate from its duties as a litigant, to protect the boundary markings that determined the border. Israel's failure to fulfill that duty before the arbitration commenced would, on that view, have made it legally responsible for Egypt's mistake in negotiating the Compromis and preparing its Memorial. Such an assumption, in turn, assumes a link between a state's substantive obligations (e.g., to share resources equitably or to preserve the markings of a border) and its duties to a counter-party in an international litigation.

What duty of candor, if any, is owed to an adversary when in litigation? You may not destroy information. You may not, subject to explicit exceptions, withhold information that is requested. But are you under any

[105] *Ibid.*, 943.

obligation to volunteer information that is otherwise accessible to your adversary? If the *Taba* award is now the law on these questions, it represents a new initiative in the subject area and requires us to consider, from a jurisprudential and policy standpoint, what the responsibility of international counsel in the future should be.

8

Qatar v. *Bahrain*: massive forgeries

On March 16, 2001, the International Court of Justice resolved a long-standing territorial and maritime dispute between Qatar and Bahrain.[1] At issue was title to the Hawar Islands, the region of Zubarah on the Qatar peninsula, and to other maritime boundaries in the Gulf.

The Court's judgment makes no reference to the fact that Qatar's Memorial largely based its case for the Hawars and Zubarah on eighty-two fabricated documents. Indeed, the forged documents scarcely exist in the ICJ's universe; the "documents" in the Qatar Memorial that are cited in the remainder of this chapter were later withdrawn and are no longer annexed to the Qatar Memorial accessible on the ICJ webpage. They have been collected in a multivolume set published by Bahrain to which reference is made here. When possible, we include quotations that were also reproduced within the text of the Qatar Memorial to enable the reader to see them printed there. For those citations marked with an asterisk, the reader should note the quoted material was not reproduced in the text of the Memorial, but rather was contained within one of the previously annexed documents, referenced in the relevant Memorial footnote. Reprints and copies of all false documents cited herein are published in the six volumes of *The Forensics of a Forgery: Bahrain's Submissions to the International Court of Justice in re: Qatar v. Bahrain*, edited by M. B. Olsen.

[1] *Maritime Delimitation and Territorial Questions Between Qatar and Bahrain (Qatar* v. *Bahrain)*, 2001 *ICJ Rep.* 40 (16 Mar.), 139 *ILR* 1.

I

Many of the essential facts were not in dispute. In 1762, the Al-Khalifa family established itself on (what later came to be known as) the Qatar peninsula, founding the town of Zubarah as a trading center. In 1796, the Al-Khalifa moved their seat of government from Zubarah to Bahrain but a local Bedouin tribe that was purportedly loyal to the Ruler of Bahrain, remained in Zubarah.[2]

In 1868, a year after the Sheikh of Bahrain's forces had overrun Doha and Wakrah, the British Political Resident intervened and brokered a peace agreement between Britain, the Sheikh of Bahrain, and the Al-Thani Sheikh of Qatar.[3] By its terms, the Sheikh of Bahrain conceded that his predecessor had committed acts of piracy and committed himself to preventing further such occurrences, while the Al-Thani promised to reside peacefully in Doha and to pay annual sums to the Sheikh of Bahrain.[4] In 1871, the Ottomans established themselves in Doha and empowered the Al-Thani as their local governors.[5] The geographic extent of the Ottoman/Al-Thani relationship became an issue in the case. In 1937, the Al-Thani ruler in Qatar expelled the Naim tribe from Zubarah and took control of the region.[6] The British, for their part, did nothing in the face of this forcible eviction.

The Hawars had a different history. The prospect of petroleum roused disputes about the Hawars which had hitherto been ignored. In the 1920s, Charles Dalrymple Belgrave, a former officer in the British colonial service, became Britain's Adviser to the Bahrain government. By April 1936, as concessions were being allocated in Qatar and Bahrain, the British Political Agent, Hugh Weightman, announced that "the Hawar group of islands lying between the southern extremity of Bahrain Island and the coast of Qatar [was] indisputably part of the State of Bahrain."[7] This decision, relayed both to the concessionaire and to Bahrain, was not reported to the Sheikh of Qatar.[8]

2 M. B. Olsen (ed.), *The Forensics of a Forgery: Bahrain's Submissions to the International Court of Justice in re: Qatar v. Bahrain*, 6 vols. (Manama, Bahrain: Jabo Publishing Group, 2003), vol. I, p. xi.

3 *Qatar* v. *Bahrain*, 2001 *ICJ Rep.*, para. 40.

4 *Ibid.*

5 Olsen, *Forensics of a Forgery*, vol. I, pp. xi–xii.

6 *Qatar* v. *Bahrain*, 2001 *ICJ Rep.*, para. 55.

7 *Ibid.*, para. 52. This decision later became a "provisional decision" during the 1939 proceeding. The effect of this was to place the burden of proving ownership on Qatar.

8 *Ibid.*, para. 54. After the 1936 decision, Bahrain occupied part of the islands and the Ruler of Qatar formally complained to Great Britain in 1938. *Ibid.*, para. 57.

In 1939, Sir Hugh undertook an investigation into sovereignty over Hawar and asked each side to substantiate its claim. Bahrain supported its position with affidavits from Dowasir tribes living on the island who affirmed their loyalty to Bahrain. Bahrain also submitted evidence of its acts of administration and governance over the island. By contrast, Qatar produced no evidence, relying on a "bare assertion of sovereignty."[9] On July 11, 1939, the British Agent informed the Rulers of Qatar and Bahrain that the Hawar Islands belonged to Bahrain.[10]

Disagreements over these issues continued to simmer. Mediation efforts by subsequent British Political Agents and, later, by the Gulf Co-operation Council in the 1970s and 1980s failed.[11] Relying on the communiqué issued at the conclusion of a 1990 negotiation session, Qatar brought the dispute to the ICJ. Bahrain contested the Court's jurisdiction. It argued that neither party had intended the Minutes[12] that they exchanged after the 1990

[9] G. Plant, "Maritime Delimitation and Territorial Questions between Qatar and Bahrain (Qatar v. Bahrain)," *Am. J. Int'l L.*, 96 (2002), 198, 201.

[10] *Qatar* v. *Bahrain*, 2001 *ICJ Rep.*, para. 57.

[11] For examples of these further attempts, see *ibid.*, paras. 59, 62–69.

[12] The Minutes were signed and exchanged following the 1990 meeting of the Co-operation Council of Arab States of the Gulf in Doha. The English translations differed slightly. Qatar's Minute was as follows:

"The following was agreed:

(1) to reaffirm what was agreed previously between the two parties;

(2) to continue the good offices of the Custodian of the Two Holy Mosques, King Fahd Ben Abdul Aziz, between the two countries till the month of Shawwal, 1411 H, corresponding to May of the next year 1991. After the end of this period, the parties may submit the matter to the International Court of Justice in accordance with the Bahraini formula, which has been accepted by Qatar, and the proceedings arising therefrom. Saudi Arabia's good offices will continue during the submission of the matter to arbitration;

(3) should a brotherly solution acceptable to the two parties be reached, the case will be withdrawn from arbitration."

Bahrain's read:

"The following was agreed:

1 To reaffirm what was previously agreed between the two parties.

2 The good offices of the Custodian of the Two Holy Mosques, King Fahd b. Abdul Aziz will continue between the two countries until the month of Shawwal 1411 A.H., corresponding to May 1991. The two parties may, at the end of this period, submit the matter to the International Court of Justice in accordance with the Bahraini formula, which the State of Qatar has accepted, and with the procedures consequent on it. The good offices of the Kingdom of Saudi Arabia will continue during the period when the matter is under arbitration.

3 If a brotherly solution acceptable to the two parties is reached, the case will be withdrawn from arbitration."

meeting to constitute legally binding instruments.[13] The Court disagreed. In examining the instrument, the Court noted that the parties had "reaffirm[ed] [their] obligations previously entered into" and "address[ed] the circumstances under which the Court could be seized after May 1991."[14] The Court thus considered the Minutes to be an international agreement that authorized it to decide the dispute, once seized. At that point, the Court also allowed the parties additional opportunity to submit the entire dispute, since only Qatar's complaints had been submitted at that time.[15]

II

In its Memorial,[16] Qatar supported its case with respect to Zubarah, Hawar, and the maritime delimitation with facially quite compelling legal theories. Many of these theories were supported by eighty-one documents comprising letters, affidavits, maps, and survey results.[17] While Qatar's theories and documents are not exhaustively recounted below, a general sampling of the documents which were later discovered to be fraudulent is described.

The parties differed over who first exercised administration over Zubarah, the scope of the Ottomans' authority in the region, Britain's reactions thereto, and how these issues bore on the significance of the 1868 Agreement.

Bahrain's story of Zubarah commenced in 1762 with the Al-Khalifa settlement.[18] Its title continued through the Naim fealty and, it contended, survived the Naim's eviction in 1937.[19] Citing the Ottomans' failed attempts after 1868,[20] Bahrain denied that Ottoman/Al-Thani power ever

Maritime Delimitation and Territorial Questions between Qatar and Bahrain, Jurisdiction and Admissibility, Judgment, 1994 *ICJ Rep.* 112, para. 19 (1 July).

13 *Ibid.*, paras. 20, 28. 14 *Ibid.*, para. 25. 15 *Ibid.*, para. 38.

16 "Memorial Submitted by the State of Qatar" in *Maritime Delimitation and Territorial Questions Between Qatar and Bahrain* (30 Sept. 1996), available at: www.icj-cij.org/docket/files/87/7057.pdf.

17 An additional map was submitted in the Qatar Counter-Memorial, bringing the total to eighty-two suspected documents. Olsen, *Forensics of a Forgery*, vol. I, pp. xvi–xvii.

18 "Memorial Submitted by the State of Bahrain (Merits)" in *Maritime Delimitation and Territorial Questions Between Qatar and Bahrain* (30 Sept. 1996), pp. 42–47, available at: www.icj-cij.org/docket/files/87/7055.pdf.

19 *Ibid.*, 8–9, 12, para. 32.

20 *Ibid.*, 74–82. One example was the Zakhnuniya affair, in 1909. Like the Hawar Islands, Zakhnuniya was considered part of Bahrain at the time. When the Ottomans invaded, Zakhnuniya residents appealed to Bahrain which, in turn, appealed to the British. The British were concerned that Zakhnuniya's status was analogous to the Hawars; and if the

extended beyond Doha and certainly not to the northwest region of the peninsula.[21]

Qatar contested this version of events. For one, it adduced evidence showing pre-Khalifa settlements in Zubarah. The Qatar Memorial claimed that "[t]here is evidence to show that a town existed at Zubarah on the northwestern coast of the Qatar peninsula from early Islamic times, and that at least by the beginning of the 17th century it was already a fortified town, with its own Sheikh and administration"[22] – that is, prior to the arrival of the Al-Utub tribe.[23]

In support of this assertion, Qatar submitted an administrative document, tallying the number of people, women and children, houses, horses, camels, ships, and levy amounts.[24] The document purported to be an account written by Hamad bin Nayem bin Sultan Al-Muraikhi Al-Zubari Al-Qatari, in April 1638, according to which Zubarah was at the time "a prosperous settlement of 150 houses with 700 inhabitants, owning boats and livestock."[25] A second document, a 1612 letter from a Sheikh of Qatar, further confirmed that Qatari tribes – not Bahrain – were in control in Zubarah. A Sheikh of Qatar told "the keeper of the Gate of the Prosperous Zubarah," that "[i]t is prohibited to receive strangers [*any person who is not a native inhabitant of Al-Zubarah*] and particularly the Al-Utub and Al-Kbisah [*Al-Kubaisi tribe*]. They are not allowed to enter Zubarah from the land or the sea."[26]

Qatar's Memorial also provided examples of regional rulers' recognition of Qatar's control in Zubarah, which supposedly indicated the full implementation of the 1868 Agreement. For Qatar, "[o]ne of the most important of the new factors [for consolidation of title] is the attitude towards a given situation of the international community, partly by the

Ottomans were permitted to annex it, they might be encouraged to make a similar grab for the Hawars. So, the British protested to the Ottoman Porte, resulting in Ottoman retreat. Presumably, this withdrawal supported the inference that if Bahrain's claim to Zakhnuniya was legitimate, so too was its claim to the Hawar Islands. J. S. Al-Arayed, *A Line in the Sea: The Qatar v. Bahrain Border Dispute in the World Court* (Berkeley, CA: North Atlantic Books, 2003), pp. 259–61.

21 "Bahrain Memorial," pp. 69–74.

22 "Qatar Memorial," para. 8.7.

23 The Al-Khalifa are a branch of the Al-Utub tribe.

24 "Qatar Memorial," pp. 22 n. 20, 64 n. 35, 191 n. 8 (citing Declaration by Hamed bin Nayem bin Sultan Al-Muraikhi Al-Zubari Al-Qatari (Apr. 1638)), reprinted in Olsen, *Forensics of a Forgery*, vol. III, p. 529.

25 *Ibid.*, para. 8.7.

26 **Ibid.*, 22 n. 20, 191 n. 7 (citing Letter from Sheikh Sultan bin Ali Al-Muraikhi Al-Zubari Al-Qatari to the Guard of the Gate of Zubarah (Apr. 1612)), reprinted in Olsen, *Forensics of a Forgery*, vol. III, p. 515.

process of recognition."[27] Appealing to this legal standard, Qatar submitted that "recognition by third countries of the extent of territory controlled by a State or other entity is highly significant in establishing title to that territory."[28] "Even more significant," Qatar argued, "is recognition by the other party to the territorial dispute."[29]

Proving that the Ottomans controlled the peninsula during the relevant time was important to that argument. Britain's recognition of Ottoman authority in Zubarah would confirm that the Ottomans were in a position as of 1868 to facilitate the Al-Thani's consolidation of power beyond Doha. Accordingly, Qatar argued that the Ottomans had extended their control in the region and the British had deferred to it. Qatar contended that Britain's passive attitude toward Ottoman expansion constituted recognition of the Ottomans' "de facto control of the peninsula."[30]

To further support that theory, Qatar emphasized that after the 1868 Agreement, Britain limited its concerns to keeping the "maritime peace" and purposefully avoided confrontation with Ottoman objectives in the region.[31] The Memorial highlighted Britain's decision not to intervene in Qatar's eviction of the Naim in 1937.[32] But the ambiguity of Britain's actions only provided an inferential argument, not a conclusive one. The British may have had short-term internal political reasons for avoiding a clash with the Ottomans in the Gulf, most likely stemming from their attention to the balance of power in Europe at the time. In any event, Qatar had produced other support for its case – letters from regional rulers.

Qatar produced a letter, written in 1870, by the Ruler of Abu Dhabi, Sheikh Zayed, to the Turkish Vali of Hasa. The Sheikh of Abu Dhabi wrote:

> [Z]ubarah is one of the meadows of Qatar. We have those who would vow to you that Bin Khalifah's people came there when it was already thickly populated. The Khalifah people did not urbanise it and did not set up any buildings there. Pay no

[27] *Ibid.*, p. 57 n. 12 (citing Oppenheim's International Law).
[28] *Ibid.*, para. 5.9. [29] *Ibid.* [30] *Ibid.*, para. 3.47.
[31] *Ibid.*, para. 8.15. "[F]ollowing the violent skirmishes between Bahraini and Qatari tribes in 1867–1868 the British took action through the Agreement of 1868 to bind the Chiefs of Bahrain and Qatar to preserve the maritime peace, with the sea acting as a buffer between them. From the time of these agreements, the British were repeatedly prepared to recognise that Qatar was effectively separated from Bahrain, and that Zubarah was part of Qatar." *Ibid.*, 8.12.
[32] *Ibid.*, para. 8.42.

heed to what opportunists say, it is useless. On the other hand if Qatar owns it, we cannot deny that. The enmity between us and Bin Thani does not entitle us to deny his rights in the seas of his country and its islands.[33]

In another document which Qatar produced, Sheikh Tahnoon bin Zayed (the immediate successor to Sheikh Zayed) wrote to Sheikh Issa bin Ali Al-Khalifah in 1909:

[I] see that if you listen to me, you will realise that what you are up to will ruin the relationship between you and Qatar . . . You see, greed – and brother, I am advising you – destroys the one who is greedy. Leave Zubarah and Hawar to their owner, Bin Thani.[34]

As the memorial stated, on the multiple occasions that the Ottoman authorities "inquired from Sheikh Zayed about the extent of Qatar's territories and about Bahrain's ambitions towards such territories," the Abu Dhabi Sheikh's descriptions "were always consistent with the Ottoman survey maps of 1867 onwards."[35]

Qatar also argued that Bahrain was aware that it had no basis for claiming Zubarah and so Belgrave was forced to "manufacture" one.[36]

Qatar produced letters showing Belgrave's attempts to manufacture that evidence, including by falsifying evidence that the Naim residents of Zubarah were loyal to Bahrain.[37] One such letter from Belgrave's office commanded the Naim to swear their allegiance to Bahrain:

whoever inhabits the lands of Al-Zubarah . . . is a citizen of Bin Khalifah, Sheikh of Bahrain. He [each citizen] has to fingerprint the paper which is with Sheikh Bin Jabor. Whoever disobeys the order shall leave [the lands], together with his children and his property; and whoever puts his fingerprint will be given a present and a monthly payment from the Sheikhs of Bahrain.[38]

Another letter from Belgrave, to Rashid bin Jabor, Sheikh of Zubarah, instructed him to create a massive affidavit to be signed by the inhabitants

[33] *Ibid.*, 193 and n. 13 (citing Letter from Zayed bin Khalifah of Abu Dhabi to Barakah bin Era'ar, Vali of Hassa (4 June 1870)), reprinted in Olsen, *Forensics of a Forgery*, vol. IV, p. 6.

[34] *Ibid.*, 69 n. 57 (citing Letter from Sheikh Tahnoon bin Zayed of Abu Dhabi to Sheikh Issa bin Ali Al-Khalifah, Ruler of Bahrain (May 1909)), reprinted in Olsen, *Forensics of a Forgery*, vol. IV, p. 76.

[35] "Qatar Memorial," para. 5.21. *Ibid.*, para. 8.30.

[36] *Ibid.*, para. 8.31. [37] *Ibid.*; see, for example, *ibid.*, paras. 8.31–8.38.

[38] *Ibid.*, 200 and n. 41 (citing Letter from Yousuf Al-Shirawi to "our friends in Qatar through Rashid bin Mohammed bin Jabor Al-Naim") (undated)), reprinted in Olsen, *Forensics of a Forgery*, vol. III, p. 5.

of Zubarah, affirming that they had lived in Zubarah under the rule of the Al-Khalifa for over one hundred years. Rashid bin Jabor was to "[h]ave the people fingerprinted without their names. Everyone is to fingerprint above and below."[39] Belgrave was clear: "We need a lot of fingerprints, even those of your slaves."[40] Rashid bin Jabor acknowledged that it would be impossible to comply with Belgrave's request without committing fraud. "How can I get you six hundred men to fingerprint," he inquired of Belgrave, "unless you send some more people from there [Bahrain] to add to those we have?"[41]

Another document annexed to the Memorial seemed to corroborate the Belgrave–Bahraini plot by showing that Belgrave attempted to bribe the Naim in return for their cooperation with his plan.[42] A letter from 1937 to Rashid Bin Jabor, relayed that "We have come to an agreement with Sheikh Hamad bin Issa regarding your stay in Zubarah. This is for your own good and to show your allegiance to your sheikh, the Sheikh of Bahrain. . . . You have authority over Bin Khalifah's properties."[43]

The Hawars presented different issues. Claims of loyalty of the Dowasir people played an important role. According to Bahrain, the Dowasir, under the rule of the Al-Khalifa, settled in Hawar in the 1800s; in 1845, they established settlements on Bahrain Island and thence migrated between their homes in Bahrain and the Hawars.[44] They were loyal subjects of Bahrain's rulers who exercised administrative power over the islands, regulating economic activities, investing in public works, exercising judicial and

[39] *Ibid.*, 200 and nn. 43, 44 (citing Letter from Belgrave to Rashid bin Mohammed bin Jabor (undated)), reprinted in Olsen, *Forensics of a Forgery*, vol. III, p. 30.

[40] *Ibid.*

[41] *Ibid.*, 200 and n. 42. (citing Letter from Rashid bin Mohammed bin Jabor to Belgrave (14 Apr. 1937)), reprinted in Olsen, *Forensics of a Forgery*, vol. III, p. 421.

[42] According to the Qatar Memorial, Rashid bin Jabor was increasingly unhappy with the task to which Belgrave had put him. A letter from Rashid purported to reveal Belgrave's poor treatment:

> O Adviser, things have gone too far . . . I have disassociated myself from my people and abandoned my acquaintances. My closest friend has become my enemy because of my love for you and my affection for the Sheikhs to the extent that they resent mentioning my name . . . I have nothing to do with your affairs and I do not want letters from you.

Ibid., para. 8.34 and n. 39 (citing Letter from Rashid bin Mohammed bin Jabor to Belgrave (5 May 1936)), reprinted in Olsen, *Forensics of a Forgery*, vol. III, p. 409.

[43] *Ibid.*, para. 8.35 and n. 40 (citing Letter from Belgrave to Rashid bin Mohammed bin Jabor (12 Feb. 1937)), reprinted in Olsen, *Forensics of a Forgery*, vol. III, p. 93.

[44] "Bahrain Memorial," pp. 156–57; 186–87; see also Al-Arayed, *A Line in the Sea*, pp. 230–31.

law enforcement authority, and regulating immigration.[45] As for Qatar, Bahrain contended, "[n]o entity claiming to call itself 'Qatar' emerged until late in the 19th Century."[46] Even then, no tribe of Doha took an interest in Hawar during the Ottoman period. And it was unlikely that anyone from Doha would have "routinely visited the Hawar Islands" before 1938.[47] In any event, according to Bahrain, the question was *res judicata* – the 1939 British arbitration had settled the entitlement question in favor of Bahrain.[48]

Qatar's Memorial, however, provided argument and evidence to the contrary. First, it appealed to geography. Qatar contended that the islands, being within twelve nautical miles of its coast, were integral to it:

> It can be seen that the island of Hawar is a direct continuation of Qatar's western coast . . . The Hawar islands appear to be the missing pieces that would be needed to complete the curve of Qatar's western coast between Ras Uwaynat and Ras Umm Hish. When fitted together, these pieces reflect the continuous geographical structure of Qatar. In fact, the Hawar Islands are physically an integral part of the landmass of Qatar.[49]

The Memorial also offered evidence of Qatar's political sovereign authority in the late nineteenth century: several of the annexed documents showed the Ottomans' authority over Hawar during this period. For example, a letter from the Ottoman Naval Captain, Mohammed Quli Abdu, to his Marine Vice-Commander on November 29, 1873, reported that:

> we have been to the intended place. We raised the flag of the sublime Sultan, may his shadow [life and authority] last on earth, on Hawar island without any objection. The English were aware of this and were present, but did not approach us.[50]

Thus Qatar could derive its title from that Ottoman authority.

The validity of the 1939 arbitral proceeding was a critical issue for the Hawar claim; Bahrain claimed it was *res judicata*.[51] Qatar, by contrast, contended that the award was biased, procedurally flawed, and the product

[45] "Bahrain Memorial," para. 556; Al-Arayed, *A Line in the Sea*, pp. 241–42; 304–05 (explaining Dowasir allegiance to Al-Khalifah in greater detail); *ibid.*, 243–53 (describing acts of administration).

[46] "Bahrain Memorial," para. 20. [47] *Ibid.*, paras. 368, 421. [48] *Ibid.*, 160.

[49] "Qatar Memorial," para. 4.2.

[50] *Ibid.*, para. 5.29 and n. 44 (citing Report from Mohammed Quli Abdu, Turkish Naval Captain, to Amir Alai (Admiral) Ahmed Basha, Turkish Marine Vice-Commander (29 Nov. 1873)), reprinted in Olsen, *Forensics of a Forgery*, vol. IV, p. 569.

[51] "Bahrain Memorial," p. 160.

of a complex conspiracy – again, with Belgrave at the helm.[52] As Qatar saw it, the conspiracy had been underway for nearly a decade prior to the 1939 arbitration; as early as 1930, Belgrave had begun to "prepare the ground very carefully," in anticipation of the negotiations for the oil concessions to the "unallotted" (e.g., Hawar) areas of Bahrain.[53]

According to Qatar, Belgrave manipulated the evidence used in the 1939 proceeding in order to support Bahrain's claim. But new documentary evidence, Qatar claimed, revealed "[t]he unpleasant *reality* . . . reflected in a number of documents dating from the mid-1930s which are in the Qatari archives."[54] The "reality" that these documents supposedly exposed included evidence that Belgrave, among other misdeeds, had fabricated proof regarding Bahrain's ownership of the Islands. One of these documents showed how Belgrave manufactured evidence of physical settlements on the Hawar islands. A letter written by Belgrave in 1938 to Abdul-Razzag Rizoogi, the Political Resident in the Trucial States – sent on the eve of the Weightman investigation – substantiated Qatar's claim that Belgrave had concocted the settlements (this letter was also cited elsewhere in the Memorial to refute Bahrain's submission in 1939 that no ruler of Qatar had ever visited the Hawar islands). In that letter, Belgrave revealed his plans:

> In five days I will leave for Hawar to see what they have done there before the committee arrives. As we have already informed you, we have set up many houses there. We have built a fort; and at the moment we are building a mosque, as you have suggested to pray in; so that the story [fabrication] is complete as you told us. But I have learnt from the Sheikh here that the people who are Hawar neither want Bahrain nor Al-Khalifah. For them it is better to be part of Qatar, especially because the Sheikh of Qatar's son visited them a month ago and he promised them plenty of presents if they did what was required. . . . Do not allow your Sheikhs to interfere in the issues of Qatar and Bahrain.[55]

Elsewhere in the Memorial, Qatar cited to additional documents to support that theory. It produced evidence that Belgrave had engineered

[52] See, for example, "Qatar Memorial," para. 5.53 and n. 86 (citing Letter from Belgrave to Abdul Razag-Rizoogi (10 Feb. 1939)), reprinted in Olsen, *Forensics of a Forgery*, vol. III, p. 197.

[53] *Ibid.*, paras. 6.51–6.52. [54] *Ibid.*, paras. 6.51–6.52.

[55] **Ibid.*, 111 n. 75, 112 and n. 76 (citing Letter from Charles Belgrave to Abdul-Razag Rizoogi, Political Resident in the Trucial States (26 Mar. 1938)) (supporting evidence of fabricated settlements); *ibid.*, 158 n. 230 (same) (showing that Sheikh Hamad of Qatar had indeed visited the islands) reprinted in Olsen (ed.), *Forensics of a Forgery*, vol. III, p. 124.

a petition in 1930 (which had been submitted in the 1939 proceeding) which falsified the Dowasir's permanent residency on the island and their allegiance to Bahrain. The true story, Qatar submitted, was that the affiants were not enthusiastic Bahraini residents of Hawar, but were coerced by Belgrave into signing the misleading petitions.[56] In a document submitted by Qatar, three of Belgrave's affiants recanted their petitions:

> we have never set foot on Hawar. It has been the country of Bin Thani for ages and we do not have anything there. The story is that the Adviser Belgrave made us put our fingerprints on a written paper on the order of the Sheikh of Bahrain. Our country is Budayia and Allah is witness to what we say, and we have no claim or home in Hawar.[57]

Qatar produced another letter, dated January 1937, in which Belgrave described his recent effort to quickly "settle" some Dowasir in Hawar. The letter discussed how Belgrave and his team "transported them there in four days with their cattle, donkeys and water, so that it will appear, when the report is written, that it is inhabited by the people of Bahrain, who wrote a document that the island is theirs from father to grandfather; that is all."[58]

Qatar asked the Court to conclude, that "[t]he evidence of the alleged 'permanent occupation' of Hawar by the members of the Dowasir tribe has been so undermined by the revelations that it can safely be ignored."[59]

With respect to Bahrain's 1939 preliminary statement Belgrave was also accused of impropriety. For example, Qatar's Memorial contended that Belgrave had misrepresented the findings of a report made by a Bahraini agent.

56 *Ibid.*, 150.

57 **Ibid.*, 109 n. 67, 123 n. 118, 150 n. 197; 127 n. 134; 150 n. 197; 160 n. 238; 173 n. 275 (citing written testimony of Ahmed bin Ali Al-Ghatam, Yousuf bin Ahmed and Irhama bin Ahmed Al-Dosari (Nov. 1930)) reprinted in Olsen (ed.), *Forensics of a Forgery*, vol. III, p. 447.

58 *Ibid.*, 148 and n. 190 (citing Letter from Belgrave to Abdul-Razag Rizoogi, Deputy Political Resident in the Trucial States (20 Nov. 1937), reprinted in Olsen, *Forensics of a Forgery*, vol. III, p. 106. This letter was cited to demonstrate that Belgrave manipulated the facts in Bahrain's 1939 preliminary statement.

59 *Ibid.*, para. 6.226. For documents cited in the Memorial that tend to prove there were no permanent residents on the Hawar in the 1870s, see, for example, *ibid.*, para. 5.8 n. 11 (citing Report from Mohammed Quli Abdu, Turkish Naval Captain, to Amir Alai (Admiral) Ahmed Basha, Turkish Marine Vice-Commander (29 Nov. 1873)), reprinted in Olsen, *Forensics of a Forgery*, vol. IV, p. 569; *ibid.*, para. 5.18 n. 24 (citing Report of Mahmood Bey, Ottoman Sultanic Marine Vice-Commander, to Saeed Effendi, Provincial Governor of Basrah (22 May 1871)), reprinted in Olsen, *Forensics of a Forgery*, vol. IV, p. 498; *ibid.*, para. 5.29 and n. 43 (citing Letter from Barakah bin Era'ar, Turkish Vali of Hassa, to Vali Hafidh Basha, Vali of Baghdad (17 Nov. 1873)), reprinted in Olsen, *Forensics of a Forgery*, vol. IV, p. 554.

The original report had described the Hawar Islands as "an island [which is connected to the mainland] as a baby camel is tied to its mother."[60] But, Qatar contended, Belgrave twisted this description and instead conveyed that the island was "locally known as the offspring of Bahrain island which it resembles somewhat in shape"[61] – this was, Qatar argued, a "complete" "distort[ion]" of the "metaphor."[62]

Qatar's Memorial also stated that Belgrave had suppressed evidence that would have been helpful to Qatar in the 1939 proceeding. Qatar claimed Belgrave had prevented testimony that would have refuted the appearance of Bahrain's permanent presence on the island. One document purportedly demonstrated how Belgrave had insured against troublesome testimony from two Sheikhs who owned huts on the island. In a May 1939 letter, Belgrave informed the former Residency Agent in the Trucial States:

> Since the issue of Hawar has been finalised for Bahrain and the Sheikhs' testimony would damage Bahrain's right to the island that they have gained by laying their hands on it [appropriating], we request you to ask your Sheikhs to mediate so as to prevent the aforementioned people from testifying; there is no objection to your threatening them as you see appropriate.[63]

As proof of further duplicity, Qatar's Memorial also submitted a document describing the way in which critical Qatari evidence had been stolen out from under the Sheikh of Qatar's father's mattress![64]

In another subset of claims pertaining to the Belgrave conspiracy, Qatar's Memorial provided evidence of Belgrave's efforts to gain regional support for Bahraini claims. Qatar adduced correspondence showing that Belgrave had sought such support from the Rulers of Abu Dhabi, in return, inter alia, for support in a territorial dispute between Abu Dhabi and Qatar in[65] Delma and Halul, areas reportedly "full of oil."[66]

[60] *Ibid.*, paras. 6.155–6.156 and n. 188 (citing Letter from Salim bin Nasser Al-Muzaire to RB (undated)), reprinted in Olsen, *Forensics of a Forgery*, vol. III, p. 636.

[61] *Ibid.*, para. 6.155. [62] *Ibid.*, para. 6.156.

[63] **Ibid.*, 152 n. 204 (citing Letter from Belgrave to Khan Bahadur Issa Abdul-Lateef Al-Sarkel, former Residency Agent in the Trucial States) (10 May 1939)), reprinted in Olsen, *Forensics of a Forgery*, vol. III, p. 228.

[64] *Ibid.*, 162 and n. 246, 163 and n. 248 (citing Letter from Hamad bin Abdullah Al-Thani to Abdul-Razag bin Rizoogi (11 Dec. 1939)), reprinted in Olsen, *Forensics of a Forgery*, vol. III, p. 608.

[65] There were alleged disputes over Udayd as well.

[66] **Ibid.*, para. 6.64 n. 71 (citing Letter from Sheikh Hamad bin Issa bin Ali Al-Khalifah, Ruler of Bahrain, to Sheikh Shakhboot bin Sultan, Ruler of Abu Dhabi (18 Aug. 1935)), reprinted in Olsen, *Forensics of a Forgery*, vol. III, p. 378.

But Qatar produced evidence showing that the Abu Dhabi Rulers had criticized Britain/Bahrain's encroachments previously. In a letter dated August 1934, Sheikh Shakhboot of Abu Dhabi wrote to Sheikh Hamad of Bahrain cautioning, "What you have done will not escape the notice of those who will come after you and, my dear [sir], injustice is a terrible thing. What you have done is too much. You have never wanted a reconciliation with Bin Thani."[67]

Belgrave was purported to have persisted in his entreaties. In a letter to Abdul-Razag Rizoogi, in February of 1939, Belgrave wrote that a royal decree would be issued in July annexing "*Hawar of Qatar to Bahrain.*"[68] Belgrave impressed upon Rizoogi "that we have prepared everything that will guarantee the right of Bahrain to it, including reports and help [other necessary things]. We ask you to give the rulers of the countries our regards and the regards of Sheikh Hamad Bin Issa Al-Khalifah who expects them to stand with him. . . . "[69] A July 1938 letter to the British Representative in Sharjah had contained another request to cooperate:

> [B]ahrain, by the approval of the British State, is going to take the Island of Hawar which belongs to Qatar. Second, we are going to give them a copy of the signed document concerning the issue when it is disclosed after it is signed by the Government. Third, we do not want anybody to interfere in the issue or to take Qatar's side until the entire issue is revealed and we do not want anybody to support what Qatar says. Fourth, the matter of taking Hawar from Qatar is over, and if anybody from any of these cited countries gives witness, the ruler will be responsible for it, and nobody else, since the people of these countries have huts in Hawar and they have been sold since olden times to the people of Bahrain. Please inform the Sheikhs of all these matters.[70]

These letters supposedly showed that Belgrave failed to secure voluntary regional cooperation.

[67] *Ibid.*, para. 5.61 and n. 97 (citing Letter from Sheikh Shakhboot bin Sultan, Ruler of Abu Dhabi, to Sheikh Hamad bin Issa Ali bin Al-Khalifah, Ruler of Bahrain (22 Aug. 1934)), reprinted in Olsen, *Forensics of a Forgery*, vol. IV, p. 114.

[68] *Ibid.*, 82 and n. 102 (emphasis added in Memorial) (citing Letter from Belgrave to Abdul-Razag Rizoogi (10 Feb. 1939)), reprinted in Olsen, *Forensics of a Forgery*, vol. III, p. 197.

[69] *Ibid.*

[70] *Ibid.* at 75 and n. 85 (supporting theory that Bahrain and Britain knew Qatar owned Hawar); 81–82 and n. 101 (supporting theory that Bahrain/Britain sought regional support for the annexation plot) (citing Letter from Belgrave to Khan Bahador Issa Abdul-Lateef Al-Sarkal, Representative of the British State in Sharjah (20 July 1938)), reprinted in Olsen, *Forensics of a Forgery*, vol. III, p. 165.

Qatar also had evidence that Belgrave had recruited spies for his cause. One was Salim bin Nasser Al-Muzaire, who served as the Imam of the mosque of Sheikh Abdullah bin Jassim (Ruler of Qatar) during this decade.[71] In 1935, Salim reported his own recruiting success to Belgrave: "the matter which you assigned to us and the people of Qatar is accomplished... and that we have secretly met the people in Hawar and they have agreed to be eyes [spies] for you in the country there."[72] Another intelligence report recounted to "Al-Balyooz" (Belgrave) the "number of Qatari and Qateefi fisherman" on the Hawar Island and confirmed that they had "burnt the huts of the Qatari people," just as Al-Balyooz had instructed them.[73]

Qatar's Memorial also challenged the assertion in Bahrain's contention in 1939 that Qatar's ruling family, the Al-Thani, had never exercised authority over the Hawar and no Al-Thani family had ever even visited the island. As proof of the Al-Thani's administrative presence in the Hawar Islands in the late nineteenth century,[74] Qatar adduced a January 1927 letter from Sheikh Sultan bin Zayed that mentioned Jassim bin Thani's visits to Hawar "in former days."[75]

Regardless of the validity of the 1939 decision, Qatar argued that long before that British proceeding, Qatar's ownership of Hawar had been widely recognized.[76] For instance, in the late nineteenth century, the sheikhs of Abu Dhabi periodically informed the Ottoman Valis of Hassa (who apparently changed with regularity at the time) of their conviction that Hawar belonged to Qatar. A July 1877 letter from the Ruler

[71] *Ibid.*, 111.

[72] **Ibid.* n. 73 (citing Letter from Salim bin Nasser Al-Muzaire to Sheikh Hamad bin Issa bin Ali Al-Khalifah (12 Jan. 1937)), reprinted in Olsen, *Forensics of a Forgery*, vol. III, p. 688.

[73] **Ibid.* n. 74 (citing Letter Salim bin Nasser Al-Muzaire to Al-Balyooz in Bahrain (15 Jan. 1935)), reprinted in Olsen, *Forensics of a Forgery*, vol. III, p. 672.

[74] One document shows that the Al-Thani had raised their banner in Hawar in 1887. See note 51 above. Another showed that Qatar had sovereignty over the Hawar Islands in the late nineteenth century, evidence by pursuit of criminals on the islands and tax collection from the fishermen. *Ibid.*, para. 6.178 and n. 222, para. 6.183 and n. 228 (citing Letter from Saeed Al-Mutawwa Al bin Hajer to Sheikh Jassim bin Mohammed bin Thani, Ruler of Qatar (16 Feb. 1891)), reprinted in Olsen, *Forensics of a Forgery*, vol. III, p. 583.

[75] *Ibid.*, para. 6.184 and n. 229 (citing Letter from Sheikh Sultan bin Zayed of Abu Dhabi to Sheikh Issa bin Ali, Ruler of Bahrain (Jan. 1927)), reprinted in Olsen, *Forensics of a Forgery*, vol. IV, p. 88.

[76] See, for example, *ibid.*, para. 5.16 and n. 21 (citing Letter from Bash Jawish, Vice Commander of the Sultanic Marine Fleet, to Hafidh Basha (5 Oct. 1870)), reprinted in Olsen, *Forensics of a Forgery*, vol. IV, p. 450.

of Abu Dhabi to the Ottoman Vali of Hassa stated, "As for Hawar, we have said to your predecessor what we know: that it belongs to Qatar."[77]

In another letter from 1930, the Ruler of Abu Dhabi, Sheikh Shakhboot bin Sultan, responded to Belgrave's "queries concerning whether the Hawar islands belong to Qatar, to Qatar and Bahrain, or to Bahrain only."[78] Sheikh Shakhboot answered "that the Hawar are uninhabited islands which belong to Qatar, as we have been told by people whom we trust, and we believe what they say. Bahrain has no right to them [the islands] neither in the past nor in the future."[79] Later, in 1939, the Saudi Arabian Ruler, Abdul-Aziz bin Abdul-Rahman Al-Faisal also, according to Qatar's evidence, supported Qatar's claim to the islands and criticized Bahrain's efforts to wrest them.[80]

Other documents were also provided to show that even Bahrain recognized Qatar's sovereignty over the Hawars. For example, in one letter, Sheikh Issa bin Ali Al-Khalifah requested access to the fishing ports at Hawar. Sheikh Issa implored:

> Sheikh, we are ready to meet your demands. But we want nothing but your permission for our people to anchor at Hawar. We, by God, ask for nothing but your satisfaction and forgiveness. Our people have pestered us in their demands to write to you and to send you a letter. We are responsible for any misbehaviour that may occur by our people on *your island and in your country*.[81]

The International Court's mandate was to "draw a single maritime boundary between the respective maritime areas of seabed, subsoil and

[77] *Ibid.*, para. 5.33 and n. 47 (citing Letter from Sheikh Zayed bin Khalifah of Abu Dhabi to Barakah bin Era'ar, Vali of Hassa (23 Dec. 1874)), reprinted in Olsen, *Forensics of a Forgery*, vol. IV, p. 52. The "original" document contains slightly different wording: "As for Hawar I cannot say more than what we have already said to your predecessors; it belongs to Qatar."

[78] *Ibid.*, para. 5.60 and n. 96 (citing Letter from Sheikh Shakhboot, Ruler of Abu Dhabi to Belgrave, Adviser to the Government of Bahrain (27 July 1930)), reprinted in Olsen, *Forensics of a Forgery*, vol. IV, p. 102.

[79] *Ibid.*

[80] *Ibid.*, para. 5.67 and n. 103 (citing Letter from Abdul-Aziz bin Abdul-Rahman Al-Faisal of Saud Arabia to Sheikh Shakhboot (2 Dec. 1939)), reprinted in Olsen, *Forensics of a Forgery*, vol. IV, p. 180.

[81] *Ibid.*, para. 5.49 and n. 79 (emphasis added in Memorial) (citing Letter from Sheikh Issa bin Ali Al-Khalifah, Ruler of Bahrain, to Sheikh Saeed Al-Mutawwa Al bin Hajer, Sheikh of the Western Ports of Qatar (July 7, 1907)), reprinted in Olsen, *Forensics of a Forgery*, vol. III, p. 345. Olsen's version differs slightly.

superadjacent waters."[82] Qatar included in its Memorial Ottoman documents and maps to show that its "jurisdiction and sovereignty" extended from Zubarah well into the seabed, including Hawar.[83] Many of these maps, which showed a maritime delimitation favorable to Qatar, were represented as demonstrating the views of the major international maritime powers of the time.[84] Qatar argued that:

> [a]lready, in 1867 the Ottomans had begun to make surveys of the area and to produce maps on the basis of these surveys. The British were aware of the existence of these maps, as witnessed by the stamps they bear. They show Bahrain and Qatar as separate entities, the Ottomans being concerned to demonstrate that the mainland, including Qatar, fell within their sphere of influence.[85]

The "image of 'Bahrain ruling the waves,'" was false, Qatar argued, and part of Belgrave's "systematic policy of maritime imperialism linked to oil discovery."[86]

None of the documents we have just reviewed was able to withstand forensic scrutiny.

Yet taken together, the documents supporting Qatar's case that we have reviewed would have presented a compelling case:

1 "[D]emonstrat[ing]" the territorial integrity of Qatar as comprising the whole peninsula and the Hawar Islands.
2 "[S]how[ing]" that this alleged territorial integrity was recognized "at least" since the mid-nineteenth century by Britain, the Ottoman Empire, local rulers, and indeed Bahrain.
3 "[S]how[ing]" the worthlessness of Bahrain's evidence regarding the Hawar Islands in the arbitration that resulted in the British Award of 1939....
4 "[P]rovid[ing] evidence" of Qatar's own "acts of sovereignty" on the Hawar Islands.[87]

[82] *Maritime Delimitation and Territorial Questions between Qatar and Bahrain, Jurisdiction and Admissibility Judgment*, 1994 *ICJ Rep.*, para. 38.

[83] "Qatar Memorial," para. 10.33 and n. 54 (citing, inter alia, Ottoman sketches, maps, and statements from the Turkish Marine Captain to the Vali in Hassa), reprinted in Olsen, *Forensics of a Forgery*, vol. IV, pp. 271–471, 613, 674–75; *ibid.*, 61 and n. 28, 193 and n. 14 (citing Letter from Medhat Basha, Vali of Hassa, to Sheikh Issa bin Ali, Ruler of Bahrain (Oct. 1871)), reprinted in Olsen, *Forensics of a Forgery*, vol. IV, p. 511.

[84] See, for example, *ibid.*, para. 5.15 nn. 17–20 (citing Ottoman maps dated June–Nov. 1867), reprinted in Olsen, *Forensics of a Forgery*, vol. IV, pp. 303, 327, 359, 387.

[85] *Ibid.*, para. 3.13 and n. 15 (citing Ottoman Map (27 June 1867)), reprinted in Olsen, *Forensics of a Forgery*, vol. IV, p. 303.

[86] *Ibid.*, para. 10.33.

[87] Al-Arayed, *A Line in the Sea*, p. 391 (citing "Counter-Memorial Submitted by the State of Qatar" in *Maritime Delimitation and Territorial Questions Between Qatar and Bahrain,*

In addition to the items that Judge Fortier noted as "the central elements" of Qatar's case, the forged documents we have reviewed were also used to support the theories that Zubarah was recognized as Qatar's by regional rulers,[88] and that "Zubarah already existed as a flourishing town" prior to the arrival of the Al-Khalifa.[89]

III

On receiving Qatar's Memorial and "historical" documents Bahrain's lawyers were stunned. For all their own intensive research, they had not discovered any of these documents.

It soon became clear that the first task was to determine the authenticity of the eighty-one annexed documents, from Qatar's Diwan Amiri Archives. Fortunately, Bahrain was in a position to engage leading historic and forensic specialists to analyze the suspected documents. Inquiries were sent to all the public archives in Bahrain, England, France, Germany, Turkey, the UAE, and the US that could plausibly have housed copies of Qatar's documents or other documents that would have confirmed their contents.[90] Using one standard method for authenticating, the archivists and researchers were asked to search for any references to the suspect documents in other, authentic documents that might have corroborated them and their contents.[91] Using another standard method for ascertaining the authenticity of any one document, the team contacted the writer, addressee, or surviving family members for confirmation.[92] Deploying all of these methods, not a trace of any of the eighty-one suspect documents was found.[93]

Historical experts in Persian Gulf and Ottoman history reviewed the documents intensively. One of the researchers, John Wilkinson, initially

paras. 1.2–1.8 (31 Dec. 1997), available at: www.icj-cij.org/docket/files/87/7061.pdf); see also *Qatar* v. *Bahrain*, 2001 *ICJ Rep.*, p. 452; paras. 8–9 (Judge Fortier, dissenting).

88 "Qatar Counter-Memorial," paras. 1.10; see, supra notes 33–35.

89 *Ibid.*, para. 1.11; see, supra notes 25–26

90 See generally Olsen, *Forensics of a Forgery*, vol. I (containing archivist reports from each of these locations).

91 See Letter from Agent of the State of Bahrain to the International Court of Justice, from the Office of the Minister of State, State of Bahrain, to Stephen M. Schwebel, President, International Court of Justice (25 Sept. 1997), reprinted in Olsen, *Forensics of a Forgery*, vol. I, pp. 5, 8, para. 15.

92 *Ibid.*, para. 16. 93 *Ibid.*

ignorant of the suspected fraud,[94] was so struck by the fact that "a sufficiently large body of [the documents], or the material they contain, ha[d] been so evidently faked" that he concluded "that it [was] not worth looking at their historical context as it affect[ed] Bahrain's case."[95] So Wilkinson shifted his efforts to "show[ing] where and how these documents are demonstrably fraudulent."[96] Qatar's documents were not only mysteriously absent from any archive besides the Diwan Amiri Archives in Doha, but they were also riddled with historical anachronisms, letters written to and from persons dead at the time of the alleged writing, letters written to and from officials whose positions did not exist, or letters written in Arabic between two English speakers – to name just a few examples of the fraud uncovered by these experts.

In addition to the research reports it had commissioned, Bahrain also retained a team of forensic experts which included Mokhtar Mohammed Amin, the former Head of the Egyptian Forgery and Falsification Identification Department of the Ministry of Justice, Mohammed Ezz-el-Din Sobhi, the former Head of the Assiut branch of another Egyptian forgery department, and Peter Tytell, a private American forensic examiner.[97] These specialists used several methods to scrutinize the documents, some or all of which disproved the documents' authenticity. Among their techniques, they searched for anomalies and irregularities in the seals, stamps, and the source of the paper used, and conducted handwriting comparisons of the suspected documents and documents already authenticated and known to have been written by the alleged author of the suspect document.[98] The specialists also contacted the manufacturers of certain stamps to ascertain whether the stamps had been designed as of the date of their purported use.

Their detailed document-by-document analysis revealed paper distortions and splices, handwriting disguises, stamp irregularities, and other flaws. Evidence of disguised handwriting, for instance, was found in the variations in the shape and formation of characters; as was evidence of inconsistent characters; "abnormal and grotesque character forms not commonly found in Arabic writing"; abnormal truncation; size variation; and retouching and overwriting.[99] Also, upon examination of the paper

[94] J. C. Wilkinson, "Historical Report" (5 Sept. 1997), reprinted in Olsen, *Forensics of a Forgery*, vol. I, pp. 27, 28 (introductory remarks).
[95] *Ibid.* [96] *Ibid.*
[97] See Olsen, *Forensics of a Forgery*, vol. II, pp. 8–9 (describing their qualifications).
[98] *Ibid.*, 7–14, for an overview of the forensic methods used.
[99] See *ibid.*, 153–55.

itself, the experts found that many of the letters had actually come from "secondary use" paper – paper originally used for other sources. Some documents were prepared on paper from old Ottoman documents, some on paper torn from larger sheets, and others on paper from blank pages of old books.[100]

The conclusion of the three forensic experts was that, "[h]aving examined the originals of 75 of the 81 suspect documents and photocopies of the remaining six, it is our expert determination that the entire Qatari Diwan Amiri Archives collection of 81 documents submitted for examination is not genuine."[101] But the lengths to which the forgers had gone and their "m.o.," to borrow a criminological term that is disturbingly apt, merits some additional discussion.

Two seventeenth-century documents with which Qatar supported the claim of pre-Khalifa settlements in Zubarah, were found to be anachronistic. First, the Arabic text referred to tribes who did not arrive in the area until 1727–28 and placed the Al-Utub on the Qatar peninsula at a time that is "impossible to reconcile with known history."[102] Second, like many of the other documents, these two documents used the term *hijri* inconsistent with "traditional practice."[103] Wilkinson concluded, "that these two documents are highly unlikely to be authentic historical records, bordering on the impossible."[104]

The collection of Belgrave documents had various badges of fraud. Several formatting aspects of the Belgrave documents were inapt. For instance, many of the Belgrave letters submitted in the Qatar Memorial contained a signature stamp. But Belgrave hardly ever used a signature stamp, and not any of the stamps found on these letters. (Belgrave was known to have used only three different signature stamps throughout his career as Adviser to the Bahrain government, none of which matched the stamp found on Qatar's documents).[105] In addition, the British blazon that was affixed to a number of the Belgrave documents would have been impossible because Belgrave was not a part of the British government or administration.

[100] See, e.g., *ibid.*, pp. 57–81.

[101] Letter from Agent of the State of Bahrain to the International Court of Justice, from Office of the Minister of State, State of Bahrain, to Stephen M. Schwebel, President, International Court of Justice (31 Dec. 1997), reprinted in Olsen, *Forensics of a Forgery*, vol. II, p. 3.

[102] Wilkinson, "Historical Report," pp. 29–30.

[103] *Ibid.*, 30. *Hijri* is loosely translated as "AD." [104] *Ibid.*

[105] State of Bahrain, Ministry of Cabinet Affairs & Information, Bahrain Archivist Statement (3 Aug. 1997) in Olsen, *Forensics of a Forgery*, vol. I, pp. 283, 284–86; *ibid.*, vol. II, pp. 88–89.

Consequently, "[i]t would have been scandalous for him to have been using such a seal and it is preposterous to suppose that Belgrave would have used them in his official or private correspondence."[106] Many of his letters featured other aspects atypical of a letter that would have been sent from a genuine adviserate; for instance, the letters were handwritten, not typewritten, did not appear on letterhead, and had no file or document number.[107]

In the Belgrave proof supporting Bahrain's claim to Hawar, some of the language and referents were, at times, confused. Belgrave wrote to another official in Arabic, which was ridiculous in the circumstances: he would not have written to Abdul-Razag Rizoogi in Arabic, for the latter was an Indian civil servant who had once been a head interpreter in Bahrain.[108] In other letters, he referred to himself by the wrong title, perceiving himself to be part of the British administration, and was referred to by different – and incorrect – titles. Some writers called him *balyoz*, which is the HMG representative in the Gulf, while another referred to him as the *mustashar balyoz*, both the Adviser to the Ruler and British Representative.[109] Neither was accurate.

Qatar's documents with respect to the Dowasir petitions were intended to prove that Belgrave forced the Dowasir residents to misrepresent their residency in Hawar. Upon examination, the mixed use of handwriting and fingerprinting in one of Qatar's "confession" documents was found odd.[110] The researcher noticed that one letter testifying to Belgrave's act was in handwriting, which meant the signer must have been literate. Strangely, however, this signer was "asked" for his fingerprint instead of a seal or signature, indicating illiteracy. The research report tied together these incongruous facts: the signer, Yusuf b. Ahmed had also made a prior public attestation about Hawar belonging to Bahrain. In this publicly recorded document, Yusuf had given his thumb impression. Because a print is hard to "fake," the forger had to make his "author" sign the letter.[111]

Documents adduced to support Qatar's claim of regional recognition of its sovereignty over Hawar were also discredited historically. The authors of these documents either directly recognized Qatar's ownership or had done so indirectly by "reporting" to the Turkish Vali of Hassa that the contested

106 Wilkinson, "Historical Report," p. 47.

107 See, for example, "Bahrain Archivist Statement," p. 285; see also Olsen, *Forensics of a Forgery*, vol. III, p. 95.

108 Wilkinson, "Historical Report," p. 50. 109 *Ibid.*, 47–48. 110 *Ibid.*, 53. 111 *Ibid.*

territories belonged to Qatar. Some of these letters had been written to and from deceased men. For instance, a letter from Sheikh Sultan bin Zayed was sent one year after his assassination.[112] As for the communications with the Vali of Hassa, which included one of the letters recognizing Qatar's authority in Zubarah,[113] there never existed a "Vali of Hassa."[114] Indeed, "there was no Ottoman official in Hassa" at that time.[115]

There were also instances of historical anachronism. Some of Qatar's twentieth-century Abu Dhabi documents (as opposed to the nineteenth-century documents from the Ottoman period) were designed to convey the impression that Bahrain had proposed to Abu Dhabi that, in return for its support for its claim to the Hawar Islands, Bahrain would support Abu Dhabi's claim in its border dispute with Qatar.[116] Such collusion over Udayd and the islands between Qatar and Abu Dhabi would have been impossible at that time given that no dispute over these areas existed in the 1920s or 1930s.[117]

A letter written in 1937 from Sheikh Shakhboot of Abu Dhabi to Sheikh Saeed bin Maktoom of Dubai, confirming Qatar's right to the Hawar Islands, had been cited by Qatar as "[a]nother important communication which demonstrates Bahrain's failure to secure support from rulers in the region for its claim to the Hawar Islands."[118] In actuality, at this time relations between Abu Dhabi and Dubai were very poor; indeed, a war broke out soon after the date of this letter. Friendly correspondence over the Hawar issue would have been extremely unlikely in 1937.[119]

[112] *Ibid.*, 42. While on the topic of letters to and from the departed, it is worth mentioning the letter to Khan Bahador Issa Abdul Lateef Al-Sarkal, referenced note 71 above; the recipient had died three years prior to this report. Moreover, Belgrave was away from Bahrain on the date and so could not have sent this letter. Olsen, *Forensics of a Forgery*, vol. III, p. 167.

[113] See note 33 above.

[114] I. Bostan and C. Finkel, "Ottoman Report" (4 Sept. 1997), reprinted in Olsen, *Forensics of a Forgery*, vol. I, pp. 67, 71; Wilkinson, "Historical Report," p. 35.

[115] Wilkinson, "Historical Report," p. 32; Bostan & Finkel, "Ottoman Report," p. 71.

[116] Wilkinson, "Historical Report," p. 38. This includes one letter from the Ruler of Bahrain, Sheikh Hamad Bin Issa Ali Al-Khalifah to the Ruler of Dubai, Sheikh Saeed bin Maktoom, dated September 21, 1926, implying such a deal, which is discussed in Olsen, *Forensics of a Forgery*, vol. III, p. 361, and cited in "Qatar Memorial," p. 75 n. 84.

[117] Wilkinson, "Historical Report," pp. 40–41. [118] "Qatar Memorial," para. 5.64.

[119] See document in Olsen, *Forensics of a Forgery*, vol. IV, p. 152. Another such letter was cited on page 83, note 106 of the Qatar Memorial, stating that the Ruler of Dubai thought Bahrain had "no rights whatsoever" to the Hawar Islands, reprinted in *ibid.*, 165.

Also, in the Abu Dhabi documents, a letter from Sheikh Sultan bin Zayed lacked some of the style and formatting characteristics found in the Sheikh's known documents.[120] Comparison of seals used in Qatar's document and documents known to be authentic revealed that the seal impression used on Sheikh Sultan's letter had never been used by Sheikh Sultan.[121]

Qatar had also relied on Ottoman maps, surveys, and letters to persuade the Court that the international community had long considered Zubarah and Hawar to be Qatar's. "Almost all of the documents in question," concluded Bahrain's Ottoman research experts, "contain[ed] a variety of obvious and ridiculous internal inconsistencies, historical errors, inappropriate seals and inexplicable anachronisms."[122]

Language anomalies presented one key marker of fraud. All of the Ottoman documents were written in Arabic, even though correspondence between high-ranking Ottoman officials would never have been in Arabic; it would have been in Osmanlica.[123] Similarly, one of the cited maps was represented as an international agreement. This too would never have been written in Arabic but rather in French or Osmanlica.[124]

Aside from the inappropriate use of Arabic, the sheer number and magnitude of mistakes and inconsistencies in the documents was astonishing. The repeated reference to the Vali of Hassa – a non-existent position[125] – would have been an absurd mistake for an Ottoman official to make. Documents were rife with bungled titles. Thus, an Ottoman naval authority who allegedly co-authored a letter from the Vali of Hassa held himself out to have a non-existent rank.[126] In a letter supposedly from the Vice-Commander of the Sultanic Marine Fleet, dated October 5, 1870,[127] a

> high-ranking Ottoman naval officer . . . referred to himself as holding a rank that did not exist. He also confused the name of the Imperial Ottoman Navy. In addition, the author erroneously described that status of the Ottoman administrative unit of the addressee. He then ascribed to the addressee a title that did not correspond with that incorrect status (a double error akin to a French official writing to the 'Mayor of the Department of the 6th Arrondissement of Paris').[128]

120 *Ibid.*, vol. II, pp. 131–32, 301–07.

121 See, *ibid.*, vol. IV, p. 90 (describing a document cited on page 70, note 58 and page 158, note 229 of the Qatar Memorial to show that Qatar had sovereignty over the Hawar Islands and that the Sheikh of Qatar had visited them).

122 Bostan and Finkel, "Ottoman Report," p. 87.

123 *Ibid.*, 70. 124 *Ibid.*, 85. 125 *Ibid.*, 71.

126 *Ibid.*, 76 (referring to a letter cited on page 229, note 54 of the Qatar Memorial and reprinted in Olsen, *Forensics of a Forgery*, vol. IV, p. 434).

127 Cited in the "Qatar Memorial," p. 59 n. 21; and p. 229 n. 54.

128 Olsen, *Forensics of a Forgery*, vol. IV, p. 453. The document is reprinted in *ibid.*, p. 450.

Similarly, the map produced by the "Exploratory Marine Captain" also baffled the Ottoman analysts; despite their extensive work in the field of Ottoman Naval history and in Ottoman naval archives, they had never encountered such a title.[129]

Also striking was the quality of the maps and the bizarre use of seals. The maps that Qatar adduced to confirm British approval of borders were of poor quality, in contrast to the high quality of genuine British maps of the same period.[130] The use of Ottoman seals was also problematic. Some of the documents contained a Sultanic *tughra* – an official personal seal, which only the Sultan was permitted to use: no "Ottoman official would have illegally used [such] a seal."[131] Additionally, the star and crescent seal, which is used in some documents, never existed as an Ottoman stamp and would never have been used to authenticate documents.[132] Taken together with the fact that none of the alleged Ottoman documents were found in the Ottoman archives, Bostan and Finkel concluded that "[a]t least 19 of the 23 documents are fakes of an extremely poor quality. Of the remaining 4, one is extremely likely to be fraudulent and the other three are in all probability also fraudulent."[133]

In an attempt to convey the degree of fraud which had been discovered by Bahrain's researchers and forensic analysts in the documents submitted to the International Court, Wilkinson summarized as follows:

> In sum, there are so many incongruities, inconsistencies, false information, anachronisms, inappropriate sheets of recycled paper and suspect seals that permeate this collection of documents that cumulatively they add up to a massive fraud. My overall conclusion, in addition to my document by document conclusions, is that absolutely no confidence may be placed that any of these suspect documents are genuine. They should be ignored and no credence placed on the veracity of any substantive matters purporting to arise from their content.[134]

Qatar was invited to respond to Bahrain's submission. In an Interim Report submitted to the Court, Qatar explained, that its "intent ha[d] always been to rely only upon documents whose authenticity is beyond question."[135]

129 Bostan and Finkel, "Ottoman Report," p. 74.

130 R. Schofield, "British Archives Report" (5 Sept. 1997), reprinted in Olsen, *Forensics of a Forgery*, vol. I, pp. 101, 103–04.

131 Bostan and Finkel, "Ottoman Report," p. 86 (referring to the document cited at page 229, note 54 of the Qatar Memorial and reprinted in Olsen, *Forensics of a Forgery*, vol. IV, p. 415).

132 See documents analyzed, *ibid.*, 85, 86.

133 *Ibid.*, 87.

134 Wilkinson, "Historical Report," p. 55.

135 *Qatar v. Bahrain*, "Interim Report of the State of Qatar" (30 Sept. 1998), para. 7.

Qatar rejected Bahrain's allegation that "Qatar itself may have fabricated the challenged documents," pointing out that "[n]ot only did the documents come from a variety of different sources, but the expert opinion . . . attached in Annex II, shows that they were written by no fewer than 57 individuals."[136]

As a preliminary matter, it explained why Qatar had produced these documents in the first place. Although the documents had been newly acquired, the reason for the acquisition was not suspicious – after the British had left Qatar, Qatar's Department of Cultural Heritage had attempted "to remedy th[e] deficiency" in its state archives by obtaining documents that should already have been there.[137] The eighty-two challenged documents were thus obtained as part of that project, between 1989 and 1993.[138] Moreover, Qatar had not submitted any of these "donated or purchased documents to the Court until it had taken the precaution of obtaining an opinion from an expert in forensic science."[139] From the representative sample that he considered, the expert had concluded "that examination using criminal investigation techniques produced no evidence raising questions as to the age of the paper and ink and their genuineness."[140] As additional assurance, Qatar noted, the documents were "considered as being consistent with other documents from the British or Ottoman archives."[141]

To respond to Bahrain's charge of forgery, Qatar retained two sets of forensic experts, as well as historic experts, to review the documents and Bahrain's allegations about them.[142] Qatar reported that the forensic experts' opinions differed as to the authenticity of the documents. Two of the experts concluded that the seventy-five documents they examined were authentic while the two others, David Crown and Brian Carney, concluded that seventy-seven out of seventy-nine of the documents examined contained "flaws."[143] Though it noted that Crown and Carney "may have been too categorical in their conclusions,"[144] "Qatar formally declare[d] to the Court that it [would] disregard all the challenged documents for the purposes of the present case so as to enable the Court to address the merits of the case without further procedural complications."[145] Nevertheless, Qatar stated that it believed Bahrain to have "vastly overstated the

[136] *Ibid.*, para. 10. [137] *Ibid.*, para. 13. [138] *Ibid.*, paras. 13–15. [139] *Ibid.*, para. 18.
[140] *Ibid.*, para. 19. [141] *Ibid.*, para. 20. [142] *Ibid.*, paras. 5–6. [143] *Ibid.*, paras. 23–25.
[144] *Ibid.*, para. 29.
[145] *Ibid.*, para. 7. Qatar also retained historical experts to examine the documents, who responded to some of Bahrain's historical experts' conclusions. *Ibid.*, paras. 31–46.

extent to which the content of the challenged documents affect[ed] Qatar's case."[146]

As such, Qatar withdrew all eighty-two challenged documents.[147] In February 1999, the Court placed Qatar's December 1998 apology on the record.[148] Qatar did not abandon its claim to the Hawars and Zubarah. Its lawyers relied on different theories to support its claim.

IV

In March 2001, the International Court unanimously rejected Bahrain's claim to Zubarah, but decided by twelve votes to five that title to the Hawar Islands was Bahrain's.[149]

Rather than focus on the competing factual versions of historical control over Zubarah, the Court relied principally on the 1868 Agreement and an unratified 1913 Anglo-Ottoman Convention. After the 1868 Agreement, the Court found, the "new rulers of Bahrain were never in a position to engage in direct acts of authority in Zubarah."[150] The 1868 Agreement had facilitated the Sheikh of Qatar's gradual consolidation of power, which was then "acknowledged in the 1913 Anglo-Ottoman Convention and was definitively established in 1937. The actions of the Sheikh of Qatar in Zubarah of that year were an exercise of his authority on his territory and, contrary to what Bahrain has alleged, were not an unlawful use of force against Bahrain."[151]

The 1913 Convention, which was signed but never ratified,[152] stated in Article 11 that the "the El-Katr peninsula . . . shall be governed, as heretofore by Sheikh Jassim-bin-Sani and his successors."[153] Qatar had maintained that it was "clear that for both the British and the Turks the reference to the Qatar peninsula meant the whole peninsula – including Zubarah."[154] The Court felt that this 1913 Convention, although never in

[146] *Ibid.*, para. 47.

[147] The eighty-second document was a map submitted in the December Counter-Memorial and also discovered to be fraudulent on March 28, 1998.

[148] Olsen, *Forensics of a Forgery*, vol. I, p. xvii.

[149] However, the Court determined that the islands of Janan and Hadd Janan were not part of the Hawar group that belonged to Bahrain, nor was the Dibal reef. The island/reef of Qit'at Jarada was found to belong to Bahrain.

[150] *Qatar* v. *Bahrain*, 2001 *ICJ Rep.*, para. 84. [151] *Ibid.*, para. 96.

[152] See W. M. Reisman, "Unratified Treaties and Other Unperfected Acts in International Law," *Vand. J. Transnat'l L.* 35 (2002), 729.

[153] "Qatar Memorial," para. 5.42. [154] *Ibid.*, para. 8.27.

force, provided "an accurate expression of the understanding of the parties" at the time;[155] that is, that the whole peninsula belonged to Qatar.[156]

The basis of the Court's decision on Hawar was the 1939 British decision. It found Qatar had, indeed, agreed to let Britain resolve the issue;[157] thus its post hoc complaints did not nullify its previous consent. Considering a confluence of factors operating at the time of the proceeding, the Court held that "[t]he 1939 decision must therefore be regarded as a decision that was binding from the outset on both States and continued to be binding on those same States after 1971, when they ceased to be British protected States."[158]

For the maritime areas of the dispute, the Court drew "a single maritime boundary" demarcating the maritime border between Bahrain and Qatar.[159] We need not consider these.

V

For purposes of our inquiry, the remarkable case of *Qatar* v. *Bahrain* raises two initial questions. One concerns the authorship of the forgeries, the other the assignment of professional responsibility.

As to the first question, no answer is available. If the Government of Qatar conducted an investigation after the exposure of the fraud, it, and its conclusions, were never published. But there is no evidence to implicate an official or officials within the Qatari government who might have engaged, consciously and intentionally, in an effort to submit a trove of forged documents in order to win the case. It is possible that freelance forgers produced documents that were likely to be purchased by the recently established archives of a new state.

The answer to the question of legal responsibility for detecting fraud is equally elusive. There are, to be sure, clear danger signals for all lawyers, whether international or domestic and whether in government or the private bar, about the possibility of forgery. If counsel, in a hotly contested case, are contacted and offered hitherto unknown documents or recordings that support the case, not to be suspicious and to take steps to verify their authenticity would be a serious lapse of professional responsibility, if not violation of the more general precept of *caveat emptor*. We are informed of an instance in which counsel, contacted in such circumstances with an offer of "winning" documents, refused even to respond. To introduce such

155 *Qatar* v. *Bahrain*, 2001 *ICJ Rep.*, para. 89. 156 *Ibid.*, para. 97.
157 *Ibid.*, para. 139. 158 *Ibid.* 159 *Ibid.*, para. 168.

documents as evidence without some effort at confirmation would be reckless of responsibility to the Court, not to speak of the interests of the client. But that is not what appears to have happened here.

In a domestic legal system, especially one in which only one language is used, counsel may be expected to be able to spot documents which turn up in the ordinary course of preparation of a case and are, for one reason or another, improbable; their improbability may derive from internal inconsistencies or incompatibility of the document's existence or content with other apparently reliable pieces of evidence. In those circumstances, counsel may turn to forensic experts in order to confirm a document's validity.

Such "seat-of-the-pants" intuition may not avail international lawyers when they are presented with translations of documents that are drawn from the archives of the State they are representing. This is especially the case when there is a substantial set of documents in issue that are internally consistent. It is even more the case when there are relatively few other documents in the record, as is often the case in obscure boundary disputes. The international lawyer's difficulty here is compounded by allocations of responsibility within a team. The international lawyer, who is retained to develop the legal theory of the case on the basis of the facts as assembled by government officials, is unlikely to know the provenance of State archival documents or whether all the relevant documents have been identified and presented. Where, however, outside counsel are also tasked with scouring archives in other capitals, and there are discrepancies between the published records and documents in many archives, and those extremely useful but inconsistent documents are available only in one of the party's archives, should not alarm bells go off?

In the instant case, the circumstances of the dispute compared with the appearance of the documents might reasonably have aroused suspicion. One of Bahrain's researchers thought these were questions worth asking. "[M]y first question," Wilkinson observed, "would be to know the supposed provenance of these documents, in particular since we know that only a few years ago the Qatar archives were very empty indeed."[160] Should Qatar's lawyers have wondered about the production of decades- and centuries-old never-before-seen documents from a national archive but a few years in existence? If these documents seemed to be bona fide, should one have asked why they were only now debuted at the International Court, rather

[160] Wilkinson, "Historical Report," p. 28.

than in the number of mediation efforts in prior decades? Then again, Qatar offered a persuasive answer to these questions in its Interim Report.

But this may put an unreasonable burden on the international lawyers. The old adage has it that if you are a carpenter, the answer to every problem is a hammer. Wilkinson was not an international lawyer but a historian for whom suspicion about documents was an essential tool of the trade. At least until this case, it appears that the general approach of international lawyers appearing before international courts and tribunals was one of almost textual reverence: the authenticity of the documents with which they worked was taken for granted. Doubts about documents' authenticity were to be raised and proved by the other side in ordinary adversarial procedures.[161]

In this respect, the *Qatar* v. *Bahrain* case might be seen as a constitutive event in international legal practice, heralding that, henceforth, the burden should be on the side producing evidence to satisfy itself of its authenticity. Precepts borrowed from other branches of the law suggest that risk should be allocated to the party who has the most information and is thus in the best position to avoid a loss. Reasoning from this notion, the risk of fraud (or put differently, the burden of containing it) should be borne by the proffering counsel. Imposing the onus on the other two available players – opposing counsel or the Court – entails higher costs and greater risk of error.

Had the International Court's decision come out differently, the regional relations in the Gulf Cooperation Council (GCC) could have veered down a less productive path. Specifically, a more Qatar-favorable decision might have incentivized neighboring states to renew or "realize" territorial disputes, hoping for a similarly favorable ruling. Taken together, it is arguable that the high costs at issue and the suggestive circumstances should have triggered counsels' duty to investigate the truth of the documents before laying them before the Court.

Proposing such a duty, however, begs the question of practicality. How far can and should a lawyer go to investigate his own client? Short of employing a group of forensic specialists and historians at the client's expense, guarantees seem hard to come by. Such manifestations of distrust – especially if only acting on a hunch – could undermine the lawyer–client relationship. These countervailing concerns are difficult to weigh.

Yet there are disadvantages to placing the burden on opposing counsel, for their ability to discover fraud will vary widely from case to case. In

[161] See discussion in Chapter 6 this volume.

Qatar v. *Bahrain*, some members of the Bahrain legal team spoke Arabic and were able to "sniff out" the possibility of fraud before the next round of pleadings. This may not always be so. In the time it takes opposing counsel to suspect something is amiss and then retain translation and expert analysis, the case may be far advanced. In addition to language constraints, the resources available to detect and investigate may also be lacking. Fortunately, Bahrain was able to spare no expense in forensic analysis. In other cases, depending on the other party's abilities, the expense of commissioning such an investigation may put it beyond the realm of the reasonable.

The majority opinion attached neither approbation nor even mild disapproval to the incident. The only place in the majority opinion where it was aired was in an introductory account of the parties' back-and-forth regarding the submissions, the challenge, and the ultimate agreement to disregard the eighty-two documents.[162] Blandly, the Court reported Qatar's decision to "disregard" the documents in order to avoid "further procedural complications."[163] Throughout, the Court carefully avoided the word "fraud" or "forgery," referring instead to the documents as those whose "authenticity had been challenged."[164]

The only significant exception to this reticence was the separate opinion of Judge Fortier, the ad hoc judge appointed by Bahrain. He commented upon the fraud, having "decided that it was [his] duty to do so."[165] His opinion highlighted two detrimental effects of the fraud. First, he pointed out how the ethos of the documents permeated the case even subsequent to their withdrawal. In his words, "these documents h[ad] 'polluted' and 'infected' the whole of Qatar's case . . . [t]hey remain in the record and some of them linger and are invoked occasionally in support of Qatar's alternative argument."[166] This is another unfortunate lesson of this case: fraud, even if uncovered, may prove a stubborn thing to expunge.

Second, Judge Fortier felt that the Court had abrogated a duty to take more affirmative action to counteract this polluting effect: "in considering the Parties' conflicting versions of the facts in this case, [the Court] had a duty to do more than merely narrate the Parties' respective exchange of letters following Bahrain's challenge of the authenticity of 82 documents which loomed as central to Qatar's case."[167]

[162] *Qatar* v. *Bahrain*, 2001 *ICJ Rep.*, paras. 15–22. [163] *Ibid.*, para. 20.
[164] *Ibid.*, para. 23. [165] *Ibid.*, 451, para. 1 (separate opinion of Judge Fortier).
[166] *Ibid.*, paras. 4–5. [167] *Ibid.*, para. 11.

There is thus no indication that the forgeries disadvantaged Qatar's prospects for success. Although ascriptions of authorship to Qatar might have served as the basis for a claim to non-suit the entire case, the essential interest of the Government of Bahrain was in winning the territorial and boundary dispute by securing the disqualification of the documents. The Court based its decision to award Zubarah to Qatar on several agreements, conventions, and diplomatic letters that revealed Britain's opinion that Bahrain was not sovereign over Zubarah (from at least 1868).[168] Reliance on these obviated reference to the fraudulent documents. In so doing, the Court avoided the challenged documents and built its judgment on unobjectionable sources. The Court may have considered it improvident to say much more on the issue of fraud.

Perhaps the Court saw itself as charged primarily with settling disputes and not with denouncing misconduct. Attempting to assume a censorial role might have come at the cost of its effectiveness in the settlement of disputes. An interesting microcosmic parallel may be found in New York City's efforts to tax part-time residents:

> According to New York tax authorities, people are rarely charged with perjury or making false statements in a residency audit. "Our job is to collect revenue and administer the tax laws," Dan Smirlock, a former New York deputy tax commissioner, said. "We do a lot of criminal referrals for tax evasion to district attorneys. But for perjury the proof is so difficult. It doesn't seem to be a high priority."[169]

In the immediate case, the Court may have been concerned that were it to put too fine a point on the fraud it might have opened the decision to future uncertainty. So, in order to maintain the integrity of the decision and to shield it from future skepticism, it cordoned off the fraud from the merits phase. Although this may have been the best institutional choice for the Court, it left unanswered the consequences of fraud and the level and nature of responsibility to actively ferret it out.

What, then, could the Court have done? At a minimum, it might have explicitly confirmed that its judgment leaned not at all on the fraudulent documents, confirming for the record what it assumed would be obvious, albeit unsaid.

[168] See *ibid.*, 66–69 (merits).

[169] J. B. Stewart, "Tax Me If You Can," *New Yorker* (19 Mar. 2012), 46.

9

Some concluding thoughts

Lawyers pride themselves on being problem-solvers so the prospect of a problem which seems insoluble, especially one which involves lawyers themselves, is disagreeable, even humbling. But for a number of reasons practicable solutions to the problem of fraudulent evidence before public international tribunals are elusive.

One reason has to do with the roles of lawyers in an adversarial process which lawyers have constructed and themselves manage. An apocryphal story has it that the renowned Oxford philosopher Isaiah Berlin wrote a letter of recommendation to a solicitor's firm for one of his philosophy students who was also a law graduate: "This is a very able, intelligent, intellectually honest candidate if that is relevant for your line of work." It was more than a mischievous interdisciplinary dig, for advocates in adversarial situations, unlike scholars, are retained to present evidence and create a record which discriminates in favor of their respective clients. And to win! Techniques which a philosopher or a historian would scorn as incompatible with their own vocational ethics, may be permissible, if not laudable, for litigators. One of the ways by which litigators maintain their self-respect is to persuade themselves of the justice of their client's cause and the injustice of that of their adversaries. Once they have won over their internal "jury," it seems to become easier to resort to techniques which they would, in the abstract, deplore. In this respect, in 1879, an English barrister, Charles Darling, wrote with a fine irony of the presentation of evidence: "much truth is spoken that more may be concealed."[1] The presentation of material, in other words, can also be used not to inform but to swarm and overwhelm the discrimination of a tribunal. What other intellectual discipline would

[1] C. J. Darling, *Scintillae Juris*, 3rd enlarged edn. (Davis & Son, 1879), 73.

tolerate such a practice? David Goodstein's work on scientific fraud[2] raises some interesting parallels:

> [s]cience is self-correcting, in the sense that a falsehood injected into the body of scientific knowledge will eventually be discovered and rejected. But that fact does not protect the scientific enterprise against fraud, because injecting falsehoods into the body of science is rarely, if ever, the purpose of those who perpetrate fraud. They almost always believe that they are injecting a truth into the scientific record ... but without going through all the trouble that the real scientific method demands.[3]

The *New York Times* has reported "[a] surprising upsurge in the number of scientific papers that have had to be retracted," with a significant proportion of these retractions attributed to fraudulent misconduct.[4] If the fraudfeasors of the law, like errant scientists, actually believe their questionable tactics are necessary efficient means to an end of truth or just outcome, then law, like "science," "needs active measures to protect it."[5]

At what point does advocacy cross to fraud? Clearly, forged documents are fraudulent. The suppression of a document which the party knows to be so material that were it discovered, it would be decisive against that party would be fraudulent. Beyond such clear examples, however, definitions are elusive. One is reminded, in this regard, of Potter Stewart's famous observation about pornography: "I shall not today attempt further to define the kinds of material I understand to be embraced within that shorthand description; and perhaps I could never succeed in intelligibly doing so. But I know it when I see it."[6] In public international tribunals, efforts to create an effective legal regime for policing and sanctioning fraudulent evidence must confront the structure of international law. Within domestic legal systems, if threats of reputational costs have proved insufficient, courts and bar associations have proved to be relatively effective agencies for policing the behavior of lawyers. Until now, no comparable institutions operate at the public international law level; although efforts are afoot to develop them, we think their chances for meaningful regulation are limited because of the unique dynamics of international politics. As we noted at the outset of this book, the notion that government lawyers owe their primary allegiance to international law and only secondarily to the government which employs them, has some resonance in Nuremburg judgments, but with respect to

[2] D. Goodstein, *On Fact and Fraud: Cautionary Tales from the Front Lines of Science* (Princeton University Press, 2010).

[3] *Ibid.*, 2. [4] Editorial, "Fraud in the Scientific Literature," *NY Times* (5 Oct. 2012), A20.

[5] Goodstein, "On Fact," p. 3. [6] *Jacobellis* v. *State of Ohio*, 378 US 184, 197 (1964).

the prosecution of cases before international tribunals, it seems to remain an aspiration. It is the apparatus of the modern state, with its awesome power to police loyalty and punish defections from it, not to speak of its ability to grant advancement and other rewards, which commands loyalty. Recall the rather tragic dilemma in which Sir Hartley Shawcross found himself in *Corfu Channel*; that distinguished international lawyer, one of the heroes of the Nuremburg trials, rejected the idea that he should express his doubts about the suppression of a potentially relevant document to the International Court if that would jeopardize the case which his government had brought. We assume that had Shawcross confronted the same dilemma in an entirely private litigation, he would have clearly perceived his duty and acted decisively.

To be fair, the government lawyer, like Shawcross, is often, at least at the initial stages of the perpetration of a fraud, a victim. In cases such as *Corfu Channel*, *Taba*, *Nicaragua*, and *Qatar* v. *Bahrain*, the lawyers for the parties on whose behalf problematic evidence was proffered were not privy to it and were then faced with the dilemma of dealing with a situation which they had not created. In none of the cases did the lawyers withdraw and many lawyers may conclude that what they did (or refrained from doing) was the proper response.

No public international tribunal we have reviewed has non-suited a party which tried to practice fraud on it. In cases between individuals, there is a measure of entirely proportional justice in non-suiting the party that has practiced fraud on the tribunal. In public international law disputes, by contrast, the interests of an intergenerational community are involved and depriving that community of an opportunity to secure or defend its rights because of the fraud practiced by those momentarily representing it may not seem just. This may explain why international tribunals before which fraudulent evidence has been exposed have permitted the party responsible for it to proceed to argue its case or, as in *Qatar* v. *Bahrain*, have allowed the lawyers for that party to develop and present alternative arguments.

Systemic concerns may inhibit international courts and tribunals from reopening and revising judgments secured by fraud. After judgment, the law has experimented with several options for treating the judgment that has later been discovered to have been based on fraud. The misled tribunal can vacate its decision, correct the mistake, and issue a new decision or preserve the judgment but acknowledge the fraud and its effect on the *ratio* to ensure that future cases will not repeat the error. In contrast to a non-suit, that option would leave the judgment and any community rights intact. It would, however, highlight the occurrence of fraud and make the consequences of perpetrating fraud more costly for those who conspired to deceive. In the stories we reviewed, we found such transparency vis-à-vis the fraud (or putative fraud) to be the exception. It is not so much that international courts and tribunals are indifferent to fraud, but rather that their methods for identifying and treating it are too understated or implicit to provide litigants with clear guidance on what conduct is demanded and clear notice that there will be meaningful consequences for behaving improperly.

The *Sabotage Cases* were an outlier in our study. There, the German–United States Mixed Claims Commission initially absolved Germany of liability for two acts of sabotage perpetrated in US factories prior to the United States entry into World War I. After its initial decision, the Commission was presented with evidence demonstrating that much of Germany's witness testimony had been suborned. Upon reconsideration, the Commission concluded that it had been "seriously misled" and reversed its prior decision. Yet one cannot ignore the context of an impending World War, that two of the three arbitrators were American, and the mounting popular antipathy toward Nazi Germany. Still, the Commission's understanding of its authority stands in marked contrast to subsequent tribunals' much more limited self-conception. The *Sabotage* tribunal had reasoned, "If [a tribunal] may correct its own errors and mistakes, a fortiori it may, while it still has jurisdiction of a cause, correct an error into which it has been led by fraud and collusion."[7] This arbitral philosophy, equating affirmative fraud and suppression with standard types of procedural irregularity, does not, in contrast to the *Weil* and *La Abra* decisions, consider finality as a goal which is weightier than accuracy and honesty. The road that the *Sabotage* Tribunal blazed for itself was one hospitable to reopening and revising awards induced by fraud. It has proved to be the road not taken by subsequent tribunals.

Another claims commission, established over forty years later, was far more restrained in its treatment of fraud. The Iran–US Claims Tribunal adopted an indirect method of dealing with fraud, that is, through the careful application of burden-shifting requirements. It developed an evidentiary rule in which the claimant bore the burden of proving a document prima facie authentic before the burden shifted to the respondent seeking to prove that a document was fraudulent. This is certainly an efficient rule for

[7] See *Decision of the Commission* (15 Dec. 1933) in *Mixed Claims Commission: United States and Germany: Decisions and Opinions from January 1, 1933 to October 30, 1939 (Excepting Decisions in the Sabotage Claims of June 15, and October 30, 1939)*, pp. 1115, 1127–28 (1940).

judicial administration but it also creates perverse incentives for claimants. If the only consequence of adducing a fraudulent document is the inability to prevail on these pleadings, the risk-reward calculus tilts in favor of fraud. The unscrupulous claimant is further emboldened by the presumption of credibility afforded official documents and by the disproportionate burden placed on respondents seeking to prove fraud.

Nicaragua v. *United States*, like *Sabotage* and several of the claims pressed before the Iran–US Claims Tribunal, featured an instance of a statement by the Agent, the Foreign Minister Father D'Escoto, that did not comport with the facts. In that case, high-ranking Sandinista government officials, including the Foreign Minister, apparently concealed the Sandinista government's active support for the insurgency in El Salvador. The International Court was not, it appears, oblivious to the possibility that the witnesses were being untruthful. But, unable to sort out the facts with certainty, the Court elected to punt rather than to confront the possibility of fraud. The Court based its decision on a legal theory that rested on grounds independent of the facts averred in the testimony. To Judge Schwebel's dismay, it "excluded, discounted and excused the unanswerable evidence of Nicaragua's major and maintained intervention in the Salvadoran insurgency."[8]

The "avoidance" approach was not unique to *Nicaragua* v. *United States*. In *Corfu Channel*, the Court wrestled with the UK's refusal to produce a potentially sensitive document, XCU. As the later-revealed internal documents show, XCU did cast doubt on the innocence of the UK's passage through the Straits of Corfu when the Albanian attack occurred; the document might have proved inconsequential but it should have been produced. Yet the Court deferred to the British Agent's explanation that national security precluded production of the document and fashioned its decision independent of the document. In this way, the Court resorted to a methodology which insulated its own decision from the possible taint of fraud by excluding the problem – be it a document suppressed or a document forged – from its reasoning calculus.

The Court again pursued that strategy in *Qatar* v. *Bahrain*. After the exchange of Memorials, many of the documents adduced by Qatar as evidence of its sovereignty claims over the Hawar Islands and Zubarah were exposed as forgeries. The documents were retracted, Qatar was permitted to develop an alternative argument and the case proceeded. This case prompted us to inquire into the extent of international counsel's duty of due

[8] *Military and Paramilitary Activities in and Against Nicaragua (Nicaragua* v. *United States)*, 1986 *ICJ Rep.* 14, p. 272, para. 16 (27 June) (dissenting opinion of Judge Schwebel), 76 *ILR* 1, 349.

diligence in ascertaining whether documents handed to it by a government client and vouchsaved to be authentic are what they purport to be. In cases such as this one, where language, timing, and resource barriers are substantial, we asked what more Qatari counsel, who had no hint that these documents had been cooked, could have done to discover the fraud before producing the documents to the Court.

Not all of our stories involved clear examples of fraud. Indeed, part of the intellectual and ethical challenge is giving content to the term "fraud." The selective presentation of facts or the failure to disclose evidence helpful to one's adversary is apparently not deemed by tribunals as clearly fraudulent behavior, as the case of *Tunisia/Libya* and the *Taba* arbitration show. In *Tunisia/Libya*, Libya's conduct was called into question for presenting facts in such a way as to create a picture that misled the Court. In its submission for the proper maritime boundary line, Libya suggested a state of de facto convergence around the 26° line, a picture the Court accepted. When Tunisia later applied to the Court for revision because of the inaccuracy of the 26° line, the Court rejected the application in part because Tunisia had failed to discover for itself the relevant coordinates during the litigation. The Court's interpretation of Article 61 of the Statute and its application to the *Tunisia/Libya* case seems to leave little or no room for consideration of whether the injured party's failure to timeously discover the relevant facts is attributable to the other party's fraud or concealment.

A different *ratio* may be inferred from the *Taba* award. The Egypt–Israel Tribunal was charged with determining the boundary between Egypt and Israel. This required a determination of where the boundary had been delimited pursuant to a 1906 agreement and subsequently demarcated by ninety-one boundary pillars. The heart of the dispute was with respect to the final boundary pillar, BP 91. One of the focal points of the BP 91 dispute was whether Israel had violated a duty of good faith in failing to disclose to Egypt that it had removed the site on which the final pillar – the "Parker Pillar" – had stood, as well as the fact that it knew that Egypt was mistaking and conflating the final pillar and the penultimate pillar. The Tribunal did not explicitly criticize Israel's silence. Yet in failing to consider the *possibility* that Egypt could have avoided its own mistake, through more diligent research and analysis of the situation, the Tribunal may have implicitly judged Israel's conduct (and perhaps considered the intergenerational interests implicated by Israel's behavior). The implicit notion that parties have an unsolicited duty to assist their adversaries in the development of their case is quite unprecedented; were it adopted as the norm, it might present serious practical problems.

In international law, it is striking that courts and tribunals are loath to denounce a state party for having submitted fraudulent evidence. It is only in the *Sabotage Cases*, as we have seen, that a tribunal explicitly castigated a state party for having suborned perjury and submitted false documents. As we suggested, even that case is unique in that the award was rendered on the eve of World War II, which may have accounted for the Commission's harsh language. In other cases and, in particular, in *Qatar* v. *Bahrain*, it was only the ad hoc judge appointed by Bahrain who even mentioned the fraudulent evidence imbroglio. The rest of the Court seemed to focus on the question of reaching the right conclusion. Are we entitled to conclude that from the perspective of international tribunals, they have no ancillary duty to police the honesty of states and their representatives but rather to rely on the cleansing dynamic of the adversarial process, to work through the evidence, as best they can, and to reach the right conclusion?

The problem we have grappled with can be viewed from the perspective of counsel as well as from the perspective of the tribunal presented with fraudulent or misleading evidence. From the perspective of counsel, different factors seem to be in play. The dilemma of Sir Hartley Shawcross, in his representation of the United Kingdom in the *Corfu Channel* case, presented, in most acute form, the conflict between loyalty to a state in what could be a critical international decision and duty to the court before whom the lawyer appears. In *Corfu Channel* it was the duty to the state that prevailed. There have been a number of contemporary efforts to reverse those poles of loyalty and to insist that the primary loyalty of counsel on behalf of a state is to the international community.[9] Their success is uncertain.

As unsettled as the normative situation appears to be, we are not persuaded, from our study of the stories in this book, that the creation of a "code of conduct for international counsel" would change practice. It would certainly make the law clear but the late Professor Grant Gilmore observed, "[t]he worse the society, the more law there will be. In Hell there will be nothing but law, and due process will be meticulously observed."[10] Without means for enforcement and without effective shaming sanctions, new codes could well become means for harassing counsel and obstructing the international judicial and arbitral processes but not for addressing the problems which the courts and tribunals in our study faced.

[9] W. M. Reisman, *The Quest for World Order and Human Dignity in the Twenty-first Century: Constitutive Process and Individual Commitment: General Course on Public International Law* (Leiden/Boston: Martinus Nijhoff, 2012), pp. 363–81.

[10] G. Gilmore, *Ages of American Law* (New Haven, CT: Yale University Press, 1977), p. 111.

Perhaps part of a solution lies in the national systems. As the *Weil* and *La Abra* cases suggested, national legal and political authorities do not encounter the same obstacles that international systems confront. Domestic systems could, therefore, concern themselves with the conduct of their lawyers who litigate abroad. Again, this is not a wholly satisfactory response. Particularly where government lawyers and sensitive political issues are involved, the competing loyalty systems will hamper the efficacy of such solution.

Truth is not always a prized commodity in international political discourse and its valuation declines even further in crisis: "in war," Aeschylus said, "truth is the first casualty." But the contribution of international courts and tribunals to world order and their very credibility depend, in no small measure, on the accuracy of the factual basis of the decisions which they render. That factual accuracy depends, in turn and in large part, on the probity of the states and state representatives who appear before them. So international courts and tribunals must be treated differently from other international political arenas. As is so often the case, Judge Stephen Schwebel, to whom our book is respectfully dedicated, said it best in the *Nicaragua* case in the epigraph with which we commenced this study:

> [T]here can be no equation between governmental statements made in this Court and governmental statements made outside of it. The foundation of judicial decision is the establishment of the truth. Deliberate misrepresentations by the representatives of a government party to a case before this Court cannot be accepted because they undermine the essence of the judicial function. This is particularly true where, as here, such misrepresentations are of facts that arguably are essential, and incontestably are material, to the Court's judgment.[11]

That is surely the proper standard. Making it effective will continue to be a challenge for international law.

[11] *Nicaragua* v. *United States*, 1986 *ICJ Rep.*, para. 27 (dissenting opinion of Judge Schwebel).

Bibliography

Cases

Application for Revision of the Judgment of 11 September 1992 in the Case Concerning the Land, Island and Maritime Frontier Dispute (El Salvador/Honduras: Nicaragua Intervening) (El Salvador v. *Honduras)* (18 Dec. 2003), 97 *ILR* 112

Aryeh v. *Iran*, 33 *Iran-US Cl. Trib. Rep.* 272 (1997)

Birnbaum v. *Iran*, 33 *Iran-US Cl. Trib. Rep.* 286 (1995)

Cal-Maine Foods, Inc. v. *Iran*, 6 *Iran-US Cl. Trib. Rep.* 52 (1984)

Continental Shelf Case (Tunisia/Libya), 1982 *ICJ Rep.* 18 (24 Feb.), 67 *ILR* 4

Continental Shelf Case, Application for Revision and Interpretation of the Judgment of 24 February 1982 in the Case Concerning the Continental Shelf (Tunisia/Libya), 1985 *ICJ Rep.* 192 (10 Dec.), 81 *ILR* 419

Corfu Channel Case (United Kingdom v. *Albania)*, 1949 *ICJ Rep.* 4 (9 Apr.), 16 *ILR* 155

Dadras International and Per-Am Construction Corp. v. *Iran*, 31 *Iran-US Cl. Trib. Rep.* 127 (1995)

Dames and Moore v. *Iran*, 8 *Iran-US Cl. Trib. Rep.* 107 (1985)

Davidson (Homayounjah) v. *Iran*, 36 *Iran-US Cl. Trib. Rep* 43 (2000)

Glamis Gold, Ltd. v. *United States (Canada* v. *United States)*, UNCITRAL Award, 8 June 2009, available at: www.state.gov/documents/organization/125798.pdf

Golshani v. *Iran*, 29 *Iran-US Cl. Trib. Rep.* 78 (1993)

Gulf Associates, Inc. v. *Iran*, 35 *Iran-US Cl. Trib. Rep.* 45 (1999)

Henry Morris v. *Iran*, 3 *Iran-US Cl. Trib. Rep.* 364 (1983)

Jacobellis v. *Ohio*, 378 US 184, 197 (1964)

Lake Lanoux Arbitration (France v. *Spain)* (Arbitral Trib. 1957), 24 *ILR* 101

Lischem Corp. Gifted, Inc. v. *Atomic Energy Organization of Iran*, 7 *Iran-US Cl. Trib. Rep.* 18 (1984)

Location of Boundary Markers in Taba Between Egypt and Israel, 20 *R. Int'l Arb. Awards* 1 (29 Sept. 1988)

Maritime Delimitation and Territorial Questions Between Qatar and Bahrain (Qatar v. *Bahrain)*, 2001 *ICJ Rep.* 40 (16 Mar.), 139 *ILR* 1

Maritime Delimitation and Territorial Questions between Qatar and Bahrain, Jurisdiction and Admissibility, Judgment, 1994 *ICJ Rep.* 112 (1 July)
Military and Paramilitary Activities in and Against Nicaragua (Nicaragua v. *United States)*, 1986 *ICJ Rep.* 14 (27 June), 76 *ILR* 1, 349
Mixed Claims Commission, United States and Germany, Administrative Decisions and Opinions of a General Nature and Opinions and Decisions in Certain Individual Claims From October 1, 1926, to December 31, 1932, with Orders of March 25 and May 7, 1925 and Appendices (Washington, DC: Gov. Printing Office, 1933)
United States ex rel. Lehigh Valley RR v. *Germany* (Mixed Cl. Comm'n 1930)
Decision of the Commission Rendered by the Umpire, Honorable Owen J. Roberts (3 Dec. 1932)
United States ex rel. Phila.-Girard Nat'l Bank v. *Germany*
Mixed Claims Commission, United States and Germany, Opinions and Decisions in the Sabotage Claims Handed Down June 15, 1939, and October 30, 1939 and Appendix (Washington, DC: Gov. Printing Office, 1939)
Certificate of Disagreement and Opinion of the American Commissioner (15 June 1939)
Decision of Commission Rendered by the Umpire (15 June 1939)
Mixed Claims Commission: United States and Germany: Decisions and Opinions from January 1, 1933 to October 30, 1939 (Excepting Decisions in the Sabotage Claims of June 15, and October 30, 1939) (Washington, DC: Gov. Printing Office, 1940)
Decision of the Commission (15 Dec. 1933)
North Sea Continental Shelf (Germany v. *Denmark/Germany* v. *The Netherlands)*, 1969 *ICJ Rep.* 3 (20 Feb.), 41 *ILR* 29
Polish Agrarian Reform and the German Minority (Germany v. *Poland)*, 1933 *PCIJ* (ser. B) No. 60 (29 July), 7 *ILR* 497
Ram Int'l Indus. v. *Air Force of Iran*, 29 *Iran-US Cl. Trib. Rep.* 383 (1993)
Riahi v. *Iran*, 39 *Iran-US Cl. Trib. Rep.* 158 (2003)
Riahi v. *Iran*, 2004 WL 2812132, *Iran-US Cl. Trib.* (17 Nov. 2004)
Uiterwyk Corp. v. *Iran*, 19 *Iran-US Cl. Trib. Rep.* 107 (1988)
Ultrasystems Inc. v. *Iran*, 2 *Iran-US Cl. Trib. Rep.* 100 (1983) (partial award)
Ultrasystems, Inc. v. *Iran*, 4 *Iran-US Cl. Trib. Rep.* 77 (1983) (final award)
United States v. *La Abra Silver Mining Co.*, 32 Ct. Cl. 462 (1897)
United States v. *La Abra Silver Mining Co.*, 175 US 423 (1899)
United States v. *Weil*, 35 Ct. Cl. 42 (1900)
Z. & F. Assets Realization Corp. v. *Hull*, 31 F. Supp. 371 (DDC 1940)
Z. & F. Assets Realization Corp. v. *Hull*, 311 US 470 (1941)

Pleadings

"A Brief of the American Agent Supplementing the Oral Argument had at Boston, Mass., July 30-Aug. 1, 1931" in *United States ex rel. Lehigh Valley RR* v. *Germany* (Mixed Cl. Comm'n 15 Sept. 1931) (No. 8102)
"American Brief for Washington Argument of Nov. 1932" in *United States ex rel. Lehigh Valley RR* v. *Germany* (Mixed Cl. Comm'n 18 Nov. 1932) (No. 8103)
"Application Instituting Proceedings" in *Corfu Channel Case (United Kingdom* v. *Albania)*, 1949 *ICJ Pleadings* 8 (13 May 1947)

"Brief on Behalf of the Underwriters' Committee" in *United States ex rel. Lehigh Valley RR* v. *Germany* (Mixed Cl. Comm'n 10 Mar. 1925) (No. 8102)
"Brief for Claimant" in *United States ex rel. Lehigh Valley RR* v. *Germany* (Mixed Cl. Comm'n 21 May 1928) (No. 8103)
"Counter-Memorial of the Arab Republic of Egypt, In the Matter of an Arbitration Between the Arab Republic of Egypt and the State of Israel" (12 Oct. 1987)
"Counter-Memorial of Israel, The Egypt-Israel Arbitration Tribunal Established in Accordance with the Compromis Signed 11 September 1986" (12 Oct. 1987)
"Counter-Memorial of the Libyan Arab Jamahiriya" in *Continental Shelf Case (Tunisia/Libya)*, 1982 *ICJ Pleadings* 147, paras. 28–30 (2 Feb. 1981), available at: www.icj-cij.org/docket/files/63/9523.pdf
"Counter-Memorial Submitted by the State of Qatar" in *Maritime Delimitation and Territorial Questions Between Qatar and Bahrain* (31 Dec. 1997), available at: www.icj-cij.org/docket/files/87/7061.pdf
Declaration of Intervention of the Republic of El Salvador, *Military and Paramilitary Activities in and Against Nicaragua (Nicaragua* v. *United States)* (15 Aug. 1984), available at: www.icj-cij.org/docket/files/70/9625.pdf
"Final Brief for the Underwriters" in *United States ex rel. Lehigh Valley RR Co.* v. *Germany* (Mixed Cl. Comm'n 22 Mar. 1930) (No. 8103)
"Memorial of the Arab Republic of Egypt, In the Matter of an Arbitration Between the Arab Republic of Egypt and the State of Israel" (13 May 1987)
"Memorial of Israel, The Egypt-Israel Arbitration Tribunal Established in Accordance with the Compromis Signed 11 September 1986" (13 May 1987)
"Memorial of the Libyan Arab Jamahiriya" in *Continental Shelf Case (Tunisia/Libya)*, 1982 *ICJ Pleadings* 455, para. 30 (30 May 1980), available at: www.icj-cij.org/docket/files/63/9517.pdf
"Memorial Submitted by the State of Bahrain (Merits)" in *Maritime Delimitation and Territorial Questions Between Qatar and Bahrain* (30 Sept. 1996), available at: www.icj-cij.org/docket/files/87/7055.pdf
"Memorial Submitted by the State of Qatar" in *Maritime Delimitation and Territorial Questions Between Qatar and Bahrain* (30 Sept. 1996), available at: www.icj-cij.org/docket/files/87/7057.pdf
"Memorial of the United Kingdom" in *Corfu Channel (United Kingdom* v. *Albania.)*, 1949 *ICJ Pleadings* 17 (30 Sept. 1947)
"Oral Arguments" in *United States ex rel. Lehigh Valley RR* v. *Germany* (24 Sept. 1930) (No. 8103)
"Petition for Rehearing" in *United States ex rel. Lehigh Valley RR* v. *Germany* (Mixed Cl. Comm'n 12 Jan. 1931) (No. 8102)
"Rejoinder of the Arab Republic of Egypt, In the Matter of an Arbitration Between the Arab Republic of Egypt and the State of Israel" (1 Feb. 1988)
"Reply Brief for the Underwriters" in *United States ex rel. Lehigh Valley RR* v. *Germany* (Mixed Cl. Comm'n 15 Mar. 1929) (No. 8102)
"Reply of the United Kingdom" in *Corfu Channel (United Kingdom* v. *Albania)*, 1949 *ICJ Pleadings* 241 (26 Mar. 1948)
"Verbatim Record" in *Continental Shelf Case (Tunisia/Libya)*, available at: www.icj-cij.org/docket/files/63/9543.pdf

"Verbatim Record" in *Corfu Channel (United Kingdom* v. *Albania)*, ICJ Doc. 1949/1, available at: www.icj-cij.org/docket/files/1/10905.pdf
"Verbatim Record" in *Military and Paramilitary Activities in and Against Nicaragua (Nicaragua* v. *United States)*, available at: www.icj-cij.org/docket/files/70/9639.pdf
"Verbatim Record" in *Military and Paramilitary Activities in and Against Nicaragua (Nicaragua* v. *United States)*, available at: www.icj-cij.org/docket/files/70/9641.pdf
"Verbatim Record of the Hearing" in *The Egyptian-Israel Arbitration Tribunal Established in Accordance with the Compromis Signed 11 September 1986* (14–25 Mar.; 11–15 Apr., 1986)
"Written Observations on the Declaration of Intervention" (10 Sept. 1984), available at: www.icj-cij.org/docket/files/70/9623.pdf

Treaties, statutes, UN documents and other agreements

Agreement for a Mixed Commission To Determine the Amount To Be Paid by Germany in Satisfaction of Germany's Financial Obligations Under the Treaty Concluded Between the Two Governments on August 25, 1921, US-F.R.G., Aug. 10, 1922, 42 Stat. 2200 reprinted in Kiesselbach, W., *Problems of the German-American Claims Commission*, E. H. Zeydel (trans.) (Washington, DC: Carnegie Endowment for International Peace, 1930), app. B, p. 132
Convention on the Law of the Sea, Dec. 10, 1982, 1833 UNTS 397
Declaration of the Government of the Democratic and Popular Republic of Algeria concerning the Settlement of Claims by the Government of the United States of America and the Government of the Islamic Republic of Iran, Article III(2)
Exec. Order No. 12170, 44 Fed. Reg. 65,279 (14 Nov. 1979)
GA Res. 1000, A/RES/394 (5 Nov. 1956)
Iranian Assets Control Regulations, 31 CFR pt. 535 (1979)
SC Res. 324, UN Doc. S/RES/324 (9 Apr. 1947)
"Special Agreement" in *Corfu Channel (United Kingdom* v. *Albania)*, 1949 *ICJ Pleadings* 8 (25 Mar. 1948)
"Special Agreement" in *Continental Shelf Case (Tunisia/Libya)*, 1982 *ICJ Pleadings* 3 (10 June 1977)
"Special Rules of March 20, 1929" in H. H. Martin, *Final Report of H. H. Martin Acting Agent of the United States Before the Mixed Claims Commission United States and Germany* (Washington, DC: Gov. Printing Office, 1941)
Treaty of Peace, US-FRG, 25 Aug. 1921, 42 Stat. 1939 reprinted in Kiesselbach, W., *Problems of the German-American Claims Commission*, app. A, p. 129

Books and collected works

Aldrich, G. H., *The Jurisprudence of the Iran-United States Claims Tribunal* (Oxford University Press, 1996)
Al-Arayed, J. S., *A Line in the Sea: The Qatar v. Bahrain Border Dispute in the World Court* (Berkeley, CA: North Atlantic Books, 2003)

Ambler, E., *Dirty Story: A Further Account of the Life and Adventures of Arthur Abdel Simpson* (New York: Charles Scribner's Sons, 1967)

Ambrosius, L. E., *Wilsonian Statecraft: Theory and Practice of Liberal Internationalism During World War I* (Wilmington, DE: Scholarly Resources, 1991)

Anderson, C. P., *Report of American Commissioner: Mixed Claims Commission United States and Germany* (Washington, DC: Gov. Printing Office, 1934)

Austen, J., *Emma* reissue edn. (New York: Bantam Classics, 1984)

Bostan, I. and Finkel, C., "Ottoman Report" (4 Sept. 1997) reprinted in Olsen (ed.), *Forensics of a Forgery*, vol. I, pp. 67

Brower, C. N., and Brueschke, J. D., *The Iran-United States Claims Tribunal* (The Hague: Martinus Nijhoff, 1998)

Carlston, K. S., *The Process of International Arbitration* (New York: Columbia University Press, 1946)

Clive, N., "British Policy Alternatives 1945–1946" in Bærentzen, L., Iatrides, J. O. and Smith, O. L. (eds.), *Studies in the History of the Greek Civil War, 1945–1949* (Copenhagen: Museum Tusculuanum Press, 1987)

Darling, C. J., *Scintillae Juris*, 3rd enlarged edn. (Davis & Son, 1879)

Gaddis, J. L., *The Cold War: A New History* (New York: Penguin Books, 2005)

Gerolymatos, A., *Red Acropolis, Black Terror: The Greek Civil War and the Origins of Soviet-American Rivalry, 1943–1949* (New York: Basic Books, 2004)

Gilmore, G., *Ages of American Law* (New Haven, CT: Yale University Press, 1977)

Goodstein, D., *On Fact and Fraud: Cautionary Tales from the Front Lines of Science* (Princeton University Press, 2010)

Hart, H. L., *The Mixed Arbitral Tribunals: An Experiment in Legal Procedure* (London and New York: Sir I. Pitman & Sons, 1932)

Holmes, O. W., "The Path of the Law" in Lerner, M. (ed.), *The Mind and Faith of Justice Holmes: His Speeches, Essays, Letters, and Judicial Opinions* (New York: Modern Library, 1954)

Kelsen, H., *General Theory of Law and State*, Wedberg, A. (tr.), (Cambridge, MA: Harvard University Press, 1945)

Ladas, S. P., *The Exchange of Minorities: Bulgaria, Greece and Turkey* (New York: Macmillan, 1932)

Lauterpacht, H., *Private Law Sources and Analogies of International Law: With Special Reference to International Arbitration* (Hamden, CT: Archon Books, 1970)

Mapp, W., *The Iran-United States Claims Tribunal: The First Ten Years, 1981–1991* (Manchester University Press, 1993)

Merriam, C. H., *Political Power: Its Composition and Incidence* (New York and London: Whittlesey House, McGraw Hill, 1934)

Miscamble, W. D., *From Roosevelt to Truman: Potsdam, Hiroshima, and the Cold War* (Cambridge University Press, 2007)

Moody, S., *444 Days: The American Hostage Story* (New York: Routledge, 1981)

Moore, J. B., *History and Digest of the International Arbitrations to Which the United States has Been a Party*, 6 vols. (Washington, DC: Gov. Printing Office, 1898)

Olsen, M. B. (ed.), *The Forensics of a Forgery: Bahrain's Submissions to the International Court of Justice in re: Qatar v. Bahrain*, 6 vols. (Manama, Bahrain: Jabo Publishing Group, 2003)

Papastratis, P., *British Policy Towards Greece During the Second World War, 1941–1944* (Cambridge University Press, 1984)

Parker, A. C., *Parker Pasha, The Diaries of Parker Pasha: War in the Desert, 1914–18, Told from the Secret Diaries of Colonel Alfred Chevallier Parker* (London: Quartet Books, 1984)

Reisman, W. M., *Folded Lies: Bribery, Crusades, and Reforms* (New York: Free Press, 1979)

The Quest for World Order and Human Dignity in the Twenty-first Century: Constitutive Process and Individual Commitment: General Course on Public International Law (Leiden/Boston: Martinus Nijhoff, 2012)

Rosenne, S., *The World Court: What It Is and How It Works*, 5th rev. edn. (Leiden/Boston: Martinus Nijhoff, 1995)

Sandifer, D. V., *Evidence Before International Tribunals*, rev. edn. (Charlottesville, VA: University of Virginia Press, 1975)

Schwebel, S. M., *International Arbitration: Three Salient Problems* (Cambridge University Press, 1987

Shai, D., *American Spectacles and Other Cultivated Illusions* (New Haven Press, 1993)

Tansill, C. C., *America Goes to War* (Boston, MA: Little Brown, 1938)

Wilkinson, J. C., "Historical Report" (5 Sept. 1997) reprinted in Olsen (ed.), *Forensics of a Forgery*, vol. I, p. 27

Journal and news articles

"Black Tom Decision Praised in Berlin," *NY Times* (16 Nov. 1930)

"Black Tom Ruling Rejected by Reich," *NY Times* (17 June 1939)

Borchard, E. M., "The Opinions of the Mixed Claims Commission, United States and Germany," *Am. J. Int'l L.*, 19 (1925)

"Opinions of the Mixed Claims Commission, United States and Germany (Part II)," *Am. J. Int'l L.*, 20 (1926)

Bowett, D. W., "The Taba Award of 29 September 1988," *Isr. L. Rev.* 23 (1989)

Carty, A., "The Corfu Channel Case – And the Missing Admiralty Orders," *L. & Prac. Int'l Cts. & Tribunals*, 3 (2004)

"Cousin Pointed Out Black Tom Suspect," *NY Times* (4 Sept. 1916)

"Du Pont Powder Plant Explosion Rocks 4 States," *NY Times* (13 Jan. 1917)

Edelist, R., "The Taba Deception Who Gave the Order? First Exposure of a Double Deception 'Exercise' and Treble Clumsy Oversight in the Affair of the Taba Border Dispute," *Monitin* (Jan. 1986) translated version reprinted in "Rejoinder of the Arab Republic of Egypt, In the Matter of an Arbitration Between the Arab Republic of Egypt and the State of Israel," Annex 3, p. 2 (1 Feb. 1988)

Editorial, "Fraud in the Scientific Literature," *NY Times* (5 Oct. 2012)

"Exploding Shells Rain Four Hours; $5,000 Loss," *NY Times* (12 Jan. 1917)

Farah, D., "Managua Blasts Rip Lid Off Secrets," *Wash. Post* (14 July 1993)

"Find German Agents in Munition Works," *NY Times* (18 Nov. 1917)

Golden, T., "New Arms Scandal Adds to Nicaragua's Woes," *NY Times* (5 Sept. 1993)

Goshko, J., "Salvadorans Accused of Hiding Arms: Guerrilla Cache Said to Be in Nicaragua," *Wash. Post* (17 June 1993)
"Held as Plotters in Black Tom Fire," *NY Times* (10 Aug. 1916)
"Held in Explosion Case," *NY Times* (3 Sept. 1916)
Holmes, O. W., Jr., "The Path of the Law," *Harv. L. Rev.*, 10 (1897)
Kelly, M., "The President's Past," *NY Times* (Magazine) (31 July 1994)
"The Road to Paranoia," *The New Yorker* (19 June 1995)
"Loss at Kingsland put at $17,000,000," *NY Times* (13 Jan. 1917)
Manchester, H., "The Black Tom Case," *Harper's Mag.* (Dec. 1939)
McClendon, R. E., "The Weil and La Abra Claims Against Mexico," *Hispanic American Historical Rev.*, 19 (1939)
"Munition Explosions Cause Loss of $20,000,000; 2 Known to be Dead, Many Missing, 35 Hurt; The Harbor Raked by Shrapnel for Hours," *NY Times* (31 July 1916)
"Munitions Explosions Shake New York; Wreck $7,000,000 Jersey Storage Plant; Many Killed; Alarm and Damage Here," *NY Times* (30 July 1916)
"Nicaragua; Suspicious Sandinistas," *Economist* (10 July 1993)
"Partisan Reflections," *Nat'l Rev.* (29 Aug. 1994)
Plant, G., "Maritime Delimitation and Territorial Questions between Qatar and Bahrain (Qatar v. Bahrain)," *Am. J. Int'l L.*, 96 (2002)
Reichler, P. S., "The Nicaragua Case: A Response to Judge Schwebel," *Am. J. Int'l L.*, 106 (2012)
Reisman, W. M., "Unratified Treaties and Other Unperfected Acts in International Law," *Vand. J. Transnat'l L.* 35 (2002)
Schwebel, S. M., "Celebrating A Fraud on the Court," *Am. J. Int'l L.*, 106 (2012)
"The Nicaragua Case: A Response to Paul Reichler," *Am. J. Int'l L.*, 106 (2012)
Stewart, J. B., "Tax Me If You Can," *New Yorker* (19 Mar. 2012)
Sztucki, J., "Intervention Under Article 63 of the ICJ Statute in the Phase of Preliminary Proceedings: The 'Salvadoran Incident,'" *Am. J. Int'l L.*, 79 (1985)
Turner, R. F., "Coercive Covert Action and the Law," *Yale J. Int'l L.*, 20 (1995)
"Washington Loses Black Tom Claims," *NY Times* (14 Nov. 1930)
Weil, P. "Some Observations on the Arbitral Award in the Taba Case," *Isr. L. Rev.*, 23 (1989)
Woolsey, L. H., "The Arbitration of the Sabotage Claims Against Germany," *Am. J. Int'l L.*, 33 (1939)
"The Sabotage Claims Against Germany," *Am. J. Int'l L.*, 34 (1940)

Press statements, letters and documentary materials

Beckett, W. E., "Report by the Agent on the Corfu Case" Dep't of State, *Press Releases* 59 (15 Nov. 1930)
Holmes, O. W., "The Path of the Law," Address Delivered at the Dedication of the New Hall of the Boston University School of Law (8 Jan. 1897) in M. Lerner (ed.), *The Mind and Faith of Justice Holmes: His Speeches, Essays, Letters, and Judicial Opinions*, reprint edn. (New Brunswick, NJ: Transaction Publishers, 1989)

Rosenne, S., Address to the United Nations Conference on Public International Law (15 Mar. 1995) (on file with authors)
Letter from the Secretary-Gen. to the Coordinator-Gen. of the Frente Farabundo Martí para la Liberación Nacional (FMLN) (June 12, 1993) in Further Report of the Secretary-General on the United Nations Observer Mission in El Salvador (ONUSAL), annex I, U.N. Doc. S/26005 (29 June 1993)
Letter from Albert Victor Alexander, First Lord of the Admiralty, to Clement R. Attlee, Prime Minister (25 July 1946)
ADM 1/22504, Admiralty Message 061551, from Admiralty to the Commander-in-Chief Mediterranean (1 Aug. 1946)
ADM 1/22504, Telegram from Admiralty to Commander-in-Chief Mediterranean (10 Aug. 1946)
ADM 1/22504, Admiralty Message 211106A/September, from Admiralty to Commander-in-Chief Mediterranean (22 Sept. 1946)
PREM 8/406, Telegram No. 2412, from Permanent United Kingdom Representative to the UN (22 Nov. 1946)
LCO 3/3217, Telegram No. 2012, from United Kingdom Delegation to Council of Foreign Ministers, p. 1 (26 Nov. 1946)
PREM 8/1312, Telegram from Permanent United Kingdom Representative to the United Nations to Foreign Office (9 Jan. 1947)
PREM 8/1312, Telegram from Foreign Office to Permanent United Kingdom Representative to the United Nations (11 Jan. 1947)
FO 371/72100 R11937/G, Letter from Sir Eric Beckett, Legal Advisor, to Ernest Bevin, Foreign Secretary (14 Oct. 1948)
FCO 371/72100, Minute from Sir Hartley Shawcross to Right Hon. Ernest Bevin (15 Oct. 1948)
PREM 8/1312, Letter from Hartley Shawcross, Attorney General, to Clement R. Attlee, Prime Minister (29 Oct. 1948)
LCO 2/4515, Minute from Hartley Shawcross, Attorney General, to William Jowitt, Lord Chancellor (1 Nov. 1948)
PREM 8/1312, Note by the First Lord of the Admiralty to the Prime Minister (2 Nov. 1948)
FO 371/72101, Minute from Eric Beckett to Sir O. Sargent (3 Nov. 1948)
ADM 1/22504, Minute from Hartley Shawcross, Attorney General, to Clement R. Attlee, Prime Minister (3 Nov. 1948)
FO 371/72101, Minute from W. E. Beckett, Legal Advisor at the Foreign Office, to Sir Orme Sargent, Permanent Under-Secretary at the Foreign Office (3 Nov. 1948)
ADM 1/22504, Minute 196/48, from Clement R. Attlee, Prime Minister, to Hartley Shawcross, Attorney General (4 Nov. 1948)
FO 371/72101 252042, Minute (5 Nov. 1948)
ADM 1/22504, Admiralty, Notes on the Attorney General's Memorandum of the 3rd November, para. 1 (5 Nov. 1948)
ADM 1/22504, Minute from William Jowitt, Lord Chancellor, to Clement R. Attlee, Prime Minister (5 Nov. 1948)
ADM 1/22504, Minute by the Lord Chancellor to the Prime Minister (5 Nov. 1948)

ADM 1/22504, Minute from William Jowitt, Lord Chancellor, to Viscount Hall, First Lord (5 Nov. 1948)
ADM 1/22504, Minute from Hartley Shawcross, Attorney General, to Clement R. Attlee, Prime Minister (6 Nov. 1948)
PREM 8/1312, Letter from Hartley Shawcross, Attorney General, to Clement R. Attlee, Prime Minister (6 Nov. 1948)
PREM 8/1312, PM/OS/48/90, Minute from Sir Orme Sargent, Permanent Under-Secretary at the Foreign Office, to Clement R. Attlee, Prime Minister (9 Nov. 1948)
ADM 116/5758, Telegram No. 429 from Eric Beckett, Legal Advisor to the Foreign Office, to Mr. Dodds, Admiralty Official (19 Nov. 1948)
ADM 116/5758, Telegram No. 480, from P. N. N. Synott, USS Admiralty, to the Admiralty Secretary (21 Dec. 1948)
ADM 116/5758, Letter from Eric Beckett to Frank Soskice, Solicitor General (22 Dec. 1948)
ADM 116/5758, P. N. N. Synott, USS Admiralty, Notes of a Meeting held on Jan 4, 1949 RE XCU
ADM 116/5758, P. N. N. Synott, USS Admiralty, Notes of a Meeting held on Jan 5, 1949 RE XCU
Minutes from John G. Lang, Permanent Secretary to the Board of Admiralty, to Viscount Hall, First Lord of the Admiralty (8 Jan. 1949)
PREM 8/1312, Sir Eric Beckett's Record of Jan. 10, 1949 Meeting
Minute from Clement R. Attlee, Prime Minister, to Viscount Hall, First Lord of Admiralty (12 Jan. 1949)
PREM 8/1312, Minute from Viscount Hall, First Lord of the Admiralty, to Clement R. Attlee, Prime Minister (12 Jan. 1949)
PREM 8/1312, Minute from Hartley Shawcross to Clement R. Attlee, Prime Minister (13 Jan. 1949)
Minute from Clement R. Attlee, Prime Minister, to Hartley Shawcross, Attorney General (14 Jan. 1949)
PREM 8/1312, Brief from Frank Soskice, Solicitor General, to the Foreign Secretary and First Lord, Corfu Channel Case (undated)

Index

Index

Lightning Source UK Ltd.
Milton Keynes UK
UKOW04n1820200714

235445UK00002B/20/P

9 781107 063396